BECOMING AN ICF
CREDENTIALED COACH

BECOMING AN ICF CREDENTIALED COACH

The Journey to ACC, PCC and MCC – Practice Insights from ICF Assessors

Jonathan Passmore and
Judit Ábri von Bartheld

First published in 2024 by Libri Publishing

Copyright © Libri Publishing

Contributors retain copyright of their chapters.

The right of Jonathan Passmore and Judit Ábri von Bartheld to be identified as the editors of this work has been asserted in accordance with the Copyright, Designs and Patents Act, 1988.

ISBN: 978-1-911451-32-7

All rights reserved. No part of this publication may be reproduced, stored in any retrieval system or transmitted in any form or by any means, electronic, mechanical, photocopying, recording or otherwise, without the prior written permission of the copyright holder for which application should be addressed in the first instance to the publishers. No liability shall be attached to the author, the copyright holder or the publishers for loss or damage of any nature suffered as a result of reliance on the reproduction of any of the contents of this publication or any errors or omissions in its contents.

A CIP catalogue record for this book is available from The British Library

Cover and Design by Carnegie Book Production

Libri Publishing
Brunel House
Volunteer Way
Faringdon
Oxfordshire
SN7 7YR

Tel: +44 (0)845 873 3837

www.libripublishing.co.uk

Contents

Contributors ix

Foreword – Marcia Reynolds and Philippe Rosinski xvii

Introduction xx

Section 1: ICF BARS and Markers 1

Section 1 Introduction 1

Chapter 1: An Assessor's Perspective on the ICF BARS –
Francine Campone 2

Chapter 2: An Assessor's Perspective on the ICF PCC Markers –
Giuseppe Totino and Ann Fogolin 9

Section 2: ICF Competencies 17

Section 2 Introduction 17

Chapter 3: Exploring Competency 1: Demonstrates Ethical
Practice – Frances Penafort, Anita Gupta, João Luiz Pasqual and
Jonathan Passmore
with contributions from Svea van der Hoorn, Sandra L. Stewart
and Lola Chetti 18

Chapter 4: Exploring Competency 2: Embodies a Coaching Mindset –
Peter J. Reding, Peter Hayward and Eileen Laskar 41

Chapter 5: Exploring Competency 3: Establishes and Maintains
Agreements – Judit Ábri von Bartheld, Karen Burke and Kaveh Mir
with contributions from Fran Fisher 65

v

CONTENTS

Chapter 6: Exploring Competency 4: Cultivates Trust and Safety –
Chérie Carter-Scott and Michael Pomije   93

Chapter 7: Exploring Competency 5: Maintains Presence –
Svea van der Hoorn and Cindy Muthukarapan
with contributions from Philippe R. Declercq   118

Chapter 8: Exploring Competency 6: Listens Actively –
Tracy Tresidder, Osama Al-Mosa and Johan van Bavel   146

Chapter 9: Exploring Competency 7: Evokes Awareness –
Karen Foy, Leda Turai, Elena Espinal and Ram S. Ramanathan   169

Chapter 10: Exploring Competency 8: Facilitates Client Growth –
Meryl Moritz, Dalia Nakar and Keiko Hirano   195

Section 3: Masterful Insights   **219**

Section 3 Introduction   219

Chapter 11: Reflective Practice – Jonathan Passmore   220

Chapter 12: Dare to be LAZY – Judit Ábri von Bartheld   223

Chapter 13: Questions at the Heart of Coaching – Elena Espinal   227

Chapter 14: Pause Gives More Time than it Takes – Janet Harvey   229

Chapter 15: Walking Home to Self – Karen Foy   231

Chapter 16: Learning for Transcripts and Recordings –
Carly Anderson   233

Chapter 17: Trust and Safety – Michael Pomije   236

Chapter 18: The Trap of the "Knower" – Michael Stratford   238

Chapter 19: The Polarity between the Science and Art –
Osama Al-Mosa   241

Chapter 20: Make Your Coaching Client Do the Work! – Peter J. Reding — 241

Chapter 21: Dancing with Polarities – Ram S. Ramanathan — 243

Chapter 22: A Beginner's Mind – Dalia Nakar — 246

Chapter 23: Graceful Steps to Mastery – Meryl Moritz — 247

Chapter 24: Learning from Feedback – Sandra L. Stewart — 249

Chapter 25: Focusing on Exploration, Partnership and Intentionality – Damian Goldvarg — 251

Chapter 26: State – Leda Turai — 253

Chapter 27: The Dynamic Process – Keiko Hirano — 255

Chapter 28: The Paradox of Asking Powerful Questions in Coaching – Johan van Bavel — 257

Chapter 29: The Power of the Pause – Teri-E Belf — 259

Chapter 30: The Magical Journey to the Center of the Self – Chérie Carter-Scott — 261

Chapter 31: Synchronizing Presence through the Three Selves – Paul Jeong — 263

Chapter 32: Letting Go in Three Steps – Karen Burke — 265

Chapter 33: Shifting from Transactional to Transformational – Tracy Tresidder — 267

Chapter 34: Client Readiness – Kaveh Mir — 269

Chapter 35: Imbalances in Power and Coaching – Lola Chetti — 273

Chapter 36: Managing Our Own Saboteurs – Frances Penafort — 275

Chapter 37: Coaching Mindset – Ann Fogolin — 277

Chapter 38: Using Silence, Pauses and Reflections – Cindy Muthukarapan — 279

Chapter 39: The Significance of Opening Coaching Sessions – Svea van der Hoorn — 282

Chapter 40: Humility – Peter Hayward — 288

Chapter 41: Bias – João Luiz Pasqual — 295

Chapter 42: Not Knowing Is Your Greatest Strength – Philippe R. Declercq — 308

References — 290

Section 4: Appendices — 293

Appendix 1: Useful Links — 294

Appendix 2: Minimum Skills Requirements for ACC Credential — 295

Appendix 3: ICF PCC Markers — 308

Appendix 4: Minimum Skills Requirements for MCC Credential — 312

Appendix 5: ICF Code of Ethics — 329

Contributors

Editors

Professor Jonathan Passmore, D.Occ.Psych, MBA, MSc, BSc (Hons), BA (Hons), FBPS, CPsychol, PCC, FHEA, MC (UK)

Jonathan is a licensed psychologist and holds five degrees and three professional coaching qualifications, with ICF, EMCC and ILM. He is Professor of Coaching and Behavioral Change at Henley Business School UK and is also Senior Vice President with EZRA Coaching, part of the Adecco Group. He has written and published widely over the past three decades, including forty books and 250 peer-reviewed papers and book chapters, making him one of the most published researchers in the field of coaching. His work has been globally recognized with multiple awards and is listed in the Thinkers50 and Global Gurus coaching lists. His most recent books include *Becoming a Coach: The Essential ICF Guide* (2024) with Tracy Sinclair and *Becoming a Team Coach: The Essential ICF Guide* (2024) with Lucy Widdowson, Paul Barbour and Katarina Kanelidouk. He shares a lot of his work for free via his website. www.jonathanpassmore.com; https://www.linkedin.com/in/jonathan-passmore-08427b57

Judit Ábri von Bartheld, MCC, ACTC (Hungary)

Judit is an executive coach, a mentor coach and a coach educator on all levels. She has been an ICF assessor since 2013 and in 2014 established, and runs, an ICF ACSTH / Level 1 coach school (CHN International Coach School). In 2024 the CHN coach school received ICF Level 3 accreditation for their MCC Mastery Accelerator program. She is an ICF accredited team coach (ACTC), in 2023 CHN coach school received the ICF AATC team coach training accreditation. In 2024 she became a GTCI Certified Systemic Team Coach Senior Practitioner among the first ones globally. Between 2017 – 2024 Judit as a mentor coach and an assessor at Henley Business School, Reading University, UK contributed to the introduction of the ICF coaching standards to the PCEC coach training program. She received her MA in coaching from Middlesex University, UK. Her program Coaching Without Borders Hungary (CHN) has, over eight years, hosted more than sixty well-known speakers from the global world of coaching. Judit developed the Hungarian version of Becoming a Coach: The Essential ICF Guide. Judit was invited several times to be an evaluator on the ICF Impact Awards. She is a contributor to the ACC and also to the MCC ICF Assessors' Guide Book, a member of the ACC Task Force for ICF Assessors and also currently a member of the task force reviewing the ACC and MCC BARS. www.becomingacredentialedcoach.com

Contributors

Carly Anderson, MCC (US; originally from Australia)

Carly has mentored more than 700 coaches since 2013 for ACC, PCC and MCC development, using recordings and transcripts. Carly has twenty years of active experience as an ICF assessor for all three credentials. https://carlyanderson.com

Johan van Bavel, MCC, ACTC (Netherlands)

Johan van Bavel is the founder of the Intention Center for Leadership and Coaching, an ICF-accredited institution based in the Netherlands. Within this capacity, he educates coaches and leaders on attaining certification as ICF professional coaches and leaders. www.iaai.nl

Teri-E Belf, MCC (US)

The first MCC, a global coaching pioneer since 1987, Teri-E collaborated in co-creating the profession and received the ICF Circle of Distinction Award. Her ancient wisdom explorations surfaced as our foundational coaching principles. Purposefully, she inspires people to take steps towards their dreams, inspiring authentic service to the sacred. https://www.healthcoachescenterforeducation.com

Karen Burke, MCC (US)

KB (Karen) Burke is an MCC, engineer, MBA, coach assessor and supervisor, and teaches and assesses coaching globally. KB specializes in guiding technical clients and their teams through intricate leadership challenges.

Francine Campone, Ed.D., MCC (US)

Francine supports coaches through supervision, mentoring and training, drawing on a three-decade career as a leadership coach and adult educator. She researches, writes and edits in the coaching field. A native New Yorker, she is currently a senior student at the Zen Center of Denver. francine@reinventinglife.net; www.francinecampone.com

Chérie Carter-Scott, Ph.D., MCC (US and Thailand)

Chérie, known as the "Mother of Coaching," pioneered the coaching industry in 1974. She founded MMS Worldwide Institute (www.mmsworldwideinstitute.com) and has trained over 10,000 coaches globally in five decades. She is a *NYT* No. 1 bestselling author of *If Life is a Game, These are the Rules*, which Oprah celebrated, and her new memoir, *Life IS a Game*, which chronicles the beginning of coaching.

Lola Chetti, MCC (Mauritius and France)

Lola is Mauritian–French. She is based in New York and has worked globally as an executive coach, team coach and organizational coach trainer for fifteen years. She is a board member of the ICF's Independent Review Board (IRB). She has a master's degree with distinction from INSEAD in leadership and systems psychodynamic coaching. https://holdingspacecoach.com

Philippe R. Declercq, MCC (Belgium)

Philippe has eighteen years of experience in individual and team coaching. Active in Europe and Africa, he cultivates a passion for personal and professional development, with a particular openness to multiculturalism. His services include coaching education, supervision and certification mentoring. He is fluent in French, English and Dutch. https://PRDcoaching.com/

Elena Espinal, MCC (Mexico)

Elena is a global coach, supervisor and mentor, specializing in diversity and future design across more than thirty countries. She collaborates with *Fortune* 500 companies as a coach. Author of *Crafting the Future*, she has contributed to more than ten coaching and philosophy books. Elena directs Team Power (www.team-power.com.mx), also working with blind coaches and social programs.

CONTRIBUTORS

Fran Fisher, MCC (US)

Fran has been an MCC and an ICF assessor since 1998. She is one of the pioneers for coaching, a visionary leader and published author. She provides advanced-level mentoring and mentor training for MCC accreditation. In 2022, Fran received the honor of the ICF Circle of Distinction Award.

Ann Fogolin, MCC (Canada)

A seasoned coach, coach educator, registered mentor coach, coach supervisor, ICF assessor and trainer of ICF assessors, Ann participated in the update of the ICF PCC-level Coaching Competency Markers and is a member of the task force reviewing the ACC and MCC BARS. www.becuzimatter.com

Karen Foy, MCC (UK)

Karen is a Master Certified Coach with over twenty years' experience, and a certified coach mentor and supervisor. Karen holds a BA Psychology from the University of Sheffield and an MSc Coaching Psychology from the University of East London. She was program director of accredited coaching programs at Henley Business School, University of Reading, UK, where she is still a visiting tutor. Outside of Henley she continues as a coach and coach educator.

Dr. Damian Goldvarg, MCC, ACTC, ESIA (Argentina/United States)

Damian has thirty years of experience providing coaching services in over fifty countries. He facilitates virtual certifications in coaching, team coaching, mentor coaching and supervision. He has been an ICF assessor for fifteen years, and was the 2013–2014 ICF global president. He has published nine coaching-related books. www.goldvargconsulting.com

Anita Gupta, MCC (India)

Anita is a Master Certified Coach deeply passionate about the entire coaching realm – whether as a coach, mentor coach, coach trainer or contributing to ICF, particularly in the realm of ethics.

Janet M. Harvey, MCC (US)

Visionary CEO of inviteCHANGE, a human-development company driving productivity and performance, Janet Harvey uses her executive and entrepreneurial experience to cultivate leaders in sustainable excellence through Generative Wholeness™ (https://vimeo.com/448672025), their signature coaching and learning process. Also a bestselling author and keynote speaker, you can contact Janet via her website. https://janetm-harvey.com/

Peter C. Hayward, MCC (Germany)

Peter is a Master Certified Coach with over thirty years of experience working in fast-changing, multicultural environments. His areas of expertise include professional development and organizational transformation. He is a strong believer in utilizing humor as an approachable coaching technique. www.baldcoach.com

Keiko Hirano, MCC (Japan)

Keiko is a founding member of COACH A, the first coaching and coach-training firm in Japan (http://www.coacha.com). Keiko was awarded the ICF Circle of Distinction in 2018 for her contribution to the global coaching industry.

Svea van der Hoorn, MCC (South Africa)

Educator. Mentor coach. Supervisor. Author. D.Ed (Ed Psych). Cultivating your unique coaching style and capability in alignment with the quality-assurance frameworks. Enabling impeccable client service and joy in your work via continuous learning and growth. Stay steady. Go beyond. Keep ingenuity alive. https://www.linkedin.com/in/dr-svea-van-der-hoorn

Dr. Paul Jeong, MCC (Korea)

Paul is the founder and president of Global Coaching Company, the largest coaching company in Korea. He provides services that include leadership coaching, energy coaching, organizational change, emotional intelligence, executive coaching and ICF Level 2 coach training.

CONTRIBUTORS

Eileen Laskar, MCC (Kenya)

Eileen is a proud African woman, a coaching pioneer committed to raising the coaching standard and scaling coaching impact in Africa.

Kaveh Mir, MCC (UK and Iran)

Kaveh has coached senior executives from international organizations such as Capgemini, Amazon, HSBC, IBM, Novartis, Unilever, Mars and Google. Kaveh is currently an ICF Global Director at the Institute of Thought Leadership. Kaveh's methodology follows the foundational knowledge of coaching: Humanistic Psychology, Constructivism, Linguistics, Positive Psychology, Neuroscience and Systemic. linkedin.com/in/kavehmir

Meryl Moritz, MCC (USA)

Meryl is a leadership and team coach, educator, coach supervisor, mentor and member of the ICF Circle of Distinction. She supports leaders to develop agile responses as they strive to stabilize their organizations and position them for post-traumatic growth.

Osama Al-Mosa, MCC, ACTC, ICTA (Jordan)

An accredited global leadership coach and consultant with a psychology background, Osama Al-Mosa coaches senior leaders and teams in more than sixty-five countries. He owns a coaching services and coach-development school, is an ICF assessor and Prism Award judge, and has held board leadership roles globally and in the MENA region. http://www.osamaalmosa.com

Cindy Muthukarapan, MCC, ACTC (South Africa)

Cindy is an internationally recognized leadership coach and mentor, holding significant roles as a director of education and a board director, where she leverages her extensive experience to contribute to elevating coaching excellence and shaping the future of coaching. Cindy is a PhD candidate in applied leadership at Monarch University, Switzerland.

CONTRIBUTORS

Dalia Nakar, MCC (Israel)

Dalia founded a coaching retirement center to coach people to design their new life chapter. Dalia is an executive and team coach, a Jungian coach, a mentor coach and an ICF assessor. She is a former president of Israel's ICF chapter and an ambassador.

João Luiz Pasqual, MCC (Brazil)

João Luiz Pasqual is a certified mentor coach and supervisor, and holds the vice-chair of development position on the ICF's Independent Review Board (IRB). His dedication to ethical coaching is unwavering, with a strong focus on ethics in practice and education. Learn more at his website. https://www.cw4u.com.br

Dr. Frances Penafort, MCC (Malaysia)

Frances is committed to progressing the level of ethical maturity and knowledge of core competencies. She contributes extensively in this field and is a much-sought-after keynote speaker on ethics and core competencies, regionally and globally. More information is on her website. https://francespenafort.com

Michael Pomije, MCC (US and Thailand)

Michael brings thirty years of diverse experience from NBC Sports to founding a global lecture agency, showcasing his commitment to leadership and communication. Now, alongside Dr. Chérie Carter-Scott, they are the sole married Master Certified Coaches jointly leading all three ICF levels of Transformational Executive Coach Certification programs. www.michaelpomije.com

Ram S. Ramanathan, MCC (India)

Ram is a spiritual systemic team master coach, mentor and trainer, helping executive CXO teams to emotionally bond to collaborative vision and OKR goals, using his decades of corporate leadership and Eastern spiritual wisdom aligned with sciences. https://coacharya.com/about/team/ram-ramanathan

Peter J. Reding, MCC (US)

Peter is a pioneer in professional coaching, globally. He is a strong advocate for knowing, living and celebrating the uniquely brilliant person you were created to be.

Sandra L. Stewart, MCC (US)

Sandra is the author of *Building the Core Competencies of Change: A Guide to Coaching in Organizations* and contributor to *Building an Organizational Coaching Culture*. She is an instructor and mentor for coaching certification and a member of the ICF IRB. www.sandraLstewart.com

Michael Stratford, MCC (US)

Michael is a champion of uniqueness, with over three decades coaching clients from rock bands to *Fortune* 100 company executives and their teams. He is the creator of MillonQuest™: 7 Realms of Self-Mastery. www.millionquest.com; www.michaelstratford.com

Giuseppe Totino, MCC (Italy and US)

Giuseppe is an executive coach and leadership development expert. He also holds the IAF CPF certification. He is committed to fostering organizational coaching cultures and raising coaching standards. He played an instrumental role in developing the ICF core competencies and assessors' training. He lives in Central Florida with his family. www.giuseppetotino.com

Tracy Tresidder, MCC (Australia)

An award-winning coach, lecturer and leader with over twenty-one years of experience, Tracy has 7,000+ coaching hours, 1,000+ mentoring hours and held leadership roles in ICF and academia. Known as the "coach's coach," she supports coaches in developing competency, capability and capacity, and clients in achieving conscious, purposeful living.

Leda Turai, MCC, ACTC (Estonia)

Leda Turai, MA, MSc, MCC, ACTC, PhD scholar, executive coach, mentor coach, supervisor, ex-ICF global board chair, ICF assessor and SME, has earned numerous coaching awards and Hungary's Knight's Cross of the Order of Merit. www.lconglobal.com; www.coachingdevelopment.com

Foreword

I remember when we agreed as a young ICF board to implement certification of coaches in the late 1990s. There was a desire to ensure the integrity of our profession by certifying that people who called themselves an ICF coach were representing the values and the definition of coaching we stand for. Most importantly, we knew we had to differentiate coaching from therapeutic practices, consulting, teaching and mentoring. We felt our young profession would not survive on its own without specifying the behaviors we call "coaching" when uplifting lives, relationships and business results.

We spent hours arguing and negotiating the definition of coaching that has stood the test of time. The key phrase – partnering in a thought-provoking and creative process – is what the competencies and then the Behaviorally Anchored Rating Scale (BARS) were built on.

Partnering represents the equal power dynamic that coaches establish to create the safety and trust needed to unlock and maximize the ability for people to expand, even create, new realities to step into. We are thinking partners, not experts, doctors, problem-solvers or healers. We know every client has the seeds of knowledge that can be nurtured so they figure out what to do and who to be with coaching.

The competencies and BARS demonstrate the thought-provoking and creative process we use to create the new awareness clients need to move forward. This process also uplifts the human spirit and expands consciousness in a way that serves the possibility of creating a world that works for all.

After reading just one chapter of this book, I had to sit quietly with my smile and open heart. I am so grateful for the amazing coaches who contributed to the work, the examples they share along with their clear explanations, and how each competency works in service of both the client and coach. The book does more than teach. It inspires us to continue our development on the path of coaching mastery that has no end. As we improve, so do our clients, and the world.

I hope you treasure this book as much as I do and use it until the pages fall out – then buy a new one! Thank you, Jonathan and Judit, for pulling this masterpiece together.

Marcia Reynolds, PsyD, MCC

Since the 1990s, the ICF has played a leading role in the professionalization of coaching. When I participated in the first Executive Coaching Summit in 1999 sponsored by the ICF, our challenge was to ensure that coaching in general, and executive coaching in particular, would become an established profession, whose societal contribution would be recognized. We have come a long way since then, with the best universities offering advanced coaching education, a boom in coaching research papers and literature, and organizations increasingly calling upon coaching to deploy their human potential to benefit multiple stakeholders. The journey continues and hopefully coaching will become one day an integral part of our education across ages and across geographies.

The growing interest in coaching and the possibility for almost anyone to call themselves a coach makes it imperative, though, to be able to distinguish professional coaches from mere opportunists. This precious book will give you a concrete sense of the basic competencies required to be considered a professional coach. The ICF has done a remarkable job in defining competencies that provide a common bedrock while also cultivating diversity. This combination of universalist coherence and particularist flexibility provides the necessary safeguards while still encouraging each coach to be the unique professional they can be.

Becoming a masterful coach is not solely a matter of acquiring knowledge, learning techniques and gaining experience. It implies striving to be congruent, embodying the human qualities we help others to develop. It necessitates openness, curiosity and humble self-confidence. It entails turning to our coachees with the intention of establishing a genuine human bond. Becoming a masterful coach also involves, in my view, the readiness to engage in life-long learning from diverse disciplines including psychology as well as medicine, management, interculturalism, politics and philosophy (among others!). Coaches may not have the expert knowledge of psychotherapists, neuroscientists or philosophers. Their unique strength is in being generalists interested in all these disciplines and integrators of multiple perspectives, helping clients address complex challenges from various angles. They help coachees discover new avenues to build more fulfilling lives for themselves and for all those they can impact.

Professional coaching is needed now more than ever. Although the 193 countries of the UN General Assembly in 2015 adopted the 2030 Agenda for Sustainable Development with 17 Sustainable Development Goals (and the associated targets and indicators), we are not on track to achieve these crucial environmental, social and economic objectives. Professional coaching promises to transform the leadership needed to bridge this gap by deploying our human multifaceted potential, evoking our sense of purpose, raising our consciousness and promoting constructive relationships and collaboration. In sum, professional coaching is not only destined to help coaching clients achieve their immediate goals. It can contribute to making our world a better place for all living species.

Delving into this book will allow you to advance on your professional coaching journey by learning directly from diverse master coaches. I want to express my gratitude to all the contributors for sharing their wisdom and to Judit and Jonathan for putting together this essential book.

Prof. Philippe Rosinski, MS, MCC

Introduction

The intention with this book is to serve all those who want to perfect their coaching skills and are committed to take it to a higher level of coach professionalism by going through the credentialing system of the International Coaching Federation (ICF).

This book came about because as ICF assessors and trainers we have been inspired by all the good coaching we have seen and the impact this makes on our world. Over the past decade, this has made us realize that coaching is colorful and diverse. We need more ways to celebrate it in its wholeness and diversity. The art of coaching manifests itself in that, while you are following the ICF quality framework represented by the ICF core competencies, you can still make your coaching human by developing your own style. You can play with the competencies in a flexible manner as you shape your own coaching style. We hope that this book helps you follow the ICF competencies in an enjoyable way when your learning is more than just a compliance exercise.

This book serves to further the transparency of our profession, so you as a coach know what assessors are looking for. Making your sessions clearer, stronger and more in line with the competencies will make for easier marking, and as we say, "a happier assessor is a high-scoring assessor!"

This book demonstrates how experienced MCC coaches can work together, with a commitment to share their knowledge and experience, to support the global coaching community and the continued development of the coaching profession.

We would like to express our gratitude to all those who have supported us on our own journeys of development. We also want to express our thanks and gratitude to Carrie Abner, our publishing team and the Master Certified Coaches who have worked on this project. Their generosity in sharing their practice has been amazing, collaborating across styles, cultures and approaches on a complex project that has brought together twenty-three different nationalities and thirty-six Master Certified Coaches.

We invite you to find your own inspiration through this book that will guide you to your own unique coaching mastery along the ICF competencies.

Jonathan Passmore and Judit Ábri von Bartheld

SECTION 1

ICF BARS and Markers

Section 1 Introduction

In this first section of the book, we start with two chapters to set the context. While most coaches are aware of, and are taught, the eight ICF competencies and the sub-competencies within each, there is little discussion of how assessors actually assess coach submissions.

In the first chapter, Francine Campone dives deep into the assessment process to explain how ICF assessors use the competencies and the Behaviorally Anchored Rating Scale (BARS). She shares the assessment frameworks and how each is marked using a detailed assessment scale from "insufficient evidence" to "exemplary evidence."

In the second chapter, Giuseppe Totino and Ann Fogolin explore the PCC Markers. They clarify what the markers are, and they share their insights on the benefits of markers and how coaches can use this knowledge in the development and assessment processes.

We hope that by openly sharing how assessors work at ACC, PCC and MCC levels, we can help you on your development journey.

CHAPTER 1

An Assessor's Perspective on the ICF BARS

Francine Campone

Introduction

While the ICF competencies and BARS statements describe what a coach does, coaches seeking the ACC and MCC credentials should also understand the rating process used in assessing those two levels. As other chapters in this book indicate, the ACC and MCC BARS are behavioral statements: they describe what the coach must do to meet the standard of competency. In this brief chapter, I will present the rating levels with a brief description of what each indicates, along with examples using selected BARS statements. I will also offer conclusions regarding the path of development to support coaches achieving ratings of sufficient and beyond.

The BARS statements describe a progression from ACC- and MCC-level coaching. The rating scale used to assess at these levels reflects not only what the coach does but the degree of proficiency with which the coach demonstrates the desired behavior. Sufficient performance by an ACC applicant indicates that the coach is technically competent and demonstrates the behaviors described in the BARS statements with a coach mindset. For an MCC applicant, a coach must go beyond prescriptive behaviors in a collaborative and emergent dialogue with the client in order to earn a rating of sufficient or higher.

If this seems a bit abstract, it might be helpful to consider an analogy. Imagine you have gone to see a performance of a classical dance performed by recent graduates of a school known for the performing arts. The dancers are quite good; poised, confident and dancing in unison with others on the stage. You leave, having enjoyed the performance. A week later, a friend invites you to see the same ballet, this time performed by an experienced professional company with two well-known and highly praised dancers in the lead roles. The dancers in the company are fluid and seem almost weightless, imparting grace and elegance to the experience of the dance. Their movements are at one with the music and your experience is of the whole rather than hearing the notes separately from the movement of the performers on the stage. The two special guest performers are exceptional. They embody music, story, emotion and you are fully absorbed in the experience with them.

This is not to suggest that the first performance was inadequate. On the contrary, the performers executed the requisite steps in a polished and professional manner. The lead performers in the second event, however, brought a grace, ease and artistry that transformed a performance into a powerful collective experience.

The Rating Scale

While it can be challenging to describe the difference, looking at the language of the BARS rating scale and competencies can help aspiring coaches understand the tone and manner that distinguish a coach who sufficiently demonstrates the BARS standard from the one who is extremely proficient or perhaps exemplary. The highlighted words in the rating scale below, along with comments I have added in italics, suggest the trajectory of the rating scale as it is applied to submissions by ACC applicants.

Table 1.1: ACC Assessor Rating Scale

Insufficient	The coach does not exhibit this behavior in response to the opportunities presented. *In other words, there is no evidence that the coach has demonstrated the behavior described in the BARS statement despite the client offering several opportunities.*

Not quite sufficient	The coach attempts to exhibit this behavior but does not do so competently. *In other words, there's some evidence the coach was aware of the required behavior but did not carry through in a way that encouraged the client to reflect or move forward. For example, A4.3 states: "Coach expresses support and concern for the client…." If the coach says "Gee, that sounds like a bad time. What do you want at the end of the session," that's not quite an expression of support or concern but at least it recognizes the client has presented something which might warrant a supportive or encouraging response.*
Sufficient	The coach exhibits the behavior. *In other words, the coach has made the inquiry, exploration or response indicated in the BARS statement. For example, A7.1 states: "The coach acknowledges the client's new awareness, learning and movement toward the desired outcomes." A coach demonstrating this sufficiently might say something like "Hmm. What does what you just said mean for you in terms of what you want to accomplish?"*
Proficient	The coach exhibits this behavior with ease. *In other words, the coach demonstrates the behavior indicated in the BARS statement in a way that is natural and fluid, not relying on a formulaic statement. For example, A7.2. states: "Coach supports the client in viewing the situation from new or different perspectives." A coach demonstrating with ease might offer "You've mentioned three other people in that meeting. How do you think they might interpret that event?"*

Extremely proficient	The coach exhibits this behavior consistently with ease in response to what the client offers. At *this rating level, the coach's skill is all the above and responding in a customized way to some aspect of what the client has offered. This way of responding is consistent throughout the course of the conversation. Taking the A7.2 response above, an extremely proficient coach might say "You've noted that Joe, your peer in marketing, and Janet from HR were both present. You seemed to take notice of their expressions when James made that statement. How do you think they might have been seeing it?"*
Exemplary	The coach exhibits this behavior completely, effortlessly and consistently in response to what the client presents. *In other words, at this level, the coach's skillfulness is all the above and is consistent throughout the course of the conversation. The coach's offers, questions and observations are fluid, specific and appropriate in the flow of the conversation. The demonstration is not a one-time response but shows the coach's alliance with and attention to the client, as well as confidence and ease in the coach's own speaking. Because this level of response is unique and contextual, any example is unlikely to adequately exemplify "exemplary."*

At the MCC level, ICF expects coaches to demonstrate fluency and authenticity in their coaching interactions and to remain client-centered and responsive throughout. So, while the rating scale is the same, the behaviors described in the BARS statements and the proficiency with which these are demonstrated indicate progression and maturity in the practitioner.

Table 1.2: MCC Assessor Rating Scale

Insufficient	The coach does **not exhibit** this behavior **in response to the opportunities presented**. *In other words, there is no evidence that the coach has demonstrated the behavior described in the BARS statement.*
Not quite sufficient	The coach **attempts** to exhibit this behavior but does **not** do so **competently**. *In other words, the coach demonstrates the described behavior but in a way that suggests a formulaic response or digression from what the client has offered. For example, BARS M3.1 directs the coach to "partner with the client to explore the topic or focus of the session at a level that is meaningful to the client." Responding to an initially offered topic with "What outcome do you want?" is a formulaic response that does not quite meet the criteria for partnering or exploration to uncover potentially deeper meaning to the client's top-of-mind issue.*
Sufficent	The coach **exhibits the behavior**. *In other words, the coach's response addresses the verbal or non-verbal content offered by the client in a way that is specific and customized to the client and the moment in the conversation. For example, M6.3 tells us the coach's reflections should be relevant to the whole person of the client. One example of this might be "You mentioned you are comfortable speaking with your manager but not with your peer. I noticed your hands moving more when you mentioned your peer and they were still when you spoke about your manager. What do you think?" The offered observation calls attention to the client's somatic response. The follow-up question invites client reflection.*

Proficient	The coach **exhibits this behavior with ease**. *In other words, the coach's comments and responses as above are made in a way that is natural and fluid, with few or no hesitancies, repetitions or lengthy, awkward sentences. For example, M5.2 directs the coach to "remain curious and attentive to the client, exploring what the client needs throughout the session." In noticing that a client is laughing while saying "I'm so frustrated, I could spit!" the proficient coach might suggest "I am noticing that there seem to be two different things going on here: laughter and frustration. What feels most important at this moment?"*
Extremely proficient	The coach exhibits this behavior **consistently with ease in response** to what the client offers. *At this rating level for MCC coaches, the coach's skill is all the above and consistently responding in a customized way to some aspect of what the client has offered. Taking the example of M6.3 again, an extremely proficient coach might mirror the client's gestures along with stating the observation, and hold a space for the client to experience the moment.*
Exemplary	The coach exhibits this behavior **completely, effortlessly, and consistently in response** to what the client presents. *In other words, as with rating ACC coaching, the coach's skillfulness is all the above and is consistent throughout the course of the conversation. The demonstration is not a one-time response but shows the coach's alliance with and attention to the client, as well as confidence and ease in the coach's own speaking. Because this level of response is unique and contextual, any example is unlikely to adequately exemplify "exemplary."*

The Path beyond Sufficient

Professional coaching practitioners are always seeking to expand and improve their coaching to better serve their clients. For both ACC and MCC certifications, the progression of the ratings from sufficient to exemplary suggests an increasing level of self- and client awareness, as well as the coach's ability to express themselves responsively and authentically.

The first key to taking this journey lies in the language of Competency 2: Embodies a Coaching Mindset. The proficient, extremely proficient and exemplary coaches have internalized the first element of that competency: acknowledging that clients are responsible for their own growth. This element of a coaching mindset is essential to deeply understand and embody the concept of partnering, which appears in the language of many of the BARS statements. In order to be a full partner, the coach must cultivate self-awareness and self-knowledge and understand how to recognize and use intuition for the client's benefit. Partnering also involves the coach's ability to regulate their own emotions and to be mentally and emotionally prepared for sessions.

The second key lies in noting that every one of the BARS statements specifically positions the client as the key partner in the coaching exchange. All of the coach's attention is focused on what the client wants and needs, how the client sees the self and the situation, the client's perceptions, emotions, non-verbal reactions, intentions and perspectives. Proficient, more than proficient and exemplary coaches are able to keep the client at the center of every response, question, offer and reaction. These coaches can bracket their own ideas, feelings and needs in order to invite, inquire, explore and reflect in service to the client.

Continual work with a coaching mentor can support the development of skills aligned with the BARS statements. Supported reflection and exploration with a coaching supervisor can encourage the development of the self-awareness and self-knowledge that are needed for ease, authenticity and fluidity in coaching practice.

Conclusion

As you review the next eight chapters, which focus on the competencies, try to keep in mind what the assessors will be seeking from you at each level. Reflect on how you believe you are evidencing the behaviors in each of your coaching sessions, as the assessors can only reward what they see, not what you may know or your potential.

CHAPTER 2

An Assessor's Perspective on the ICF PCC Markers

Giuseppe Totino and Ann Fogolin

Introduction

Coaching is a profession in which clients' growth and transformation often measure success. A framework is invaluable for evaluating and enhancing coaching skills. The International Coaching Federation (ICF) recognizes this need and provides a roadmap for professional coaches through its credentialing programs. One of the essential tools for assessing coaching competencies and guiding coaches toward excellence is the ICF PCC (Professional Certified Coach) Markers.

This article delves into the intricacies of the PCC Markers, exploring their significance and purpose. Understanding these markers is not just about meeting a set of criteria but about empowering coaches on their credentialing journey, giving them the tools to shape their professional development.

What Are the PCC Markers?

To understand the PCC Markers, it is essential to comprehend their fundamental nature. These markers are a set of specific behaviors and skills that professional coaches should possess to attain the PCC level of coaching competence. The ICF's PCC credentialing requires coaches to demonstrate these behaviors, as organized into eight core competencies. Each competency comprises several markers that outline the behaviors and skills expected from a coach at the PCC level.

The language used in the markers reflects the competencies, but it is modified for observing behaviors. Coaches can improve their effectiveness and credibility by understanding and embodying these coaching behaviors.

The ICF PCC Markers are organized as follows (ICF, n.d.):

Competency 1: Demonstrates Ethical Practice

Familiarity with the ICF Code of Ethics and its application is required for all levels of coaching. Successful PCC candidates will demonstrate coaching that is aligned with the ICF Code of Ethics and will remain consistent in the role of a coach.

Competency 2: Embodies a Coaching Mindset

Embodying a coaching mindset – a mindset that is open, curious, flexible and client-centered – is a process that requires ongoing learning and development, establishing a reflective practice and preparing for sessions. These elements take place over the course of a coach's professional journey and cannot be fully captured in a single moment in time. However, certain elements of this competency may be demonstrated within a coaching conversation. These particular behaviors are articulated and assessed through the following PCC Markers: 4.1, 4.3, 4.4, 5.1, 5.2, 5.3, 5.4, 6.1, 6.5, 7.1 and 7.5.

As with other competency areas, a minimum number of these markers will need to be demonstrated to pass the PCC performance evaluation. All elements of this competency will also be evaluated in the written assessment for ICF credentials.

Competency 3: Establishes and Maintains Agreements

3.1: Coach partners with the client to identify or reconfirm what the client wants to accomplish in this session.

3.2: Coach partners with the client to define or reconfirm measures of success for what the client wants to accomplish in this session.

3.3: Coach inquires about or explores what is important or meaningful to the client about what they want to accomplish in this session.

3.4: Coach partners with the client to define what the client believes they need to address to achieve what they want to accomplish in this session.

Competency 4: Cultivates Trust and Safety

4.1: Coach acknowledges and respects the client's unique talents, insights and work in the coaching process.

4.2: Coach shows support, empathy or concern for the client.

4.3: Coach acknowledges and supports the client's expression of feelings, perceptions, concerns, beliefs or suggestions.

4.4: Coach partners with the client by inviting the client to respond in any way to the coach's contributions and accepts the client's response.

Competency 5: Maintains Presence

5.1: Coach acts in response to the whole person of the client (the who).

5.2: Coach acts in response to what the client wants to accomplish throughout this session (the what).

5.3: Coach partners with the client by supporting the client to choose what happens in this session.

5.4: Coach demonstrates curiosity to learn more about the client.

5.5: Coach allows for silence, pause or reflection.

Competency 6: Listens Actively

6.1: Coach's questions and observations are customized by using what the coach has learned about who the client is or the client's situation.

6.2: Coach inquires about or explores the words the client uses.

6.3: Coach inquires about or explores the client's emotions.

6.4: Coach explores the client's energy shifts, non-verbal cues or other behaviors.

6.5: Coach inquires about or explores how the client currently perceives themself or their world.

6.6: Coach allows the client to complete speaking without interrupting unless there is a stated coaching purpose to do so.

6.7: Coach succinctly reflects or summarizes what the client communicated to ensure the client's clarity and understanding.

Competency 7: Evokes Awareness

7.1: Coach asks questions about the client, such as their current way of thinking, feeling, values, needs, wants, beliefs or behavior.

7.2: Coach asks questions to help the client explore beyond the client's current thinking or feeling to new or expanded ways of thinking or feeling about themself (the who).

7.3: Coach asks questions to help the client explore beyond the client's current thinking or feeling to new or expanded ways of thinking or feeling about their situation (the what).

7.4: Coach asks questions to help the client explore beyond current thinking, feeling or behaving toward the outcome the client desires.

7.5: Coach shares – with no attachment – observations, intuitions, comments, thoughts or feelings, and invites the client's exploration through verbal or tonal invitation.

7.6: Coach asks clear, direct, primarily open-ended questions, one at a time, at a pace that allows for thinking, feeling or reflection by the client.

7.7: Coach uses language that is generally clear and concise.

7.8: Coach allows the client to do most of the talking.

Competency 8: Facilitates Client Growth

8.1: Coach invites or allows the client to explore progress toward what the client wanted to accomplish in this session.

8.2: Coach invites the client to state or explore the client's learning in this session about themself (the who).

8.3: Coach invites the client to state or explore the client's learning in this session about their situation (the what).

8.4: Coach invites the client to consider how they will use new learning from this coaching session.

8.5: Coach partners with the client to design post-session thinking, reflection or action.

8.6: Coach partners with the client to consider how to move forward, including resources, support or potential barriers.

8.7: Coach partners with the client to design the best methods of accountability for themself.

8.8: Coach celebrates the client's progress and learning.

8.9: Coach partners with the client on how they want to complete this session.

What Is the Purpose of Having PCC Markers?

The existence of PCC Markers serves several vital purposes within the coaching profession:

- **Standardization:** PCC Markers provide a standardized framework for evaluating coaching competencies, ensuring consistency and fairness in credentialing. Coaches and assessors can align their expectations and assessments more effectively by adhering to common standards.

- **Quality Assurance:** PCC Markers are crucial in maintaining quality standards within the coaching profession. Coaches who meet these markers demonstrate a certain level of proficiency and effectiveness in their coaching practice, enhancing the overall credibility and reputation of the profession. This assurance can instill confidence in coaches and clients, knowing they are part of a profession that upholds high standards.

- **Professional Development:** PCC Markers serve as a roadmap for professional development, guiding coaches in identifying areas for growth and improvement. By understanding the specific behaviors and skills associated with each competency, coaches can target their development efforts more effectively, ultimately enhancing their coaching effectiveness and impact.

- **Client Confidence:** The existence of PCC Markers benefits coaches and clients. When clients become aware that their coach follows a recognized set of standards and competencies, they have increased confidence and trust in the coaching process. Clients can feel assured that their PCC coach has the skills and expertise to support them effectively on their journey toward growth and transformation. This reassurance highlights the significance of the coaches' role in their clients' lives.

- **Continual Improvement:** PCC Markers encourage coaches to engage in ongoing learning and development. Even experienced coaches can benefit from revisiting these markers periodically to ensure they align with best practices and evolving industry standards. This commitment to continual improvement ultimately benefits both coaches and their clients.

In essence, PCC Markers are a cornerstone of professional excellence within the coaching profession, driving standardization, quality assurance and ongoing development for coaches worldwide. These markers are not static but are developed and updated by the ICF in collaboration with industry experts to ensure their relevance and applicability in the evolving coaching landscape.

How Knowledge of the PCC Markers Helps PCC Credentialing Candidates

For PCC credentialing candidates, a thorough understanding of the PCC Markers is essential for several reasons:

- **Credentialing Preparation:** Understanding the specific behaviors and skills associated with each competency enables candidates to prepare effectively for the credentialing process. By aligning their coaching practice with the PCC Markers, candidates can demonstrate their readiness to meet the credentialing requirements and showcase their proficiency as coaches.

- **Self-Assessment:** PCC Markers provide a valuable framework for self-assessment and reflection. Candidates can evaluate their coaching practice against the markers to identify strengths, areas for improvement and development priorities. This self-awareness enables candidates to focus on enhancing their coaching competencies and addressing gaps or shortcomings.

- **Feedback Interpretation:** During credentialing, candidates receive feedback from assessors based on their demonstration of the PCC Markers. This feedback is specific to the coaching behaviors assessed and provides detailed insights into the candidate's strengths and areas for improvement. A solid understanding of the markers allows candidates to interpret this feedback effectively, recognizing areas of success and areas needing further development. By leveraging this feedback constructively, candidates can refine their coaching practice and enhance their overall effectiveness as coaches.

- **Professional Growth:** Beyond the credentialing process, knowledge of the PCC Markers supports ongoing professional growth and development. PCC-credentialed coaches can use the markers to guide setting goals, planning development activities and measuring progress over time. By continually striving to embody the behaviors and skills outlined in the markers, coaches can elevate their practice and make meaningful contributions to their clients' lives.

To sum up, a comprehensive understanding of the PCC Markers is indispensable for PCC-credentialed candidates seeking to excel in coaching. By embracing these markers as a guide for practice, reflection and development, coaches can elevate their effectiveness, credibility and impact in supporting clients on their journey toward growth and transformation.

Conclusion

The ICF PCC Markers are a fundamental framework for achieving coaching excellence by identifying the behaviors and skills associated with proficient coaching practices. Understanding the purpose and significance of these markers can help PCC-credentialed candidates unlock new opportunities for growth, mastery and impact in their coaching journey. As the coaching profession continues to evolve, adhering to the PCC Markers is crucial. They ensure coaches maintain the highest standards of ethics, competence and client-centered excellence, and play a pivotal role in fostering trust and confidence in the coaching process and profession.

SECTION 2

ICF Competencies

Section 2 Introduction

In this book we have sought to bring together more than thirty of the world's leading ICF coaches. Most of these coaches have been actively involved in developing and reviewing the behaviors under the competencies, the markers and the BARS, and in assessing coaches at ACC, PCC and MCC levels against them. What better than to draw on their expertise to help you understand the ICF competencies, how they manifest in behaviors expressed in the markers and BARS used in assessing your credential coaching session recordings.

In this section of the book, we dive deep into each competency statement. Each chapter starts with an exploration of definitions. As we say, it's "words that create meaning," so understanding the meaning of the phrases and words used in this context is an important starting point.

Each chapter then explores the markers and the BARS at the three relevant levels: ACC, PCC and MCC. In each case we ask what types of behavior might the assessors be looking for during the detailed assessment process. In each case, we have provided several examples that provide good evidence for the right coach behavior.

Finally, in each chapter we look at the contribution the competency makes, through the eyes of both the client and the coach.

Each section ends with ten reflective questions to support your developmental journey using this competency

CHAPTER 3

Exploring Competency 1: Demonstrates Ethical Practice

Frances Penafort, Anita Gupta,
João Luiz Pasqual and Jonathan Passmore
with contributions from Svea van der Hoorn,
Sandra L. Stewart and Lola Chetti

Introduction

"Ethics" refers to the study of moral principles and values that guide human behavior and decision-making. It provides a framework that enables us to examine and evaluate our actions and choices, and gives us the rational justification for our moral judgments. The ultimate aim of ethics is to serve as a foundation for creating a harmonious and just society.

In this chapter, we will explore how this competency guides all coaches to understand that coaching is not a solo sport. Coaching involves various stakeholders and the coaches' actions have an impact on them. This core competency serves as a guide and provides professional coaches the "soul" of who they are, how they show up and how they interact with their stakeholders, sponsors, the ICF system and also the community at large. (For a discussion of Competency 1, see Passmore and Sinclair, 2024.)

This chapter is designed to provide an overview of what this core competency is. We take a deep dive into each of the seven elements, coupled with the sharing of real case examples, which help to add a deeper perspective on the respective element. We also share a series of case studies as a way of deepening our understanding of how ethical practice can serve both coach *and* client. We close the chapter with a set of reflective questions that enable you to foster a deeper connection to this core competency.

Table 3.1: Competency 1: The ICF Definition of Demonstrates Ethical Practice

Definition: Understands and consistently applies coaching ethics and standards of coaching.

Table 3.2: Competency 1: Demonstrates Ethical Practice

1.1 Demonstrates personal integrity and honesty in interactions with clients, sponsors and relevant stakeholders.

1.2 Is sensitive to clients' identity, environment, experiences, values and beliefs.

1.3 Uses language appropriate and respectful to clients, sponsors and relevant stakeholders.

1.4 Abides by the ICF Code of Ethics and upholds the Core Values.

1.5 Maintains confidentiality with client information per stakeholder agreements and pertinent laws.

1.6 Maintains the distinctions between coaching, consulting, psychotherapy and other support professions.

1.7 Refers clients to other support professionals, as appropriate.

Definitions

Ethics

Ethics is concerned with the moral principles and values that guide human behavior and decision-making. It helps us discern what is right or wrong, good or bad, just or unjust. It provides a framework that enables us to examine and evaluate our actions and choices, and gives us the moral justification for our judgments. It reflects our interaction with other humans, as well as our choices in the world. It involves the exploration of concepts such as justice, fairness, honesty and responsibility. All these empower us to foster a sense of moral responsibility and accountability in personal and professional conduct. The ultimate aim of ethics is to serve as a foundation for creating a just society.

Unlike the majority of the competencies, Competency 1 does not contain specific behavioral indicators which can be used to judge its presence. Instead, it is best assessed through ethical breaches, when a coach may act, either within or outside a session, in a way which is judged to be unethical.

This chapter is designed to provide an overview of what this core competency is, at a detailed level, as we take a deep dive into its significance and impact. This competency has a set of seven elements. We will explore each element through a case study, to help the reader better understand how that competency and the element can come alive in their work.

As the behavioral anchors are not used for this competency, we have included an exploration of how this core competency serves the client and how it serves the coach. Finally, a reflective piece is inserted to explore how this competency can be lived in the daily life of a coach, as well as touching on parts of its evolution, where appropriate.

Finally, this chapter ends with succinct case studies that enable coaches to secure a broader and deeper appreciation of what happens in the real life of coaches. This understanding will provide a solid base for coaches in their coaching career while establishing their coaching practice.

Competencies Under the Microscope

1.1 Demonstrates personal integrity and honesty in interactions with clients, sponsors and relevant stakeholders

The professional ICF coach needs to have a clear understanding that once they are engaged as a coach, they are in a relationship with a set of people – which includes the client and sponsors, as well as a wider set of stakeholders – who may have opinions or expectations about the coach, the client or the coaching process. This competency outlines what the professional coach needs to work on themselves before they enter into a coaching relationship, such as the level of honesty and integrity they want to bring. If, for whatever reason, they do not put in effort and focus on building honesty and integrity, they may risk not demonstrating ethical practice.

Real Case Example

While serving as a director on the ICF Independent Review Board (IRB), we received a complaint from a client who felt that their coach displayed a low level of honesty and integrity. Prior to commencing the coaching sessions, both they and the coach agreed on various aspects, such as: the duration of the coaching program, the duration of each session, some initial session dates and times, and the platform to be used, among others.

During the first coaching session, the client (for whom this was their first ever coaching session) arrived on the digital platform at the agreed date and time. While the client honored their commitment, the coach did not turn up. The client waited for a total of thirty-five minutes before the coach finally arrived and shared that they were late because their previous coaching session had over-run.

The client noticed this recurrent pattern of the coach, who did not honor their part of the coaching contract. The coach did not make any effort to showcase their level of honesty and integrity. The client felt disrespected by the coach.

1.2 Is sensitive to clients' identity, environment, experiences, values and beliefs

The professional ICF coach needs to have an attribute of gentleness that will embrace the vulnerabilities and sensitivities that each client brings with them. The professional coach is tasked to *work on building their relationship with their client*. When they put effort into this relationship, the outcome the coach will see is that they will display more care, kindness, empathy and sensitivity towards the beliefs, values and identity of who the client is, and will appreciate the client's values and experiences, and the environment in which the client operates. If, for whatever reason, they do not put effort and focus on building their relationship with the client, then they may risk not demonstrating ethical practice.

CHAPTER 3

Real Case Example

While serving as a director on the ICF's Independent Review Board (IRB), we received a complaint from a client who felt that their coach displayed a low level of embracing the client's vulnerabilities and sensitivities. Prior to commencing the coaching sessions, both they and their coach agreed on various aspects, notably covering how the coaching sessions were to be held: in person. Their coach also knew their religion and some sensitivities around it.

On one of their scheduled coaching sessions, as they left their office and were making their way to their coach's office, they received a call from their coach saying that that day's coaching will be conducted over the phone and not in person. This upset the client, who protested that they had specifically requested that they did not want their coaching sessions to be held over the phone, which was agreed and documented in the coaching contract. The coach insisted. The reason was that the client had been late for a couple of previous coaching sessions and, for today's coaching sessions, the coach did not want to wait in their office, but to have the session over the phone. This upset the client even further and eroded their trust in the coaching contract as well as in their coach.

In another coaching session, when the client arrived, the coach had their dog in their office. The client shared that due to their religious sensitivities, they felt uncomfortable being in the same room as the dog. The coach insisted that the dog would not be a nuisance as the dog was a quiet dog. The client felt distressed as they felt their coach was disrespecting their sensitivities around their religion. The client lodged a complaint with the IRB.

The coach failed to nurture the relationship with their client. The coach did not show sensitivity around the client's identity, their religious beliefs, their values around having in-person coaching sessions or their vulnerabilities around a safe and trusting environment.

1.3 Uses language appropriate and respectful to clients, sponsors and relevant stakeholders

The professional ICF coach needs to be respectful to their clients. One of the most obvious signals to the clients is their language – their choice of words, their tone, their pauses, their silence, and their facial and body language. By putting effort in building their communication skills, the professional coach will be working on building their relationship with their client, sponsors and relevant stakeholders. When they put effort into these skills, the outcome the coach will see is the building of a strong rapport and trust with the client, who will feel a higher level of psychological safety; they will thus be more open, more willing to try out new initiatives and appreciate that the coach is being client-centered. If, for whatever reason, the coach does not put effort and focus on building their communication skills and building a relationship with their client, then they may risk not demonstrating ethical practice.

Real Case Example

While serving as a director of the ICF's Independent Review Board (IRB), we received a complaint from a client who felt that their coach displayed poor communication skills. The role of the coach was to support them to realign back to their studies, which were experiencing below average scores.

During the coaching sessions, the coach used vulgar language that included profanities. The client felt uncomfortable and disrespected by the coach. Their trust and respect for their coach deteriorated. The client lodged a complaint, stating that the language used by their coach was totally inappropriate.

When the review team from the IRB interviewed the coach, the coach responded that their main intention was to be in-sync with the client's kind of language and help to make them feel comfortable, as the client was a university student and for most university students, this would be normal.

The coach failed to nurture the relationship with their client. The coach did not show sensitivity around who the client was, the needs of the client, what impact their choice of words would have on the client, whether trying "to be like the client" was enabling the client or derailing the client, and whether they were there to serve their own needs or the needs of their client.

CHAPTER 3

1.4 Abides by the ICF Code of Ethics and upholds the Core Values

The professional ICF coach needs to be aware of and understand the ICF guiding system, including the Code of Ethics and Core Values, so as to build their relationship and partner with the client. Since coaching is not a solo sport, all professional coaches need the support of the guiding system, notably in ethical dilemma cases.

The coach needs to showcase the four core values of professionalism, collaboration, humanity and equity. In addition, the coach must know, understand and appreciate that the twenty-eight standards of the ICF Code of Ethics act as their support system. All parties receive protection from this guiding system. All are held accountable for their own actions and will be protected from any false accusations by others.

One of the ways that the professional coach can show support and endorse the ICF guiding system is by sharing a signed copy of the Pledge of Ethics of a professional coach (Table 3.3) with their clients and other stakeholders. By this process, they will be educating their clients and stakeholders about the seriousness of the guiding system.

If, for whatever reason, the coach does not honor the four core values and the twenty-eight standards of the Code of Ethics, then they may risk not demonstrating ethical practice.

Table 3.3: The ICF Pledge of Ethics

> As an ICF professional, in accordance with the standards of the ICF Code of Ethics, I acknowledge and agree to fulfill my ethical and legal obligations to my coaching client(s), sponsor(s), colleagues and the public at large.
>
> If I breach any part of the ICF Code of Ethics, I agree that the ICF in its sole discretion may hold me accountable for so doing. I further agree that my accountability to the ICF for any breach may include sanctions, such as mandatory additional coach training or other education, or loss of my ICF membership and/or my ICF credential.

Real Case Example

In this case, the coach undertakes online work with international clients. They regard themselves as well versed in taking care not to plunge into coaching without inquiring about issues and life circumstances that the client would like them to keep in mind during the coaching. They do this as part of their contracting process. They see this as upholding the ICF Core Values. They undertake regular reflective practice, including checking of bias and blind spots. They are known in their professional community as a resource when it comes to diversity and inclusion dilemmas. They are taken by surprise when a colleague brings to their attention that they are named in a social-media post as "unprofessional," "over inquisitive about things I regard as personal" and "having unconscious bias." The social-media post is in the public domain and the comments and analytics indicate there have been a significant number of views. Despite much advice to take legal action, the coach hopes to talk with the client. They cannot as the client cancels the next session, and does not respond to the coach's attempts to reschedule. They decide to alert the ICF via the ethics hotline and request advice in relation to Standard 14.

1.5 Maintains confidentiality with client information per stakeholder agreements and pertinent laws

Despite the ICF Code of Ethics having three standards (3, 5 and 7) around maintaining confidentiality, this element is deliberately introduced here. This indicates the level of importance that the ICF places on maintaining confidentiality over what transpires between the coach and client. The information captured can take many forms, such as audio recordings, files on a computer or handwritten notes on paper. Whatever the form, it is the responsibility of the coach to maintain this confidentiality. However, there could be circumstances in which the coach may be required by the relevant authorities to disclose confidential information that transpired between coach and client. This may be in cases where there is a risk of harm to the client or others, or serious illegality such as financial fraud or corruption. The coach needs to ensure their client becomes aware of this deviation from ICF standards 3, 5 and 7, and the valid reasons for doing so. A statement should be included in the Coaching Agreement between the coach, client and stakeholder, explaining confidentiality and possible exceptions to this rule.

If, for whatever reason, the coach does not honor standards 3, 5 and 7, and instead divulges or shares information (either verbally or in writing) to the client's stakeholders, or society at large, then they may risk not demonstrating ethical practice.

Real Case Example

In this case, the coach became aware that the agency that manages the contract between the coaches and the sponsor required reporting on the client's progress in such a way that did not sufficiently take confidentiality into consideration (standards 3, 5 and 7). This was brought to the coach's attention by one of the clients, who objected to filling in the required pre- and post-session forms. The coach had a number of clients with this agency and viewed it as an important contract. It would be a significant loss of income and professional credibility if something happened that interrupted this contract. The client quoted "integrity" from the ICF Core Values as part of their objection. They preferred the coach not to raise the matter, as they had "no faith that these large institutions would close the gap between their walk and their talk." The client simply wanted to end the coaching contract in a way that did not create career-limiting damage for themselves. The coach referred to ICF standards 8 and 9 for guidance and partnered with the client to design an exit that could take care of all the parties' interests. The client was satisfied.

1.6 Maintains the distinctions between coaching, consulting, psychotherapy and other support professions

The professional ICF coach needs to be aware of and understand the sensitive distinction between when a client is a coaching client and when a client will be better served via other helping professionals such as a therapist, mentor, facilitator, trainer or consultant. One way of thinking about this distinction is Passmore's Three 'D's Model: Diagnosis, Distress and Desire. Psychotherapy tends to focus on working with clients with a specific diagnosis. Counseling is accessed by many people at specific points in their life (for example, during bereavement or relationship breakdown) and helps us navigate distress.

In contrast, coaching focus is on working with non-clinical populations and working with a focus on the future (Passmore and Sinclair, 2024).

We can extend these ideas to include other forms of intervention, such as mentoring, training and consulting, using the Future–Past and Ask–Tell continuum. We have illustrated this in Diagram 3.1. Let's start by exploring the upper-left quadrant of consulting, training and mentoring.

Diagram 3.1: Coaching and Other Interventions

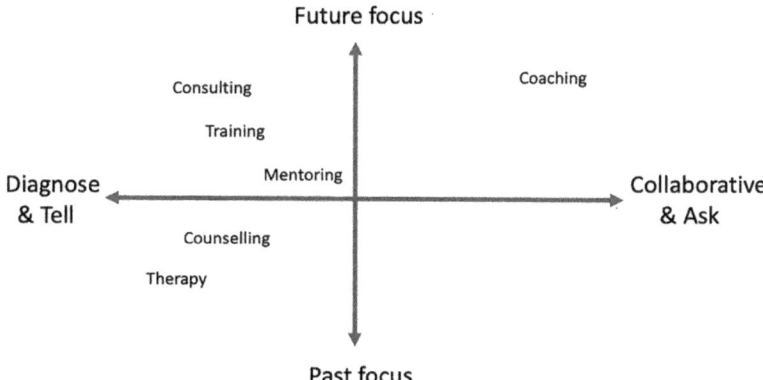

The potential client may be seeking the support of a mentor, a trainer or a consultant when they want to improve their current level of skills, as these professionals are "subject matter experts." They have the relevant knowledge, skills and experience.

For example, young employees in an organization may need someone who can support them to assimilate successfully into the organizational system, structure, culture and process. Hence, mentors are the professionals they seek, as mentors can provide advice and share their experiences.

In another scenario, consultants with many years of experience in similar industries are the right fit for a client who is seeking solutions to their current problems. They can do analysis and prescribe plausible solutions.

In another situation, clients who are seeking to learn new skills, in order to function more effectively and efficiently, need a facilitator or trainer who has the knowledge to transfer to them.

CHAPTER 3

As can be seen from the above scenarios, coaches need to be sensitive and observant as to what the client's needs are. If they fall into the top-left quadrant, then the coach needs to share their observation that the client's needs will be better served through other professionals.

If, for whatever reason, the coach fails to be observant and does not recommend other professional support, the coach may risk not demonstrating ethical practice.

Secondly, we focus our attention on the top-right quadrant. In a coaching discovery call, the coach may ask questions, seek clarity on the outcome, explore meaning and review obstacles standing in the way of success. The client is deemed to be "whole, resourceful, creative and capable" when the client is able to think and respond well (Whole), is able to share how well they acted in previous scenarios (Resourceful), is able to come up with new action steps (Creative) and, finally, is able to implement agreed-upon action steps (Capable). The coach can support the client in their journey of self-discovery and enable them to unleash their full potential.

If, for whatever reason, the coach fails to draw distinctions between who will best serve the client, then they may risk not demonstrating ethical practice.

1.7 Refers clients to other support professionals, as appropriate

The professional ICF coach needs to be aware when a coaching client will be better served by other helping professions such as therapists, counselors, psychologists and psychiatrists, for example.

In these situations (and others) we have a wider duty to society and may need to break our confidentiality agreement. This may be when we are legally obliged to do so by the courts, in cases of serious illegality (such as major financial fraud or terrorism), or where there is a risk of harm to the client or others. In most situations, this is best done collaboratively with the client, but in rare situations this may not be possible.

The coaching client may be seeking the support of other helping professionals, when certain indicators are obvious. These can be seen as "red-flag" situations, examples of which are given in Table 3.4.

Table 3.4: Signs and Symptoms

- Expressed desire and a plan to take one's own life
- Withdrawal from social relationships, changing interactions during the coaching relationship
- Significant changes in weight or appearance
- Disturbed sleep patterns
- Decline in concentration, focus or presence
- Excessively or repeatedly tearful during sessions
- Issue or topic from the past continually arises and prevents progress

(Adapted from Passmore, 2021)

In these "red-flag" circumstances, the coach can reassure the client that coaching may not serve the client effectively, as they need the support of other helping professionals. The coach can refer to their next of kin or the human resource personnel in the organization, or recommend names of therapists to seek out, and contact the police if they are threatening to harm themself or others. This is best done in the session with the client, so the client is able to access the help they need immediately, as opposed to the coach terminating the session with advice on taking action.

In addition, the ICF Code of Ethics Standard 28 guides coaches to be "doing good" versus "avoiding bad." The coach needs to acknowledge that they do not have the capacity, training or qualifications for this situation, and refrain from supporting these clients while wearing the hat of a coach.

Another ICF Code of Ethics standard (Standard 8) encourages the coach to remain alert to indications that there might be a shift in the value received from the coaching relationship. If the coach notices that a client who was previously engaged and enthusiastic in the coaching sessions suddenly does not seem engaged, then there is a clear indication of a shift in value. In this circumstance, the coach may need to refer to another professional who may be able to support the client better.

CHAPTER 3

Finally, in ICF Core Competency 6, the coach is encouraged to observe and notice if there are any trends in the client's behaviors and emotions across sessions, to discern themes and patterns. For example, if there is an emotional outburst from the client and it appears once in a while, then the coach need not classify it as a "red-flag" situation. However, if there is a recurrent pattern of emotional outburst, then the coach should refer to another professional who may be able to support the client better.

The four supports given by the ICF guiding system can be used by the coach to make a decision as to whether to refer the client to other professionals or not. If, for whatever reason, the coach fails to decide that coaching may not be the best helping profession to serve the client, then they may risk not demonstrating ethical practice.

Case Studies

Case 1: Role as Internal Coach – Wearing the Hat of Coach and HR Professional

An HR professional engaged a leader in their organization in a six-month coaching engagement. There was no written contract, but the coach explained coaching to the leader and discussed that information would not be shared from their sessions. During the coaching the client shared personal information including that they were going through significant problems at home and had trouble keeping up with the work. They coached on strategies to assist the client with this among other topics. Six months after their coaching terminated the HR professional was asked to give their thoughts on this same leader's readiness for promotion. The HR professional couldn't recuse themselves from the process as the HR department contained only two people. The HR professional carefully examined any bias they might have against the promotion due to the personal information they had on the leader and recommended the leader for promotion. Eventually, the executive decided not to promote the leader and to hire another candidate for the job. The internal leader who didn't receive the promotion accused the HR professional of a biased judgment and unethical use of private information.

In this case, while the HR professional felt they had acted in an ethical way, the client still perceived their actions otherwise. This points out the ethical challenge of perceived wrongdoing. It is important to guard against perceived wrongdoing as well as actual ethical breach. An area that was cited as a breach was the contracting phase of the engagement. In this case a written document for the agreement would have established clear protocols on confidentiality. Additionally, if the HR professional cited situations where they might be engaged in the future with decisions such as promotion, it would have allowed the client greater agency to restrict how much they shared in the coaching.

Key Takeaway: Contract with transparency and account for the unknown to the best of your ability.

Case 2: Multiple Roles – Coach and Instructor/Trainer

An ICF-certified coach was an instructor for an ICF-accredited coach-training program. During the program the instructor participated in some instructional techniques that included physical touch. The student objected to the activity as too scary and said that they wanted to stop. The coach made it uncomfortable for them to refuse by chiding them into continuing with the activities. They complained that the program had not revealed these physical-touch techniques in their contract and that they were not allowed to withdraw as requested.

Breaches were found for the following codes:

> Standard 2. Create an agreement/contract regarding the roles, responsibilities and rights of all parties involved with my Client(s) and Sponsor(s) prior to the commencement of services.
>
> Standard 9. Respect all parties' right to terminate the coaching relationship at any point for any reason during the coaching process subject to the provisions of the agreement.
>
> Standard 11. Am aware of and actively manage any power or status difference between the Client and me that may be caused by cultural, relational, psychological or contextual issues.
>
> Standard 23. Hold responsibility for being aware of and setting clear, appropriate and culturally sensitive boundaries that govern interactions, physical or otherwise.

The coach could have clearly stated in the contract more specifics about the training and what agreements were in place if the student didn't want to participate in some of the activities. The coach must recognize that as an instructor they may have greater influence over the student. The coach must be sensitive to the fact that what is comfortable to others may not be comfortable for everyone.

A second version of this case would be where a coach had promoted themselves as an ICF coach but the program itself was not ICF accredited. Most likely, because the ICF credential was clearly stated to the participants, this would still qualify as a breach.

Key Takeaway: When promoting yourself as an ICF professional, you are accountable for your behavior to the code.

Case 3: Multiple Roles – Consultant and Coach

An ICF coach contracted with a client as coach and consultant. After completing the ten-month contract, the client filed a complaint citing that they didn't think the consulting services had met the contract terms. The technical advice didn't include a one-on-one walkthrough of setting up a social-media site, as described in the contract. The complainant accused the coach of breach of the following standard:

> 21. Make verbal and written statements that are true and accurate about what I offer as an ICF professional, what is offered by ICF, the coaching profession, and the potential value of coaching.

No breach was found in this case because the ICF does not adjudicate the contracting of services outside their purview. This also applies in the case of copyright infringement where complaints of legal matters are to be first adjudicated in a legal context. If a legal breach of contract is determined in the courts, then ICF may review the implications for the ICF member.

Key Takeaway: The coach is not bound by the ethics code for quality of other services.

Case 4: Confidentiality versus Credibility

An ICF PCC coach was hired by an organization to work with one of their senior executives on their team-leadership skills. The HR director was the sponsor.

All went well with the coaching engagement until the middle of the assignment, when the client brought a conflict issue to the session. The client's objective was to find a way to get back at their colleague. In an emotional rant, the client told the coach of a plan to set the colleague up to fail. When the coach reminded the client of the positive objectives of coaching, the client continued to explore their plan of retribution. The coach reframed the language of the client, inviting them to reflect on their role as a leader and on their leadership responsibilities. The client, however, remained in an offensive mindset. The coach then gently invited the client to take time to reflect on their leadership ethical responsibilities.

At the end of the session, the coach asked for permission and shared feedback to the client on their observations on the negative focus of the latter's approach. The coach reminded the client of the objective of coaching and that they also had contracted responsibilities towards the sponsor. They acknowledged that this was a highly emotional event for the client; but they had also contracted to preserve the interests of the company and going forward were bound to divulge any information that they felt to be against the company's interests. They also reminded the client of their remit to support them in strengthening their leadership skills, especially when facing challenging situations. The coach delivered this feedback with the utmost care.

To their surprise, the coach was called later by the director of HR and given feedback that the client had reported officially to their sponsor that they felt pressured and uncomfortable in the session, were not getting value from their sessions anymore and wished to "pause" the coaching. The HR director wanted to understand what had happened to derail the coaching relationship. The coach felt their credibility was at stake and felt embarrassed by the client's misrepresentation of events.

There are several ethical elements to consider here. Firstly, can the coach contact the client about their feedback to the company? The intent would be to understand where the client is coming from and help them to recognize the negative impact of their action. Secondly, to protect their credibility, can the coach reveal to the HR director the tenor of the conversations and that they had to give challenging feedback to their client and draw boundaries by citing their duty to report to the organization any information that they felt went against its interests?

With respect to the first question, Standard 9 of the Code of Ethics states that the coach should "[r]espect all parties' right to terminate the coaching relationship at any point for any reason during the coaching process subject to the provisions of the agreement." As a result, reaching out to the client at this point is not advisable.

Furthermore, the client indicated receiving less value: Standard 8 of the Code states that coaches should "[r]emain alert to indications that there might be a shift in the value received from the coaching relationship. If so, [they should] make a change in the relationship."

With respect to the second question, confidentiality is defined in the Code of Ethics as "protection of any information obtained around the coaching engagement unless consent to release is given."

Standard 3 demands the strictest levels of confidentiality: if their contract has not expressed provision to the limits of confidentiality, the coach is not at liberty to reveal their conversation even if it is to protect their reputation.

Standard 28 refers to the coach being "aware of my and my clients' impact on society." A further point to note is that it is tricky for the coach to prove the motivation of the client – at best, it is their judgment around the person's motivation.

The best course of action is thus for the coach to terminate the coaching relationship pursuant to Standard 9. Divulging the conversation would breach coaching confidentiality.

Case 5: Ethical Dilemma in Career Coaching – Balancing Guidance and Integrity

An ICF coach who was an experienced career coach worked with a client who was a mid-level executive seeking careers advice. Across sessions, the coach repeatedly criticized the client's employer, highlighting limitations they believed to be hindering the client's growth. The coach suggested that the client's potential was stifled by their workplace and hinted at their (the coach's) connections in other industries, with the suggestion that these could help the client get a better job.

This approach breached coaching ethics. The coach's behavior eroded the client's confidence. Lack of transparency and honesty emerged as the coach failed to disclose potential conflicts of interest arising from their industry connections.

A different approach for the coach could have involved refraining from negative remarks and empowering the client within their current role. Transparency about their connections and refraining from unsolicited job suggestions could have aligned better with ethical standards. The coach's actions might have caused the client stress and confusion, potentially influencing their career choices.

Addressing concerns about the coach's approach is important. The coach should explore the discomfort and seek clarity on the client's intentions. If unsatisfied, terminating the coaching relationship in favor of being an ethical coach is an option.

Case 6: Empowering Autonomy – Navigating Ethical Quandaries in Coaching

An experienced ICF coach worked with a client who was struggling with work-related stress. The client started to rely on the coach's guidance, even for minor decisions. In a session, the client admitted regret over a significant job choice influenced solely on the coach's advice.

This created an ethical dilemma for the coach, leading them to prioritize support while honoring the client's autonomy. Recognizing the importance of empowering clients for informed decisions, the coach aimed for a client-centric approach with clear boundaries.

To tackle this issue, the coach engaged in an open conversation with the client, stressing the significance of autonomous decisions aligned with their values. They refrained from providing direct guidance, focusing instead on empowering them to explore alternatives and fostering self-reliance and ownership.

Throughout their conversation, the coach emphasized seeking diverse opinions, conducting thorough research and considering outcomes before deciding. Their aim was to nurture the client's accountability and critical thinking. The coach's goal was to balance guiding the client while respecting their autonomy, upholding ethical standards and fostering their personal growth.

Ethical dilemmas in coaching often revolve around offering guidance while safeguarding client autonomy. This balance involves supporting individuals in exploring options and critical thinking, enabling them to make choices that align with their values and aspirations.

Maintaining ethical standards requires refraining from dictating decisions but rather facilitating a process where clients own their choices. Coaches create supportive environments that encourage introspection, research and the consideration of diverse perspectives.

The primary objective isn't imposing solutions but equipping individuals with the tools and confidence necessary for autonomous navigation through challenges, respecting autonomy and ensuring informed decisions reflecting personal values and goals.

How "Demonstrates Ethical Practice" Serves the Client

Ethical coaching is rooted in integrity and transparency, forming the bedrock of trust and openness in the client–coach relationship, allowing the coach to openly share thoughts and feelings that may arise during or between sessions. Coaches who practice high ethical standards create a sanctuary for clients, honoring their diverse backgrounds, cultural nuances, beliefs and personal narratives. Such an environment not only encourages self-discovery but also fosters a progressive pathway towards personal growth.

In addition to integrity and transparency, a coaching ethos is critical in that it appreciates and acknowledges each client's individuality as being pivotal. It is through this lens of respect that a coach can empower clients, validating their unique life experiences and perspectives, and paving the way for genuine self-expression and personal evolution. These elements nurture a strong relationship between coach and client.

Another aspect of ethical coaching is effective communication. When this is present, it facilitates dialogue grounded in respect and mutual understanding. This establishes a trusting alliance where clients feel valued and heard, inspiring them to confidently articulate their aspirations and actively participate in the coaching journey. Part of this effective communication is the use of appropriate language by the coach. This will help to reinforce the viewing of clients as being resourceful and decision-capable, encouraging them to take control of their goals and chart their own course.

To serve the client better, the vow of confidentiality is a sacred component that coaches use as part of their coaching commitment. This value of confidentiality upheld by the coach is a clear demonstration of the coach's adherence to the Code of Ethics. It is a pledge that ensures personal client details remain secure, establishing a deep-seated trust that empowers clients to fully immerse themselves in the transformational experience of coaching. Adhering strictly to professional boundaries fortifies this trust and ensures that the coach's focus is always aligned with the client's welfare.

Clients have a need to have clear professional boundaries. This will help to eliminate confusion and fortify the coach's role as a guide attuned to the client's unique needs. This delineation ensures that all interactions and information exchanged are handled with the utmost discretion and professionalism.

When the coach maintains clear distinctions between the various helping professions, this helps them to mitigate professional risks, as they are less likely to encounter ethical challenges related to practicing outside the scope of their expertise, reducing the potential for disputes or misunderstandings. In addition, coaches can collaborate effectively with consultants, therapists and other specialists, ensuring a multidisciplinary approach when needed. Moreover, strategic referrals underscore the ethical commitment to client-centered care, exemplifying a coach's dedication to the client's holistic success and well-being. This aspect of ethical practice is crucial in facilitating access to broader resources and specialized expertise when required.

How "Demonstrates Ethical Practice" Serves the Coach

For coaches, ethics are the compass that directs the cultivation of mutual trust and respect within the coaching dynamic. This foundational trust is integral to fostering an environment where clients can delve into profound self-exploration and gain diverse insights into their situations, enhancing the coaching alliance.

To do this effectively, the coach can strengthen their cultural sensitivity, which will consequently enrich their coaching experience, bridging gaps between differing worldviews and enhancing the collaborative bond. Such competence in navigating diverse cultural landscapes fosters trust and effectively supports the client's journey towards their goals.

Besides deepening their cultural sensitivity, coaches need to uphold the ICF's value of professionalism. Here coaches employ context-appropriate language that bolsters the coaching integrity, enhances credibility and builds trust, ultimately fostering lasting client relationships and future collaboration opportunities.

Moreover, adherence to the ethical code elevates a coach's professional reputation and safeguards their practice. This level of integrity is essential in navigating the complexities of the coaching profession and minimizing legal risks. In addition, ethically minded coaches will actively take responsibility, learn from their actions, enhancing both their self-awareness and the overall ICF coaching community's trust and credibility.

Another critical aspect is confidentiality. This is not just a policy but a pillar of credibility for coaches. When clients are assured of the safeguarding of their disclosures, they are more likely to engage deeply and sustainably in the coaching process, establishing lasting coaching relationships and success.

One other key component is ethical clarity. When coaches have ethical clarity as they fulfill their role, it helps them to sharpen their professional identity, steering clear of ethical quandaries and nurturing a respected presence in the multidisciplinary spectrum of client support.

Finally, coaches need to sharpen their knowledge on when referrals need to be made to other professionals. This will help to reflect the coach's integrity and adherence to ethical standards, maintaining client trust, especially by acknowledging the coach's own limits and ensuring clients receive optimal support. This practice, indicative of a client-centric mindset and professional prudence, serves to enhance the coach's reputation and fosters collaborative partnerships with other experts.

Your Evolution as a Coach

Your transition journey into becoming a great coach is highly dependent on your mastery over each core competency and its behaviors. To continue to support you on this journey, a set of reflective questions is provided to enable you to dive deeper into your thoughts, mindset and beliefs.

Reflective Questions

1. Am I honest in sharing observations when addressing sensitive topics/sharing by my client?
2. Am I aware of my unconscious bias and implicit associations that might impact my ability to morally uphold my principles and provide equitable support?
3. In what ways do I actively seek to understand and respect the cultural background and identity of my clients? How do I ensure that my coaching approach is inclusive and respectful of diverse identities?
4. Am I open to exploring and understanding perspectives that may differ from my own? How do I self-manage as I navigate these differences in a coaching session, without it affecting my coaching presence?
5. What do I need to do to create a safe and confidential space for my clients to discuss their environment and challenges?

6. Am I mindful of the tone and language I use in all my interactions, both at personal levels as well as in professional settings, to ensure it is respectful and appropriate for everyone? How can I improve the effectiveness of my language and communication?
7. Do I actively seek feedback from clients about their experience with my communication style?
8. Am I aware of potential triggers or sensitivities based on a client's background? How do I reflect and navigate these with empathy?
9. What ethical challenges or dilemmas have I encountered in recent coaching engagements? How did I navigate these challenges, and what did I learn from those experiences?
10. What steps can I take to deepen my understanding of ethical considerations?

Conclusion

This chapter has provided a detailed overview of what this core competency is by taking a deep dive into its significance and impact. We gained further insight by looking at it through the lens of real case examples, which added a deeper perspective, meaning and understanding. This chapter is rich with succinct case studies that enable coaches to secure a broader and deeper appreciation of what happens in the real life of coaches. This understanding will provide a solid base for coaches in their coaching career, supporting them in their journey of developing ethical maturity.

This core competency also acts as a baseline, on which each of the three credential levels (ACC, PCC and MCC) is anchored. This chapter outlines that ethics is the essence of how a professional coach shows up, at whatever credential level – although there could be subtle differences in the application of ethics for PCC and MCC credential holders. The increased experience of PCC and MCC credential holders invites them into more varied contracting opportunities to apply coaching ethics in their ethical decision-making as compared to the ACC credential holders.

CHAPTER 4

Exploring Competency 2: Embodies a Coaching Mindset

Peter J. Reding, Peter Hayward and Eileen Laskar

Introduction

Competency 2 focuses on the essence of the coach's being: who they are. This competency is the foundation for all subsequent competencies which focus on what the coach does, and who the coach is being in the coaching session. This is the starting point for good coaching: without being a coach in our mind, we will never act like a coach in our behaviors.

Competency 2 is advocating – in equal measure – for the continuing learning and growth of the coach both as a human being and as a coaching professional.

In this chapter we will first explore the meaning of this competency. In the second part we explore, step by step, each aspect of the competency, reviewing how this shows up at each level: Level 1 (ACC); Level 2 (PCC); Level 3 (MCC); and at a fourth level which we have described as "Growing MCC," reflecting that even MCCs have growth and development musts and needs. As in the chapter on ethical practice, there are no BARS which relate to this competency and so we have used the competency framework to structure our discussion in this section. For each, we highlight which are possible to observe and those which are not possible to observe in a session. Finally, we will consider how a coaching mindset can serve the coach and how it can serve the client, before closing with ten self-evaluation questions for personal reflection.

CHAPTER 4

Table 4.1: Competency 2: ICF Definition of Embodies a Coaching Mindset

Definition: Develops and maintains a mindset that is open, curious, flexible and client-centered.

Table 4.2: Competency 2: Embodies a Coaching Mindset

2.1 Acknowledges that clients are responsible for their own choices.*

1.2 Engages in ongoing learning and development as a coach.**

1.3 Develops an ongoing reflective practice to enhance one's coaching.**

2.4 Remains aware of and open to the influence of context and culture on self and others.*

1.5 Uses awareness of self and one's intuition to benefit clients.*

1.6 Develops and maintains the ability to regulate one's emotions.*

1.7 Mentally and emotionally prepares for sessions.**

1.8 Seeks help from outside sources when necessary.**

* Can be observed/assessed during a coaching session.

** Cannot/unlikely to be observed/assessed during a coaching session.

There are four of the eight elements of Competency 2 that are very important to the coach's continuing development as a professional coach and as a human being that may not be seen in an individual coaching session. These four elements will be addressed in this chapter from the viewpoint of how one could go about fulfilling the need for ongoing learning, reflecting, preparing and seeking that are called out in these elements.

    1.2   Engages in ongoing learning and development as a coach.

    1.3   Develops an ongoing reflective practice to enhance one's coaching.

    1.7   Mentally and emotionally prepares for sessions.

    1.8   Seeks help from outside sources when necessary.

(All the above cannot or are unlikely to be observed/assessed during a coaching session.)

The remaining four of eight elements of Competency 2 that can be observed within a coaching session will be addressed with explanations and examples at the three ICF competency levels – ACC, PCC and MCC – as well as Growing MCC, continued learning and development.

- 2.1 Acknowledges that clients are responsible for their own choices.
- 2.4 Remains aware of and open to the influence of context and culture on self and others.
- 2.5 Uses awareness of self and one's intuition to benefit clients.
- 2.6 Develops and maintains the ability to regulate one's emotions.

(All the above can be observed/assessed during a coaching session.)

Let's begin our journey now through each of these eight elements of Competency 2: Embodies a Coaching Mindset.

2.1 Acknowledges that clients are responsible for their own choices

(Can be observed/assessed during a coaching session.)

Significance of Element 2.1

The profession of coaching is founded on the principle that clients are responsible for their own choices. The belief that the client is resourceful, whole and complete, and has the potential to access the best options for their own life. If the untrained coach steps in with good ideas, advice, options, and so forth, that untrained coach has moved away from coaching. Instead, they may be parenting, managing, teaching, consulting, bullying or mentoring.

What can be observed in relating to this competency is the coach asking the client for their perspectives and choices on the best course of action.

Baseline examples of a coach who knows and honors the client's choices:

- "What is your goal in this session?"
- "What is most important to you?"

- "How would you like to proceed?"
- "How do you want to spend our final ten minutes in this session?"
- "What steps, if any, are you willing to take?"

Competencies Under the Microscope: Behavior Anchored Rating Scale (BARS) and Markers

At the ACC Level

1. Prior to taking on a coaching client, ask the prospective client: *"To what degree (scale of 1–10) do you take responsibility for your own life and life choices?"*
2. Know that some potential coaching client's want/need/desire some other supportive professional (mentor, teacher/trainer, therapist).
3. Remind yourself you are shifting from your other authoritative roles to a coach – *"I do not have the answers for this coaching client!"*
4. Aim for about 80% or more listening, balanced with about 20% or less talking.
5. Educate and remind the client that you do not give advice. *"As discussed earlier and noted in our Coaching Agreement, as your coach, I do not give advice. I do ask you questions and hold a safe space for you to explore what actions or decisions work best for you."*

At the PCC Level

1. Prior to taking on a coaching client, determine if there is a good chemistry, rapport and trust for each of you. *"Am I a good fit for this client and their agenda?" "Can I maintain my role as a coach, without bringing in my bias of how I navigated (or am still navigating) a similar issue in my own life?"*
2. Absolutely know your coaching client has their own best answers:
    a. Even when I am an expert in their area of discovery or challenge,
        - *"I understand."*
        - *"I hear the magnitude of this decision."*

- "My question to you is: What is best for you (your company, your family)?"
   b. Even when they are struggling and saying they really don't know, I ask
      - "What does your gut/heart want from this decision?"
      - "If your child came to you with a similar issue, what advice would you have for them?"
      - "I am here for you to explore your options more deeply or, if you desire to go on to a different topic today, to explore your choice."
   c. Even when they ask you directly for your experience! If the client insists a shortened version can be shared – just for the sake of expressing even more empathy – but the coach refrains from giving tips, sharing ideas with the aim for the client to follow.
      - "Yes, I too have gone through a very similar issue in my life. As your coach, I can relate and empathize, but I absolutely know that you and I are unique, and I have committed to you that I will fully support your exploration for a solution that you will find for yourself and your own set of unique needs and wants. What part of this would you like to start with?"
3. Aims for about 80% or more listening, and about 20% or less talking, summarizing and asking.
4. Keep reminding the client that you do not give advice but are there to support their exploration of what would best work for them.

At the MCC Level

1. You absolutely trust the coaching process, regardless of how long it seems to take the client to progress.
2. You are 100% comfortable having the client be uncomfortable in and during their coaching journey.
3. You feel comfortable in challenging the client, the client's beliefs, the client's assumptions and even the client's goals – from a place of being of service to the client's stated goals, and from a place of absolute non-attachment to your own beliefs, conditioning or how they should decide.

Growing MCC Level

All masters of any knowledge or skill share the following sage advice: "I know so much about my area of mastery, that I have so much more to learn, to explore, to practice!" I have heard masters refer to this as the circle of learning or circle of mastery. At the beginning, my circle of learning was very small. I just needed to learn how to do this. As I continued to learn, my circle of learning grew larger and larger, a circle of how much more there is to learn. Do not let this discourage you. Being a master coach has a direct correlation to your own self-mastery. And your self-mastery has a direct correlation to your coaching mastery.

To what degree am I honoring all people for their differences and similarities without judgment? What types of people, with whom I have had very limited interaction, would I like to know, understand and grow a deeper relationship with?

How Does this Element of "Embodies a Coaching Mindset" Serve the Coaching Client?

The process of coaching is about empowering and developing the coaching client from the inside out, developing them personally and/ or professionally. This inner development can only be accomplished by the client working through their own options, and knowing they are the one to decide – without advice or being told what and how to do it.

This coach, coaching space and coaching process may represent the first time in a client's life that they are required to do this. The outcome may or may not be great. But regardless of the outcome, the outcome will be owned by the client, and it will accelerate the client's learning and development.

The client has been mostly told for their entire lifetime "here is who you are! This is what is expected of you and from you! This is how to behave to be accepted! This is what you need to learn to get ahead!" – and a thousand other messages that have been stored away in that person's subconscious. Coaching empowers the client to know they can, as well as how to, decide for themselves.

How Does this Element of "Embodies a Coaching Mindset" Serve the Coach?

The coach is not burdened with the responsibility of knowing what is in the client's best interest. The coach can listen in a deeper, more holistic way without having to come up with the client's answer. The coach is free from the responsibility of the outcome being "good" or "favorable" or "pleasing" for the client.

The coach can be very pleased when the outcome represents a "win" for the client – we are human above all else. And we can know for both ends of the outcome spectrum that it was solely the client's choice.

Box 4.3: Reflective Questions for the Coach

As a coach, I practice self-awareness of my own choice-making. I have found journalling of great value. The kind of questions I ask in my private journaling as well as post-coaching session reflections include:

1. Was that choice a conscious and aligned choice or an unconscious choice driven by old programming?
2. How might I remember the next time?
3. How much of my current life is a product of alignment with my innermost being?
4. In what areas of my life am I aligned (or not aligned) with my innate core values (versus my conditioned values from society or peer pressure)?
5. What's next in the acceptance of my unique human expression?
6. How can I replace self-recrimination with self-acceptance?
7. How can I replace having to be perfect with "I only need to be true to myself"?
8. How can I replace meeting others' approval with celebrating my unique self?
9. How can I honor all people's differences, without judgment?
10. Where, if any, did my agenda or biases come into this coaching session?

1.2 Engages in ongoing learning and development as a coach

(Cannot/unlikely to be observed/assessed during a coaching session.)

This element of Competency 2 is very important to the coach's continuing development as a professional coach and as a human being that may not be seen in an individual coaching session. This element will be addressed here from the viewpoint of how one could go about fulfilling this element of Competency 2 at each level of one's coaching mastery journey.

Overview

As coaching continues to evolve, it has become multidimensional. It's a profession, a leadership practice and, for many coaches, a way of life. All these dimensions are dynamic in nature. As a result, continuous learning and development are essential. As a profession, coaching continues to evolve based on practice and research. For example, the ICF has continued to review and update the competency model and the Code of Ethics, and researchers are deepening our understanding of the psychology of human behavior, learning and change. It is therefore the responsibility of a coaching practitioner to be intentional about learning as well as contributing to the coaching body of knowledge.

Competencies Under the Microscope: Behaviorally Anchored Rating Scale (BARS) and Markers

Level 1 Journey

This is the foundational level of professional development as the coach invests in their first coach training. The coach should explore and enroll in a school that gives them a holistic experience of coaching as well as adequate coaching practice support to hone their newly learnt skill. Part of the crucial learning at this stage also involves peer learning, especially during the mentor coaching process. It is for this reason that ICF has made the mentor coaching process mandatory for all coaches pursuing their ICF credentials.

Level 2 Journey

Learning and professional development in this phase of growth are more specific. The coach would be having the benefit of coaching practice, feedback from the mentor coaching process as well as the reflective practice (see more of this under 2.3 below). The coach is therefore pursuing further training to deepen their coaching mastery, get more training hours towards the PCC requirements, as well as exploring specific areas of specialization that are of interest to them. CCE programs come in handy as well as further mentor coaching, supervision and peer coaching.

Some reflection questions to guide the choice of learning to engage in include:

1. What has been the consistent feedback from the mentor coaching sessions?
2. What are some of the struggles when it comes to addressing certain client scenarios?
3. Which of the competencies might be challenging to explain to others?
4. What areas of coaching do you want to specialize in?

Level 3 Journey

This growth towards the mastery level is usually the longest development stretch for a coach, and the steepest and most demanding. It is also the refining phase in the life of a coach. The learning here shifts from "How can I deliver the best coaching?" to "How do I become the best coach for my clients?" The coach is therefore seeking to become more grounded and centered, fully confident in who they are, and their coaching becomes an outflow and outward expression of who they are. Some of the guiding questions for a coach in this phase of growth include:

1. Who have I become along this journey of coaching?
2. Who do I want to become in order to serve my clients in the best way possible?

3. How can I be more comfortable in letting the client be, yet challenge them to achieve their goals?
4. What further training should I pursue? Luckily, the ICF has now come up with advanced Level 3 training targeting those on their journey from PCC to MCC and this is going to be handy for those on this developmental path.

Growing MCC

This is a very interesting phase of a coach's lifecycle. The core message is that even after attaining the highest credential (MCC), the learning does not stop. The coach needs to continue entrenching the coaching mindset in their life beyond the coaching spaces. Coaching becomes a way of being beyond professional practice. Coaches at the MCC level would also benefit a great deal from sharing their knowledge with other coaches and peers for cross learning and mastery. It is also a phase of learning through innovation and thought leadership.

Some crucial questions to explore here include:
1. How do you continue to live out coaching in the highest essence possible?
2. What innovations could you add to the coaching profession?
3. What could you challenge in the coaching arena?
4. In what forums could you share your learning and ideas?
5. What additions can you make to the coaching profession?
6. Which peers can you connect with for peer learning?
7. Which publications could you contribute to and subscribe to?

2.3 Develops an ongoing reflective practice to enhance one's coaching

(Cannot/unlikely to be observed/assessed during a coaching session.)

This element of Competency 2 is very important to the coach's continuing development as a professional coach and as a human being that may not be seen in an individual coaching session. This element will be addressed here from the viewpoint of how one could go about fulfilling this element of Competency 2, at each level of one's coaching mastery journey.

Overview

Intentional reflection is one of the most important practices that a coach can develop, and this is cross-cutting regardless of whether one is a new coach or an experienced coach. The learning and mastery reflections take multiple dimensions depending on the stage/phase of growth for the coach.

Competencies Under the Microscope: Behaviorally Anchored Rating Scale (BARS) and Markers

Level 1 Journey

This being the initial phase of the coach's development journey, there's so much for the coach to learn, including solidifying their resolve to pursue coaching and do it with excellence. At this point, they are still seeking to understand coaching and how it differs from other people's development initiatives, as well as how it fits within their grand scheme of things and their life mission. The following might be good reflective questions:

1. Why have you chosen to become a coach?
2. What purpose does coaching serve for you?
3. What does coaching really mean to you?
4. Who do you really want to coach and why?
5. How are you doing as a coach and how can you become even better?
6. What is working well? What are you struggling with?

Level 2 Journey

At this phase of a coach's growth, the reflections become more focused on mastery of practice and profession of coaching. At this point the coach must have experienced coaching, both as a provider and a recipient, for a more wholesome understanding of coaching. The following might serve as good springboard questions for reflections:

1. What are you learning about yourself along this journey of coaching?
2. What is the thread of feedback from your mentor coaching sessions and what does this mean?
3. If you were to elevate your coaching to the next level, what would that look like?
4. What's the anchor to your coaching strengths and how can you leverage that more?
5. How does coaching fuel your spirit? How does coaching fit into your grand scheme of things?
6. What are you learning from your clients and their feedback?

Level 3 Journey

The reflective practice at this level ought to be the deepest and most transformative for both the coach and the clients they serve. Some springboard questions for reflection include:

1. What is the core transformation that you want to bring to the world?
2. What would scale your coaching impact to the next level?
3. Who do you need to continually become to serve your clients?
4. How can you serve the coaching world better?
5. What does the next level of growth look like for you?

2.4 Remains aware of and open to the influence of context and culture on self and others

(Can be observed/assessed during a coaching session.)

Overview

Our cultural background informs how we see and interpret the world. Context is like a backdrop that determines how we respond. Both culture and context determine what we think is possible and not possible. This sub-competency therefore has two angles: being aware of and being open to the influence of context and culture on both how the coach perceives things and the world, as well as how they may perceive the client, their situation, and the entire exploration coaching journey. The coach has therefore to be super conscious of any biases and lenses through which their own context and culture might carry and how that might influence the free flow of the coaching journey. A word of caution here: being aware and open to the influence of culture and context does not mean that the coach cannot challenge the client on those lines; it just means that even this comes with awareness and sensitivity.

Competencies Under the Microscope: Behaviorally Anchored Rating Scale (BARS) and Markers
The Journey from ACC to PCC to MCC and Growing MCC

It is hard to have clear markers for growth from ACC to PCC to MCC because self-awareness and mastery are a life-long journey. As a result we have compressed the comments here into a single section.

At the initial stages of growth of a professional coach, it would be advisable that the new coach invests in self-awareness. This awareness goes beyond the personality profiles to understanding the narrative behind the way one has a certain personality, certain emotional profile, and so forth. Most importantly, understanding their core identity, core beliefs, values and worldview, as well as their emotional triggers. Investing in this process serves the coach in two ways. Firstly, the coach gets to understand their anchors and how they serve them. In the process, they start to embrace the empowering beliefs for their own personal growth. Secondly, the coach becomes aware of the possible biases they may come with based on their past, their culture, sub-cultures and multiple contexts. As the coach matures to mastery, they become more open to being challenged and to having their clients express themselves fully without attachment and judgment.

Important Reflection Questions for Coaches

The following questions might be beneficial to coaches in helping them live out this sub-competency:

1. How much have I invested in my self-awareness?
2. What would investing further in understanding myself look like?

3. What are my significant cultural backdrops and context that I need to be aware of as I work with my clients?

4. What's my default posture and internal response when I am coaching clients whose cultural background is different from mine? What about those where there is a cultural alignment?

5. What might my areas of growth be for this sub-competency?

2.5 Uses awareness of self and one's intuition to benefit clients

(Can be observed/assessed during a coaching session.)

Significance of Element 2.5

The profession of coaching has embraced the concept that every human being has a capacity for intuition. Research evidence suggests that intuition is related to experience; so those with more experience tend to be more accurate in following their intuition, while those with less experience need to be cautious about jumping to follow their intuitive feelings.

The following are baseline examples of a coach who knows and honors their own intuitive connection with their client:

- "I sense an inkling of that. What might this mean for you?"
- "My gut feeling is there might be more to this than you are sharing. If so, what is it?"

Competencies Under the Microscope: Behaviorally Anchored Rating Scale (BARS) and Markers

The Journey to ACC

1. Do not call or label your good ideas and/or advice as intuition.

The Journey from ACC to PCC

1. You may wish, cautiously, to share intuitions.
2. You practice complete silence that allows for your client to process, accept or decline the insight, and to move on.

The Journey from PCC to MCC

1. You draw on intuitions and share these sensitively with clients
2. You are 100% OK when the client indicates that your shared intuition is not about them or their situation. You are 100% unattached to needing them to "Get it now!"

Growing MCC

1. There is yet another level of mastery that we have witnessed, as highly experienced coaches may be unable to articulate why something "feels" this way, but they openly share these insights with clients when it is in the client's interest to do so.

How Does this Element of "Embodies a Coaching Mindset" Serve the Coaching Client?

Coaching is about creating a space for learning and reflection. When the skilled professional coach can draw on their intuition, these insights can provide further opportunities for client learning and development.

How Does this Element of "Embodies a Coaching Mindset" Serve the Coach?

The coach who has developed a capacity to trust their intuition is in flow and can be wholly in service of their client.

Post-session Reflections and Evolution

1. To what degree was I prepared to receive my client-generated intuition(s)?
2. To what degree were my questions informed by my client-generated intuition(s)?
3. To what degree did I tune into my client-generated intuition(s)?
4. When did I ask what seemed like a completely unrelated question? And what might have been the genesis for that question, observation or acknowledgement?

2.6 Develops and maintains the ability to regulate one's emotions

(Can be observed/assessed during a coaching session.)

As a coach, understanding and effectively managing our own emotions is a fundamental competency for creating a positive and productive coaching relationship. Emotions are an integral part of being human, and recognizing this truth is essential in the coaching process. We believe that if we fail to acknowledge and regulate our emotions, we hinder our ability to effectively coach others who are experiencing their own emotional states.

Vulnerability plays a crucial role in developing this competency. Being honest and vulnerable with ourselves allows us to explore our emotional landscape, enabling us to relate authentically with our clients. It is through this emotional self-awareness that we can better understand the impact of our emotions on the coaching process and the client's experience.

While there are no official markers or definitive measures for this competency, it is a journey of continuous growth and mastery. Understanding and embracing our emotions does not imply eliminating them but rather recognizing their presence and learning how to manage them in a constructive way. Now, let's delve into the different skill levels we associate with this competency.

Competencies Under the Microscope: Behaviorally Anchored Rating Scale (BARS) and Markers

The Journey to ACC

At the basic ACC level, you need to develop the ability to self-reflect on your own emotions. This involves taking the time to identify and understand your feelings, acknowledging their presence and finding ways to articulate them verbally. By gaining proficiency in these skills, you will avoid becoming sidetracked or overwhelmed by your own emotions during coaching sessions, ensuring that you can stay focused on your client's needs. Additionally, you must be comfortable handling emotional topics without becoming uneasy to appreciate the power of emotions in the coaching process and recognize them as valuable insights that can lead to breakthroughs for your clients.

The Journey from ACC to PCC

As you progress to the PCC skill level, you will start to delve deeper into understanding what triggers different emotions for you. This involves examining the specific situations, people or circumstances that evoke emotional responses. The journey toward mastering this skill can be achieved and enhanced through frequent and regular self-reflection, meditation, yoga and other mindfulness practices that help provide insights into emotional patterns and triggers. Embracing curiosity and openness to discover more about your own emotions will help you foster a deeper level of empathy and connection with your client.

The Journey from PCC to MCC Level

At the MCC skill level, you need to be able to articulate your emotions with ease and also be able to confidently share them with your client. This level of emotional mastery will allow you to meet your clients at eye level and engage in productive emotional reflections together. Rather than feeling the need to "correct" emotions, you begin to appreciate the emotional landscape as a natural part of the coaching journey. Journaling and regular self-reflection are valuable tools for further honing this skill and will help you to continue your own growth and development.

Summary

As you embrace and develop this competency you will create a safe and trusting space where your clients can explore their own feelings openly. This self-awareness and emotional intelligence lays the foundation for successful coaching partnerships, fostering growth and transformation for both yourself and your client.

1.7 Mentally and emotionally prepares for sessions

(Cannot/unlikely to be observed/assessed during a coach session.)

Mentally and emotionally preparing for coaching sessions is a critical competency that sets the foundation for impactful coaching relationships. As a coach, it is essential to recognize the importance of creating the right space for the client at the right time. This involves filtering out distractions around you and ensuring that you show up with full energy and are focused when meeting your client. Taking ownership of your mindset and approach to each session is key. Viewing coaching sessions not only as an opportunity to support your client, but also as a personal growth and development opportunity will allow you to bring your authentic self into the coaching space. Being emotionally and mentally prepared means understanding the importance of taking breaks before and after coaching sessions and maintaining mental alertness. Prioritizing self-care and well-being will help you to be fully present and attentive during coaching sessions, enhancing the overall coaching experience for both you and your client.

Competencies Under the Microscope: Behaviorally Anchored Rating Scale (BARS) and Markers

Level 1 Journey

At the ACC skill level, you can begin by reflecting on your notes from previous sessions with the client before the next scheduled session. Having a clear understanding of the client's journey helps you track progress and identify areas for exploration and growth in the forthcoming session. Creating a comfortable environment, free from distractions, is vital to establish a safe and focused space for coaching sessions. Making others aware that you cannot be disturbed during coaching hours will help foster an atmosphere conducive to open and honest conversations.

Level 2 Journey

To reach the PCC skill level, you can integrate additional techniques into your daily routines. Taking walks before sessions or undertaking a short body scan can help clear the mind and reduce stress. These practices can help ensure we show up with a fresh perspective each time for a client meeting. Implementing structure into your daily practice and adhering to a calendar can help maintain a sense of organization and preparedness. Flexibility and adaptability are also important. Recognizing that clients may not always be in the right emotional space for coaching and being willing and flexible to reschedule sessions when necessary help build a trusting relationship.

Level 3 Journey

At the MCC level, coaches connect with their clients on a deeper level. Meeting the client at eye level means understanding their needs and meeting them where they are, emotionally and mentally. Having the ability to recognize when a client needs more or less energy to move forward will allow you to adjust and customize your coaching approach accordingly. Being attuned to your client's emotional state enables you to provide the support and encouragement they require at any given moment. Self-reflection is an integral part of the coaching journey. After each session, take the time to reflect on the insights gained and consider how they can inform future sessions. Continuous self-calibration is essential for personal and professional growth, allowing you to refine your coaching skills and enhance the impact you have on your clients' lives. Incorporating these advanced skills into your coaching practice will foster a transformative coaching experience, creating a powerful space for growth, exploration and positive change. As a coach who is mentally and emotionally prepared, you possess the means to guide your clients through their unique journeys and empower them to reach their full potential.

1.8 Seeks help from outside sources when necessary

(Cannot/unlikely to be observed/assessed during a coaching session.)

As coaches, you may experience situations where you encounter challenges and complexities beyond your expertise. As a professional coach, it is vital to acknowledge that seeking help from outside sources when needed is not a sign of weakness but a demonstration of wisdom and self-awareness. This competency involves recognizing your own limits, understanding the limits of coaching and being willing to refer clients to seek additional support when necessary. This is the skill of delegation. By embracing this skill, you will help your client learn not to shoulder the burden of solving everything on their own and foster a growth mindset for their personal and professional development. Being aware of your strengths and limitations is the first step towards becoming an effective coach and this is about knowing your own limits. By recognizing both what you excel at and the areas where you may require support, you can make informed decisions about where and when to seek help from others. And it is always important to recognize the limits of coaching and understand that coaching has its boundaries. As a coach, you may encounter clients dealing with complex challenges that surpass your coaching expertise, or where a different intervention is required such as training or maybe counseling. In such cases, being able to refer them to the appropriate resources or professionals is essential for their well-being and progress.

Competencies Under the Microscope: Behaviorally Anchored Rating Scale (BARS) and Markers

Level 1 Journey

Developing a solid foundation in seeking help is crucial for every coach. Basic skills in this area involve creating a support network and being comfortable with seeking assistance when required. This is likely to include an accredited coach supervisor, as well as maintaining a resource list for you to make referrals to, including a counselor. Having a network of professionals to collaborate with ensures you are ready to act when needed. Finally, it helps to reflect on your own personal triggers and areas that might challenge your objectivity as a coach and become comfortable with seeking help from others, as such referrals are a sign of strength and self-awareness as opposed to a sign of weakness.

Level 2 Journey

As coaches progress in their career, intermediate-level skills come into play, emphasizing the need for agility and proactive professional development. Agility is the capacity to respond quickly and effectively to evolving situations. Coaches should be adaptable and open to learning from diverse sources, including external training and workshops. To enhance coaching proficiency, maintaining a well-structured professional development plan is crucial. This demonstrates a commitment to continuous growth and improvement. Seeking coaching supervision from an accredited supervisor will provide you with valuable insights and feedback that will support your professional development as a coach.

Level 3 Journey

At the advanced level, coaches exemplify a deep commitment to personal and professional growth, cultivating a mindset of openness and curiosity. I believe this can be achieved by maintaining an open mind and being willing to explore new perspectives and approaches to enrich your own coaching practice continually. Even at this level, you should treat yourself with the luxury of having a personal coach! Even as a master coach, seeking guidance from a personal coach enhances self-awareness and provides an opportunity for ongoing development. Nurturing a professional network is also key, this is about staying connected with other coaching professionals through communities, educational events and peer learning. All this will help foster a rich environment for learning and reflection.

Overview

There are two significant themes that are addressed in Competency 2:

1. To be a professional coach you must have a coach's mindset, that believes the coaching client has their own best answers or the client has the capacity and resourcefulness to discover their own best answers.

2. To be an evolving professional coach you must have a life-long commitment to your own self-mastery, learning and development.

Each of these two themes reinforces the other. By holding the mindset that my client is responsible for their own life, choices, commitments, and willingness to move forward or not, as the case may be, then I too as the coach and fellow human being in this relationship also have the obligation and responsibility to know myself, be myself and honor myself to the best of my personal capacity.

Our experience of this journey has been a life-long endeavor. It most certainly did not stop at the achievement of being credentialed as an ICF MCC. As you progress in your journey you will note that you probably became more tolerant, more forgiving and generally more compassionate with yourself. This tolerance allows you to hold a wider space for your clients to explore, find and reflect on the topics they have brought to coaching. In short, you will find a relationship between your developing self-mastery and your coaching mastery.

This competency is all about being loving, caring, compassionate and celebrating yourself and your coaching client as the unique human beings you both are. You are on your way to becoming a brilliant coach. As you navigate your way through these behaviors and markers, you are continuing to grow.

How Competency 2: Embodies a Coaching Mindset Can Serve the Client

The Coaching Client can only be served as a "Coaching Client" if and when their coach is making the client do their own inner and outer work – rather than being told, taught or directed on how to do something or how to be a certain way. It is the coach's resolve to stay in the coaching role that creates a safe, supportive and non-judgmental environment that allows, invites, even insists that the client does the work that only they can do for themselves. When the (untrained or improperly trained) coach interrupts the client from doing their inner work or inner-beingness by giving the client the coach's answer, we rob the client of experiencing and strengthening their ability to develop.

How Competency 2: Embodies a Coaching Mindset Can Serve the Coach

For the coach, Competency 2: Embodies a Coaching Mindset is a necessary first step in your coaching mastery journey. The coach's evolution of self-awareness and self-mastery is amplified by you as the coach holding the safe space for the client to discover who they really are, because the coach too is in the sacred, safe space.

Without this specific mindset you are calling yourself a coach, but are continuing to be the mentor, teacher, parent, consultant that you have been in your past. The profession of coaching does not replace any of these support professionals. However, when you become a trained professional coach, the coach–client relationship shifts both the responsibility and working dynamic from the old "the expert has the answers" to "the coaching client now has the answers." That is, the client is expected to be the expert on their own life, their own journey and their own speed – without pressure from their coach.

The coach facilitates the client's journey of discovery, without giving the client "The Answer."

To conclude this competency, we have provided ten questions for you to use as part of your reflective practice. By reflecting on your practice, and specifically by using a reflective journal to do so, you will enhance the value of your coaching hours, learning and developing with each coaching session that you conduct. We celebrate your desire to continue your learning to become a better coach and a more self-aware human being.

The following are ten reflective questions to ask yourself after each coaching session:

1. What was my predominant mindset in this coaching session?
2. How might I strengthen my "coaching mindset" pre-session and during the session?
3. What triggered me, or what did I have a strong judgment about, in my coaching session? (It is very likely that whatever the judgment is, it is a self-judgment that is unresolved inside of you.)
4. When was the last time I chose to take care of myself? What is calling me that will support my well-being: physically? emotionally? spiritually? intellectually?
5. Have I outgrown my client(s), where they are not ready to benefit from my best work as a coach? Has this client outgrown me, where I am holding them back or not holding a big enough space for their continued growth?
6. How did I prepare for this session? How can I prepare better to be even more present?
7. What part of coaching am I most curious about and want to learn more about next?
8. What is it about this coaching client that I most and/or least appreciate? (Begin to formulate or re-formulate your ideal client profile. Do an ideal client profile every twelve-to-eighteen months at the beginning of your coaching career, and every three-to-five years as a master coach practitioner.)
9. How are my cultural biases helping and/or hindering this coaching client? (This is a call for greater self-awareness, not self-judging.)
10. What aspect of my client's life have I been afraid to ask about? What do I need to learn to support all parts of my client's life in an honorable manner?

Conclusion

In this chapter we have explored Competency 2: Embodies a Coaching Mindset. We have reviewed in detail how this competency shows up at ACC, PCC, MCC and Growing MCC levels as the coach works to "become" a coach (embodiment), as well as acting like a coach (behaviors).

This concludes Competency 2. The next chapter focuses on Competency 3: Establishes and Maintains Agreements.

CHAPTER 5

Exploring Competency 3: Establishes and Maintains Agreements

Judit Ábri von Bartheld, Karen Burke and Kaveh Mir
with contributions from Fran Fisher

Introduction

In this chapter, we look at Competency 3 and note that there are two sides to the Coaching Agreement: the Engagement Agreement and the Session Agreement. Our primary focus will be on the Session Agreement, as this is the aspect assessors can observe, scrutinize and evaluate for evidence during the assessment of a coaching recording. However, this chapter would not be complete without an overview of the Engagement Agreement that highlights the agreements for the entirety of the coaching contract and is the part of ICF Competency 3: Establishes and Maintains Agreements.

A critical reminder when establishing a Coaching Agreement is that clients may not always know their wants and needs. Often, the client lacks conscious knowledge of what they want in a specific coaching session or struggles to express it clearly. It is our responsibility as coaches to assist them in partnership in gaining this awareness, which serves to set the goal for the session. Once the goal is defined and clarified, it is crucial to work together on devising a plan for the client to achieve results during the session and consequently during the coaching program. This plan should be articulated in words encouraging action and moving towards the complete clarity that the client desires.

Table 5.1: Competency 3: ICF Definition of Establishes and Maintains Agreements

Definition: Partners with the client and relevant stakeholders to create clear agreements about the coaching relationship, process, plans and goals. Establishes agreements for the overall coaching engagement as well as those for each coaching session.

Table 5.2: Competency 3: Establishes and Maintains Agreements

3.1 Explains what coaching is and is not, and describes the process to the client and relevant stakeholders.

3.2 Reaches agreement about what is and is not appropriate in the relationship, what is and is not being offered, and the responsibilities of the client and relevant stakeholders.

3.3 Reaches agreement about the guidelines and specific parameters of the coaching relationship, such as logistics, fees, scheduling, duration, termination, confidentiality and inclusion of others.

3.4 Partners with the client and relevant stakeholders to establish an overall coaching plan and goals.

3.5 Partners with the client to determine client–coach compatibility.

3.6 Partners with the client to identify or reconfirm what they want to accomplish in the session.

3.7 Partners with the client to define what the client believes they need to address or resolve to achieve what they want to accomplish in the session.

3.8 Partners with the client to define or reconfirm measures of success for what the client wants to accomplish in the coaching engagement or individual session.

3.9 Partners with the client to manage the time and focus of the session.

3.10 Continues coaching in the direction of the client's desired outcome unless the client indicates otherwise.

3.11 Partners with the client to end the coaching relationship in a way that honors the experience.

Definitions

The Coaching Agreement is indispensable as it provides the foundation for the whole session. Hence, a well-established Coaching Agreement carries the power to lead to a potentially rewarding outcome by the end of the session or for the overall coaching project, as required by the client.

What Do We Mean When We Say "Establishes Agreements?"

The Engagement Agreement

"Establishes agreements" is about bonding and co-creating the structure that will be the scaffolding for the session and the overall assignment. The Coaching Agreement sets the course of the session in partnership between the coach and client. At this stage, it is best when coach and client, jointly identify, formulate and confirm what the client wants to achieve in the session and overall. This process is led by the client and supported by the coach.

This process begins with setting expectations (duration and frequency of meetings, fees, location, etc.), addressing challenges and opportunities (information gathering, stakeholder involvement, ethical guidelines for reporting) and creating a means to navigate uncertainties (goal setting, what successful behavior looks like, how will success/challenges be shared and what does confidentiality look and feel like, etc.). This upfront work supports safety, transparency and clarity, involving all parties. The absence of this upfront agreement for the entire engagement leads to confusion and possible interruptions that can impact coaching. Assessors may note that in less-effective collaborations, the sessions may be interrupted with queries that should have been clarified and agreed upon at the outset of the coaching program.

The Session Agreement

The phrase "establishes agreements," in relation to the session, signifies that the coach's objective is to assist the client by partnering in determining or confirming their session goals as soon as the coaching starts. While it's primarily up to the client to generate content, the coach is responsible for facilitating this process.

The Session Agreement demonstrates how the different competencies are interwoven and supported by other competencies such as "embodies a coaching mindset," "maintains presence," "listens actively" and "cultivating trust and safety." "Evokes awareness" can also play a role since new insight can emerge early in the coaching process as the client shares and searches for what is important for them to explore.

What Do We Mean When We Say "Maintains?"

"Maintains agreements" indicates that it falls within the coach's duties to keep track of initial objectives and support clients in staying focused or changing the focus on their goals as they think best. This implies that there could be alterations or adaptations in what has been initially agreed during the coaching sessions. Within this, re-contracting can happen if the client wishes it. The re-contracting means Competency 3 can be applied multiple times throughout the session.

Comparing the Coaching Engagement Agreement and Coaching Session Agreement Levels

Competency 3 covers both the Coaching Engagement Agreement and the Coaching Session Agreement levels. For this reason, they are separated out to highlight what happens at the session level, and what happens at the engagement level prior to the coaching sessions. We have summarized these distinctions in Table 5.3. (Note that sub-competency 3.8 appears under both headings.)

The Coaching Session Agreement competencies are covered by the ACC and MCC BARS and the PCC Markers. These are the sub-competencies where evidence is sought by the ICF assessors through the BARS and the Markers, where the assessors are looking at the coach behaviors through the statements of the BARS and the Markers.

Table 5.3: Dividing Competency 3 between the Engagement and the Session Agreements

For the Coaching Engagement Agreement **Not Observable by the Assessors**	For the Coaching Session Agreement **Observable by the Assessors**
3.1 Explains what coaching is and is not and describes the process to the client and relevant stakeholders.	3.6 Partners with the client to identify, or reconfirm, what they want to accomplish in the session.
3.2 Reaches agreement about what is and is not appropriate in the relationship, what is and is not being offered, and the responsibilities of the client and relevant stakeholders.	3.7 Partners with the client to define what the client believes they need to address or resolve to achieve what they want to accomplish in the session.
3.3 Reaches agreement about the guidelines and specific parameters of the coaching relationship, such as logistics, fees, scheduling, duration, termination, confidentiality and inclusion of others.	3.8 Partners with the client to define or reconfirm measures of success for what they want to accomplish in the session (for the duration of the session).
3.4 Partners with the client and relevant stakeholders to establish an overall coaching plan and goals.	3.9 Partners with the client to manage the time and focus of the session.
3.5 Partners with the client to determine client–coach compatibility.	3.10 Continues coaching in the direction of the client's desired outcome unless the client indicates otherwise.
3.8 Partners with the client to define or reconfirm measures of success for what they want to accomplish in the Coaching Agreement (for the period of the coaching engagement).	
3.11 Partners with the client to end the coaching relationship in a way that honors the experience.	

As with each of the chapters, we will review each of the BARS for this competency at the ACC and MCC levels as well as the PCC Markers. Finally, we will consider how Competency 3: Establishes and Maintains Agreements serves the coach and clients. We also include suggestions for how to continue to grow, including beyond the MCC level with reflective questions to guide your ongoing learning.

Coaching Behaviors that Support the Coach to Establish and Maintain Agreements

While "establishes agreements" concerns goal-setting exercises, "maintains agreements" revolves around goal-management tasks. The act of maintaining here shouldn't be confused with preserving the original agreement only; instead, it emphasizes always having an agreement and noticing that preliminary agreements tend to shift during coaching interactions.

Competencies Under the Microscope: Behaviorally Anchored Rating Scale (BARS) and Markers

The BARS and Markers only apply for the Coaching Session Agreement. The coaching engagement sub-competencies are not differentiated according to levels, but apply equally to all levels.

Coaching Behaviors that Cultivate, Establish and Maintain Agreement

Establishing a Coaching Agreement for each session is not a mechanical or repetitive task. It requires the intention and action to be carried out with full awareness.

The Journey from ACC to PCC to MCC

The distinctions between ACC-, PCC- and MCC-level coaching become evident through the different depth of inquiry and direct communication tools used in the interactions between coach and client, as these mirror the coach's maturity.

At the ACC level, the coach focuses mainly on identifying the topic of the client, the "what." The coach's job is to show curiosity for what the client wants to share, be it a challenge, a story or their life.

At this level, the coach is often responsible for thinking hard about what to ask the client. This approach essentially may lead the client and set the direction of the conversation by the coach making assumptions based on what they heard regarding what is important for the client to address to achieve their goal.

When the coach leads the conversation, there is less partnership with the client. In full partnership, the coach is not making assumptions or acting on their biases or agendas based on previous experience.

In ACC coaching, there are times when the topic and outcome occasionally merge in one question as the coach works to identify the goal of the session, instead of the two (topic and outcome) being explored in detail as separate components. At this stage, curiosity is the fundamental behavior that the coach demonstrates.

At the PCC level, coach–client partnering is evident as they agree upon the topic, outcome, success measures and the co-creation of the session. The coach looks beyond the "what," the topic, to see and explore the person behind the issue. Through reflective inquiry, the "who," the essence of the client's being, their identity will surface.

The topic and outcome are covered as described at the ACC level of coaching. At the PCC level, the conversation deepens, allowing for learning more about the person and the client's being. The dance between coach and client continues to evolve, but it becomes more and more evident that the client leads and the coach follows. The coach works with what the client offers on two levels: the "what" and the "who." Coach curiosity dominates, and it extends beyond simply learning more about the topic and about how the client relates to the topic: the coach is also seeking to understand the essence of the identity of the client and the triggers that might be hidden behind the issue or challenge that the client is facing. There is yet more space created by the coach for the client, for deeper exploration and reflection about the client's inner world.

As we learn more about the client's perspective, the client will gain more understanding about themselves concerning their situation and the challenges they face.

Here, we understand the outcome and introduce the measure of success (3.2). Additionally, we are also looking here to uncover the client's motivation and commitment, indicating that the client is willing to work on this situation and is ready to find a solution (3.3). At this stage, the coach can trust that the client knows how to tackle their issue and will guide the coach where to begin their exploration and where the priority lies. This allows the coach and client to decide, in partnership, how to best use the time available.

At the MCC level, the Coaching Agreement further elevates the conversation, taking it to deeper levels, spread across more dimensions. The coach aims to find the issue beneath the issue; and this underlying issue is likely to be connected to the client's beingness. MCC coaches spend more time on the Coaching Agreement, as more time is dedicated to learning about the client, about their identity, issues, concerns and/or the challenges they face.

With attention to more details uncovered in the Coaching Agreement, a sharper focus for the whole session can be achieved, leading to greater insights at this early stage and throughout the session, as well as more meaningful outcomes at the end of the session. Greater specificity is achieved through deeper exploration. The topic may be segmented into chunks – lead by the client – that will "guarantee" a more achievable outcome and secure a feeling of success at the end of the session. The conversation is taken to further levels, the coach applying multiple-angle approaches to explore multiple perspectives. The coach explores different dimensions of the identity of the client. The coach is ready to react and respond to the client with a refined sensitivity. This experience helps the coach to recognize that the first topic that crops up often may not be the real one. Usually, the coach finds an underlying agenda with the actual issue hidden behind a story or a belief. A simple story provided at the outset is something that the client is more willing to share; but however convincingly this is presented and however much it seems to be significant, this only scratches the surface of what is hindering the client from making progress with their life and achieving greater success.

EXPLORING COMPETENCY 3: ESTABLISHES AND MAINTAINS AGREEMENTS

Coach sensitivity, combined with coach presence and listening to the coach's intuition, is needed by the coach to pick up what the client says and really means, and contract for that. It often takes courage for the coach to reflect openly, or at times even challenge, the client regarding what the coach observes as emerging from under the surface.

New insights for the client are as likely to happen here as at any other point in the session. The coach must observe not only the words and language the client uses to describe their issue but also how emotions shade these, as well as what other data the body language of the client reveals.

The coach must recognize incongruencies in the client's language, emotions and embodiment. This allows for deeper explorations, which can result in a better definition of the focus among the issues that the client puts on the table. To discern the real important topic, the coach can rely on cues like the tone of voice, the energy level and the emotional shifts that can be observed, in addition to the body language accompanying the client's verbal expressions. The coach's role is to hear the alternatives that emerge and present them back to the client, allowing the client to choose which topic or direction they want to pursue to work on. The client determines the direction of the coaching. Partnering is very strong at the MCC level, so every step of the session can be jointly created and agreed upon.

As the client makes choices, the client can change the coaching course at any time.

When a new choice is made, a new direction for the coaching can emerge; this calls for re-contracting in partnership between coach and client. The Coaching Agreement needs to be replayed during the contracting phase, fully or at least in part, to ensure that the coach and client agree on and are aware of the session's original or revised expected outcome.

BARS and Markers

For the Coaching Engagement Agreement, we look at sub-competencies 3.1, 3.2, 3.3, 3.4, 3.5 and 3.11, which are not part of the ICF assessment system. For the Coaching Session Agreement, we will look at sub-competencies 3.6, 3.7, 3.8, 3.9 and 3.10 through the eyes of the ACC and MCC BARS and the PCC Markers, since these are the ones that the assessors are observing. We review these as aligned to levels 1, 2 and 3 for the Coaching Session Agreement.

Coaching Engagement Agreement Sub-competencies

Sub-competencies 3.1 to 3.5 kick-off before launching the coaching program, and sub-competencies 3.8 and 3.11 stay open for discussion and the refinement of the program throughout the coaching engagement. At the Coaching Engagement Agreement stage, the preparation for the coaching session is identical on all three levels.

3.1 Explains what coaching is and is not and describes the process to the client and relevant stakeholders

This behavior can be demonstrated through the following actions:

- Coach and client in partnership coordinate a meeting – one or more – involving pertinent stakeholders (such as sponsors, human resource managers, clients, managers, business partners and other relevant individuals) to ensure a collective understanding of the parameters and boundaries of coaching.

- The coach can effectively convey the following message: "In preparation for our coaching engagement, I propose a meeting where I can elaborate on the concept of coaching, outline the expected coaching process as we collaborate and provide you with an opportunity to address any questions you may have. We need to agree whether coaching is needed or any other form of human and/or leadership development."

For example:

- "Can we schedule a pre-coaching meeting to clarify the coaching process and address any questions or concerns from all involved parties?"

- "Let's set up a meeting to delve into the coaching concept, go over the expected process and provide an opportunity for questions."

3.2 Reaches agreement about what is and is not appropriate in the relationship, what is and is not being offered, and the responsibilities of the client and relevant stakeholders

This behavior can be shown through the following actions:

- The coach, client and stakeholders engage in candid conversations to outline the expectations, given that individual responsibilities are also agreed on. This includes understanding the distinctions between coaching, consulting, mentoring and therapy. These insights serve as a guidepost for the upcoming coaching journey, providing insight on potential scenarios. Additionally, the dialogue identifies who is responsible for completing the development plan and goal attainment.

- An approach is established, offering a clear resolution pathway if any party encounters confusion or concerns within the coaching relationship.

- Embracing a commitment to ethical conduct, the coach will share a copy of the ICF Code of Ethics. This encompasses Part 4: Ethical Standards and examines the areas of Responsibility to Client, Practice and Performance, Professionalism, and Society in sections I–IV. These discussions highlight the landscape of ethical integrity and professional accountability for all parties. This will also determine the reporting scheme, the ethical rules and the obligation of confidentiality applicable to the coach's behavior.

For example:

- "Can we collaboratively clarify your [the client's] role and primary responsibility for ensuring the attainment of our coaching goals?"

- "If any concerns arise in our coaching relationship, how should we effectively address and resolve them?"

3.3 Reaches agreement about the guidelines and specific parameters of the coaching relationship, such as logistics, fees, scheduling, duration, termination, confidentiality and inclusion of others

This behavior can be shown through the following actions, in which the coach, client and stakeholders confirm:

- **Logistics:** Practical details of the frequency of coaching, on which platform (virtual) or location (in person). Discussion of implications if coaching must be delayed or rescheduled.

- **Fees:** Agreement on fees for the coaching, including the total cost, payment schedule, how additional charges will be managed and cancellation guidelines.

- **Scheduling:** Agreement on a cadence of coaching sessions and how/if stakeholders will be included – for example, in a tri-party meeting.

- **Duration:** Clarification of the length of the overall coaching program, the number of sessions and the duration of each session.

- **Termination:** Discuss and confirm the terms under which either party can end the coaching relationship and the notice required. (Explain to clients that confidentiality continues even after program termination.)

- **Confidentiality:** This sub-competency also connects to Competency 1: Demonstrates Ethical Practice, and the reader should refer to the chapter describing that competency. The behaviors that exhibit this competency are to discuss and agree upon the level of confidentiality that will govern the coaching sessions. This information may include what information shared by the client will be kept private if there are any exceptions to confidentiality. These should be discussed and agreed upon before starting any coaching program. An example might be: "360 assessments are to be confidential to the client and coach, while the cadence of coaching or ceasing coaching before the program ends is not confidential."

- **Inclusion of others:** This sub-point addresses whether other individuals (such as the client's manager, team members, human resources personnel, colleagues or family members) will be involved in the coaching process, to what extent and at what point.

For example:

- "Confidentiality extends to all aspects agreed upon by both parties, even after the coaching collaboration ends or terminates, including 360 results and psychometric test outcomes. However, information related to the coaching pace, schedule or any early termination of the program can be considered not confidential if a joint communication plan is agreed upon."

- "How do you envision involving other individuals, like your manager, team members, colleagues, family members and friends, in the coaching process and to what extent?"

3.4 Partners with the client and relevant stakeholders to establish an overall coaching plan and goals

Vital elements of partnering include:

- **Discovery:** This process typically starts during the initial chemistry meeting between the coach and client. Ultimately, the client has the final say in selecting who they want to work with. This dialogue serves to uncover the goals and challenges of both the client and the relevant stakeholders and sponsors of the coaching engagement. The coach, client, stakeholders and sponsors must collectively address and align their expectations for the coaching journey. A thoroughly discussed Coaching Agreement between all parties enhances and upholds the reputation of the coaching profession.

- **Program Goals:** The program goals should be closely aligned with the overall life and business goals of the client, stakeholders, sponsors and, in the context of corporate coaching, the company. For all coaching modalities, the program goals must harmonize with the client's overarching objectives and be something the client is motivated to work on.

- **Coaching Plan/Development Plan:** Informed by input from the client, stakeholders, sponsors and applicable assessment tools, a collaborative process ensues to develop a coaching plan. This plan encompasses goals, strategies, milestones, responsibilities and key actions.

- **Communication:** Maintaining transparent communication with the client, stakeholders and sponsors throughout the coaching process is a vital part of partnering and of top importance to align perspectives, expectations and objectives. Clients and stakeholders should understand you are committed to partnering with them to foster open and effective communication.

- **Regular Check-ins:** Schedule regular check-ins so that stakeholders/sponsors are fully included in the coaching program and are informed about its progress in line with what the Code of Ethics and agreements between the parties permit. For example, "to be most successful in this Coaching Agreement, a best practice is to have a mid-point check-in with client, coach and stakeholders. This helps to ensure the coaching engagement is in alignment with the client's, sponsor's and organization's goals."

- **Securing Buy-in and Coachability:** Ensuring consensus amongst all parties regarding the coaching plan, coaching frequency, confidentiality protocols and the path forward is vital. In cases where continuing coaching poses challenges for the client, coach or organization, transparent discussions are crucial. These conversations determine the optimal course of action for potentially pausing or concluding the coaching engagement if that turns out to be necessary.

3.5 Partners with the client to determine client–coach compatibility

This sub-competency highlights that the coach collaborates with the client to assess whether a good fit exists between the client and the coach. This process often involves chemistry meetings or similar preliminary connections to ensure that both parties are comfortable working together and, in partnership, can build a solid foundation for their coaching sessions. The coach's attitude, style and experience must match the client's needs, learning style, preferences and expectations of coaching.

Examples of partnering with clients and stakeholders:

- "Our six-month program will have twelve meetings, usually spaced every two weeks. However, we can adjust the meeting schedule to suit your needs. What works best for you?"
- "What are your main goals and challenges, and how can we ensure everyone's expectations align for our coaching journey?"
- "How can we create a coaching plan that reflects your goals and needs and ensures clear responsibilities and milestones along the way?"
- "How can we demonstrate our commitment to fostering open and collaborative communication?"
- "How can we ensure our communication remains transparent and effective throughout this coaching journey?"
- "How can we proactively address any potential communication challenges during the coaching process?"
- "Are there specific channels or regular check-ins to help us align our perspectives, expectations and objectives?"

- "How would you like to conduct our mid-point review session of how things are going in this coaching program?"
- "I hear you [the client] and the stakeholder identifying potential additional outcomes. Would you like to explore some other goals now?"

Examples of compatibility checking:

- "Have you worked with other coaches before? What worked well, and what was less effective?"
- "How will you know if we are a good fit working together?"
- "Do you feel that my coaching experience and attitude are a good fit for your needs and goals?"
- "Does my approach meet your learning needs?"

To be coachable, clients need several critical success factors:

1. **Topic:** The client has a topic or focus area. If the client is unsure of a topic, the coaching process can begin with clarifying the topic. If the client does not find a topic important enough to work on, then that client, at that point, may not be coachable.
2. **Knowledge of Coaching:** The coach and client assess the client's understanding of coaching and ensure there is clarity between coaching and other helping professions such as therapy, mentoring or consulting. Ensuring the client knows the coaching process is critical to help manage expectations and align the coaching relationship.
3. **Willingness and Commitment:** The coach gauges the client's willingness to engage in the coaching process actively and their commitment to make the necessary changes in their lives. Stress and/or other external influences can sometimes impact a person's readiness for coaching, so motivation to reflect and readiness for change are important indicators.
4. **Key Traits:** Traits typically associated with coachability include, among others, openness to reflection and to receive feedback, self-awareness, a growth mindset, a desire to work on self-improvement and a willingness to change.
5. **Coach–Client Compatibility:** The coach and the client need to assess compatibility, a mismatch in personalities, beliefs or a

difference in the set of values which can hinder client progress, though if handled transparently, it can be managed. Suppose coach-client rapport declines for either known or unknown reasons. In that case, exploring alternative coach support for the client is essential.

6. **Flexibility:** The coach should acknowledge that adjustments to plans may be necessary due to evolving client or organizational needs and goals. Suppose the coaching plan needs to be adapted when changing the original objectives. In that case, involving stakeholders and sponsors beyond the client in the adjustment process is critical.

3.8 Partners with the client to define or reconfirm measures of success for what the client wants to accomplish in the coaching engagement or individual session

Here, "success" means that of the whole coaching program. Prior to starting the coaching engagement, all parties involved in the program agree on what success will look like at the end of the program.

Coach behaviors at this stage, in reference to the coaching engagement:

- Coach curiosity to learn about the needs of all the parties.
- Listening skills to hear the views and needs of all parties involved.
- Being a good observer and making observations as needed to reach a common understanding on the goal of the program.
- Sharing ethical practices for clarity on the roles and for the transparency of the program.

3.11 Partners with the client to end the coaching relationship in a way that honors the experience

Various circumstances can lead to the termination of a coaching relationship, such as the conclusion of the agreed period or reaching the goals agreed on. Upon reaching the end of coaching, the coach must reflect upon and adhere to the terms of the Coaching Agreement and ethical code. When the client is ready or expresses the will to terminate, it is important to honor their wish. This is especially important when ending the agreement prematurely. In addition, a coach needs to discern the appropriate forms of communication necessary at this stage to engage with sponsors and other stakeholders involved effectively.

For example:

- "I acknowledge your request for termination and wish you success in your future goals. I want to request that you complete the feedback questionnaire."

At the end of the engagement period, the coach invites the client to review progress, goals achieved and lessons learned and to explore what might be next for the client. The coach pays attention to the relationship and how the client feels about ending the support relationship.

The coach invites the client to reflect, renew and recommit to the goals achieved during the engagement period. The coach invites the client to share their perception of the outcome and relationships.

For example:

- "I am curious to know how you would describe your feelings now we are approaching the end of our engagement."
- "I propose that we review our feelings and perceptions of how we partnered during the sessions."
- "I am interested to hear how you integrate the learning from the sessions."
- "What were the top key coaching moments in our session?"
- "Knowing what you know now and given our progress in the sessions, what is next for you?"

Before the end of the engagement period

When multiple stakeholders are involved, the coaches at all levels must adhere to the ethical guidelines even when the Coaching Agreement prematurely terminates, such as when a client expresses a wish to exit their organization.

For example:

- "I want to invite you to share your views about our progress and then, with your permission, share my feelings on our progress."

- "Listening to what you share and observing previous sessions, I feel something is not working. I am interested to hear your views."
- "Now that we have both agreed to terminate the relationship, how would you like us to act on it?"

Level 1 Aligns with Associate Certified Coach (ACC)

Competency 3: Establishes and Maintains Agreements

Definition: Partners with the client and relevant stakeholders to create clear agreements about the coaching relationship, process, plans and goals. Establishes agreements for the overall coaching engagement as well as those for each coaching session.

Coaching Session Agreement Sub-competencies

3.6 Partners with the client to identify, or reconfirm, what they want to accomplish in the session.

3.7 Partners with the client to define what the client believes they need to address or resolve to achieve what they want to accomplish in the session.

3.8 Partners with the client to define or reconfirm measures of success for what they want to accomplish in the coaching engagement *or individual session* (for the duration of the session).

3.9 Partners with the client to manage the time and focus of the session.

3.10 Continues coaching in the direction of the client's desired outcome unless the client indicates otherwise.

ACC BARS

A3.1 Coach invites the client to identify their desired coaching outcome.

A3.2 Coach and client reach an agreement on what the client wants to accomplish in the session.

EXPLORING COMPETENCY 3: ESTABLISHES AND MAINTAINS AGREEMENTS

A3.3 Coach shows curiosity about the client and how the client relates to what they want to accomplish.

A3.4 Coach attends to the agenda set by the client throughout the session, unless the client indicates otherwise.

A3.1 Coach invites the client to identify their desired coaching outcome

- "You mentioned earlier several things including: the state that you want to be in, how you want to approach your husband, how you approach and observe others, and how to manage the studio. Where would you like to focus today?"
- "If you were to narrow in on the outcome that would be valuable to you today, what would that outcome be?"
- "What is your topic for this session?"

A3.2 Coach and client reach an agreement on what the client wants to accomplish in the session

- "What would you like to accomplish today in our session?"
- "What would you like to come out of this coaching session with?"
- "What will you be happy with in this session as an outcome?"
- "What would success look like for you today?"
- "What would you want to take away from this session?"

A3.3 Coach shows curiosity about the client and how the client relates to what they want to accomplish

- "'Resentment' – that's an interesting word choice. Can you share more about what that means to you in relation to your topic?"
- "I noticed a shift in your energy as you were talking about some of the things that come up when you outlined your topic. I'm curious – is there a bigger issue to explore for you here?"
- "How do you envision involving other individuals, like your manager, team members, colleagues, family members and friends, in reaching your goal, and to what extent?"
- "How is this relevant to you today in relation to what you want to achieve?"

- "What meaning does this hold for you now?"

A3.4 Coach attends to the agenda set by the client throughout the session, unless the client indicates otherwise

- "You mentioned you wanted to come up with a plan for reducing procrastination and I am noting you just mentioned you wanted to speak up more in meetings. Is that something you would like to shift to?"

Box 5.4: Reflective Questions for the Coach at the ACC Level

1. Did you ask the client to identify the topic?
2. Did you confirm what the client identified to be the topic?
3. Did you ask about the expected outcome?
4. Did you show curiosity about the client's issue?

Level 2 Aligns with Professional Certified Coach (PCC)

Competency 3: Establishes and Maintains Agreements

Definition: Partners with the client and relevant stakeholders to create clear agreements about the coaching relationship, process, plans and goals. Establishes agreements for the overall coaching engagement as well as those for each coaching session.

3.1 Coach partners with the client to identify or reconfirm what the client wants to accomplish in this session

- "I heard you saying you want to talk about how to delegate more to your team. Is that the topic you want to cover, or would something else be more useful for you in our time together now?"
- "I heard you say you want to have a clearer plan for finishing your PhD. What would be most helpful to talk about?"

3.2 Coach partners with the client to define or reconfirm measures of success for what the client wants to accomplish in this session

- "Wanting a definite direction for 2024, how will you evaluate that we have reached this outcome?"
- "You said you wanted to feel energy towards beginning to exercise again. What would you like as an outcome when we are complete today?"

3.3 Coach inquires about or explores what is important or meaningful to the client about what they want to accomplish in this session

- "How is this relevant for you today?"
- "Where is your motivation/commitment to solve this issue today in our session?"

3.4 Coach partners with the client to define what the client believes they need to address to achieve what they want to accomplish in this session

- "I noticed a shift in your energy as you were talking a bit about some of the things that come up in your working relationship. Would you like to explore that first or how should we get started?"
- "Where is your priority here?"
- "What is the best approach we can adopt for our discussion of your issue?"

Box 5.5: Reflective Questions for the Coach at the PCC Level

1. Did you explore what the client wanted to accomplish?
2. Did you check how it would be clear for the client that they have reached the desired outcome in the session?
3. Did you explore why that topic is relevant for the client?
4. How did partnering appear at the contracting stage?

CHAPTER 5

Level 3 Aligns with Master Certified Coach (MCC)

Competency 3: Establishes and Maintains Agreements

> **Definition:** Partners with the client and relevant stakeholders to create clear agreements about the coaching relationship, process, plans and goals. Establishes agreements for the overall coaching engagement as well as those for each coaching session.

Regarding the examples given below for the MCC BARS, please take into consideration that in order to meet the requirements for MCC-level coaching, the contextual and relational aspects of the coaching conversation need to be taken into account. These in their wholeness serve as evidence for whether, in the given coaching, a sufficient depth and variety of dimensions of the client's life, purpose and identity have been fully explored and responded to by the coach.

M3.1 Coach partners with the client to explore the topic or focus of the session at a level that is meaningful to the client

1. Coach: "Planning the future sounds like a wonderful topic, especially when I look at your video background – it gives me a sense of lightness shining through."

    "Planning for 2024 is an inspiring topic. What aspects would you like to focus on?"

2. Coach: "I will try to capture what you said and use the metaphor of balls in the air. It sounds that it's like you're being a masterful acrobat by juggling all these balls, with one of these balls being your practice as a coach and you want to bring your whole self into coaching to be the best coach for them. Is this session about creating more of that best coach in you, or revealing more the best coach, or… something else?"

3. Coach: "So would it be accurate to note three parts? One is the deep, meaningful, transformational impact you would like to have on people; the second is the way you do that in a meaningful inquiring, I think you said an "invitational" way; the third element

is who are you being as a coach with them in that process, and how you bring your whole self into that process?"

Client: "Yeah. It's a really good summary."

Coach: "So, if we are addressing this important question for you, what would be a good outcome in this conversation? The who and the what and the how?"

Client: "Yeah."

Coach: "And you said that, that might be too much for one conversation. If we use our time well, and if we have a meaningful and impactful conversation for you, then what do you think might be possible?"

M3.2 Coach partners with the client to keep the desired outcome as a guide to the coaching conversation in a flexible, gentle and natural manner

1. The coach is still working on the Coaching Agreement fifteen minutes into the conversation: Coach: "What would you like us both to be listening for as we move through our conversation?"

2. Coach at length explores the feelings emerging for the client in the session and afterwards says: "How might the lingering sadness and acknowledgement of those feelings be supported in our time today?" Follow-up question from Coach: "Yeah. What do you think would be the most meaningful conversation we could have around this to support you, in not bringing these sorts of lingering feelings of disappointment into your upcoming offsite?"

3. Coach: "What specifically is important for you in becoming that whole person coach with all the ingredients you have just listed now?"

M3.3 Coach notices subtle shifts in the conversation and invites the client to change direction if the client desires

Coach: "I'm wondering if there's another story within that, that your peer is not a strong teammate. What comes up for you?"

Coach: "I heard you say that might require a lot of meditation or pre-empting. I understood that to be a lot of preparation."

Client: "Yep."

Coach: "I'm wondering if that's the only way into compassion, or if there's another place that we might explore?"

Coach: "Okay, and I noticed that now you reversed the order, because before it was who, what and how. And now it sounds like this is the who. Which one shall we explore?"

Box 5.6: Reflective Questions for the Coach at the MCC Level

1. How deeply did you explore what the client named to be in their focus for the session?
2. Through how many lenses did you explore the desired outcome of the session?
3. How did you achieve partnering at the contracting phase of the coaching?
4. What shifts in the conversation did you notice as the client went deeper into exploring what they wanted to work on during the session?

Growing MCC

You are on your way to becoming a masterful coach. As you navigate your way through these behaviors and markers, you are continuing to grow. A coach who achieves their Master Certified Coach (MCC) accreditation recognizes this is not a destination. They will continue honoring the competencies, maintaining their self-reflective practice and demonstrating a commitment to ongoing learning and development.

Case Study

At the beginning of the session, the client expressed her concern about her lack of professional advancement within her organization. She noted that some of her former mentees, who are younger, are surpassing her in their careers. The client doubts her ability to reach Level 7, as she has remained at Level 6 for over three years.

The coach started by acknowledging the emotional state of the client then went into asking an open-ended question: "How best can we use our time together?" The client mentioned that she "would like you to help me with my next promotion review." The Coach inquired about the words the client used: "What kind of help are you expecting to receive from me?" The client replied, "I am concerned about my lack of achievement in the organization. Some of my former mentees, who are younger, are surpassing me in their careers."

The coach empathizes with the client by saying, "I acknowledge hearing that it is hard to see your mentees surpassing you in their careers." The coach inquired about the client's words: "What do you think the feeling of 'concern' is telling you?" The client replied, "Well, it has been three years since I have received any promotion, and I can see other people younger than me getting promoted." The coach inquires how the client perceives their world and reflects on what the client communicated to ensure the client's clarity and understanding of what has been heard. "Tell me if I am hearing you correctly. It seems you are comparing yourself to others, believing they are doing something better or different from you." The client replied, "Yes, I am constantly doubting that I am good enough to get a promotion."

The coach partnered with the client to reconfirm what the client wanted to accomplish in this session. "It sounds like you want to explore in this session how your doubt about yourself being good enough might be connected to the topic you mentioned at the beginning, which was about your promotion." The client replied, "Yes, I am doubting myself, and now that you said it, I think it is my doubt in self that I need to explore in the session." The coach then explored what is important or meaningful to the client and what they want to accomplish in this session. "Let's say you do not do anything about the doubting self; what could happen?" The client confirmed how much she thinks the topic of doubting herself is vital to her goal. The coach partnered with the client to define the outcome of the session and the measure of success for the client's goal in this session. "By the end of the session, what could we achieve that would be useful for you in clearing your doubting self?" The coach then partners with the client to define what the client believes they need to address, where the client's priority lies regarding what they want to accomplish in this session. "Where is a good place for us to start exploring your self-doubt?"

The coach can several times play back and confirm what the client says to qualify working in the partnership as expected in coaching, and to facilitate the client's understanding of what is really relevant for them to work on in the session.

How "Establishes and Maintains Agreements" Serves the Client

During the formation of our Coaching Agreement, clients can express themselves freely and share what's on their mind, downloading their joy and sorrow in a safe environment. They also get the space to think and reflect on the session's purpose with the possible outcome, which can lead to client progress to personal and professional growth. Clients experience the coach's undivided attention, judgment-free listening and unconditional acceptance during this stage. The coach's curiosity and listening skills dominate here.

As clients share their stories and challenges, new insights and discoveries emerge for them, leading to the identification of priorities and increased clarity around their goals. If clients are stuck, the Coaching Agreement helps them uncover desired and possible outcomes, which can energize them and offer them a positive perspective.

The Coaching Agreement serves as the professional structure or framework for initiating and encouraging the client's reflections, providing a safe and structured environment for clients. It's the initial evidence that coaching brings immediate value to the client when practiced with the competencies – in this case with the Coaching Agreement.

How "Establishes and Maintains Agreements" Serves the Coach

The Coaching Agreement supports the coach with a structure that gives the backbone to the session. It presents a logic that establishes a professional bond that holds the whole session and is key to a successful coaching conversation.

The Coaching Agreement competency is like opening a treasure chest for the coach. Through the different stages of this competency, a whole and creative human being emerges in the person of the client, whom the coach empowers to lead the dance in the coaching process.

As the client shares, placing their trust in the coach, the coach's curiosity grows and they learn more about the different dimensions of the client's life. The conversation naturally deepens as the coach gains a deeper understanding of the client's issues, emotions and identity. This phase allows the coach to experience the essence of the coaching profession: to support an individual in their development.

If a Coaching Agreement lacks the necessary specificity, this can impact the rest of the session: the coach may encounter difficulties such as leaving enough time for the closing part of the session, including time for designing accountability, co-creating closure or excessive circling around issues that are not pointing to the agreed outcome – especially if no outcome is agreed – and not contributing to the session's success.

A solid Coaching Agreement saves time for the coach by covering sufficient details while identifying and confirming the focus of the client's goal.

There is a tool coaches can refer to that sets the sequence for the coaching inquiry, known as STOKERS.

Table 5.7: STOKERS

Subject	What would you like to focus on in this session?
Timing	Given that we have thirty minutes today, what would be a good use of that time?
Outcome	What would you like to have achieved by the close of the session?
Knowledge	How would you know you have that outcome?
Energy	What is making this topic important for you today?
Role	How best can we partner to achieve this?
Start	Where would you like to start?

(Pedrick, 2020)

This framework supports the coach and at the ACC level it can be helpful; but applying these questions formulaically can be counter-productive. It can seem like an AI ChatGPT talking to the client. This formulaic structure is valuable to start with, but it is often better to use the above questions freely as you continue to grow your coaching skills and incorporate in your own style at the PCC and MCC levels.

Reflective Questions

1. How effectively did the Engagement Agreement assist the client's readiness for the coaching session?
2. How curious and patient was I in listening at the start of coaching to support the client in articulating the session's goal?
3. How well did we partner to identify and reconfirm the session's goal and outcome?
4. How well did I discover deeper roots beneath their goals rather than merely dwelling on surface narratives?
5. How well did I restrain my preconceptions on what the client should or needs to focus on compared to partnering to identify the session's focus?
6. How well did I partner with the client, identifying the root motivation for the session's goal?
7. How proactive was I in holding us accountable for the session goal and the outcome of the session, including possible shifts in the focus, as identified by the client?
8. How well did I partner with the client to decide on the session's direction at the contracting stage?
9. To what depth did I follow the Coaching Agreement?
10. How well did I respond to the client rather than being occupied with following my script?

Conclusion

In this chapter we have explored Competency 3: Establishes and Maintains Agreements. We have reviewed in detail how this competency shows up at ACC, PCC and MCC levels as the coach works at both the assignment level and the session level to create and maintain an agreement for the coaching work. The next chapter is focused on Competency 4: Cultivates Trust and Safety.

CHAPTER 6

Exploring Competency 4: Cultivates Trust and Safety

Chérie Carter-Scott and Michael Pomije

Introduction

Embarking on the journey to become an accomplished, certified coach necessitates considerable dedication, as well as an investment of time, energy and resources. It demands a relentless commitment to personal growth, striving continually to manifest the best version of yourself.

To effectively facilitate this transformative journey, coaches must cultivate an environment of trust and safety – these elements form the bedrock of the coaching process. In essence, the coach not only facilitates the journey but also ensures a supportive, secure space for the client's personal exploration, revelation and continued development.

Trust and safety involve the creation of an empowering space where clients feel wholly supported and free from judgment or criticism, ensuring they can navigate their path to growth in a trusting environment. To excel in this competency, a coach must cultivate a sense of self-trust, ensuring that clients feel safe and supported. Furthermore, it's about creating a space where clients can express vulnerabilities with confidence, knowing their coach will handle them with care and discretion.

Safety extends beyond the emotional; it involves setting clear boundaries and maintaining a professional demeanor that makes clients feel secure in their coaching relationship. By embedding the principles of trust and safety into every aspect of your coaching practice, you enable a transformative experience that allows clients to explore their potential fully and authentically.

In this chapter we will firstly explore the meaning of this competency. In the second part we explore, step by step, each aspect of the competency, reviewing how these show up at each level: ACC, PCC, MCC and at a fourth level which we have described as Growing MCC, reflecting that even an MCC has growth and development needs. Like the authors of the previous chapters, we have used the ICF BARS and Markers.

Table 6.1: Competency 4: The ICF Definition of Cultivating Trust and Safety

Definition: Partners with the client to create a safe, supportive environment that allows the client to share freely. Maintains a relationship of mutual respect and trust.

Table 6.2: Competency 4: Cultivates Trust and Safety

4.1 Seeks to understand the client within their context which may include their identity, environment, experiences, values and beliefs.

4.2 Demonstrates respect for the client's identity, perceptions, style and language and adapts one's coaching to the client.

4.3 Acknowledges and respects the client's unique talents, insights and work in the coaching process.

4.4 Shows support, empathy and concern for the client.

4.5 Acknowledges and supports the client's expression of feelings, perceptions, concerns, beliefs and suggestions.

4.6 Demonstrates openness and transparency as a way to display vulnerability and build trust with the client.

Given your aspiration to become a certified coach, now is an opportune moment to delve into the competency of cultivating trust and safety. These twin pillars of the coaching relationship are rooted in the profound and empowering connection that forms between coach and client. Beyond that, they extend to encompass the broader environment, confidentiality and the coach's absolute abstention from any negative judgments.

Trust and safety encapsulate a realm where clients are encouraged to express themselves openly, knowing that their disclosures will be treated with the utmost respect and discretion. This kind of environment sets the stage for deep empathy – the capacity of the coach to fully understand, resonate with and respond to the client's experience. The cultivation of trust and safety enables a bond that not only promotes sincere dialogue but also paves the way for meaningful growth and transformation.

Definitions

What Do We Mean When We Say "Trust?"

Trusting your client means that you believe in your heart that they will be honest, transparent and will fully disclose their challenges to you, their coach. Trusting your client means that you don't need to second guess them, to read between the lines or to figure out their motives, capability or solutions. Trusting your client means that you believe that they are honorable, and will come to you if and when they have an issue with you as their coach; it also means that your client will communicate whatever their issues are with you, including: your approach, your style, your tone, your pace, your tolerance and patience, and/or your methods. You, as their coach, also trust your client to have sufficient knowledge, experience and wisdom to work on their topics in order to transform their concerns and themselves into ideal outcomes.

What Do We Mean When We Say "Safety?"

Safety, in its broadest sense, is a state of being protected from harm. Safety, in coaching, means that the coach will abide by and honor the ICF Ethical Guidelines; in addition, the coach will absolutely respect and hold sacred the confidentiality in the coaching relationship. In addition, the coach creates an environment where the client feels secure, respected and comfortable when fully expressing themselves without any fear of negative judgment, ridicule, criticism or harm.

Safety in the coaching context comprises three essential dimensions: physical, emotional and psychological.

1. **Physical safety** pertains to the tangible environment where the coach and client engage, virtually and in face-to-face sessions. It is the coach's responsibility to ensure that this physical space is not only comfortable but also devoid of any threats to the client's well-being. This includes mitigating risks of physical harm or injury, and in the era of pandemics, maintaining rigorous health protocols to prevent illness.

2. **Emotional safety**, a cornerstone of the coaching relationship, is characterized by the freedom for clients to voice their emotions without reservation. It implies a promise from the coach that the client can openly share their feelings and thoughts without fear of negative repercussions. This environment of unconditional acceptance, free from any risk of ridicule, rejection or emotional shaming, facilitates open communication and uncovers the client's deepest sentiments. In fostering this level of trust and profound connection, emotional safety is instrumental in the coaching process.

3. **Psychological safety** embodies a sense of mutual respect that paves the way for partnership, candid disclosure and cooperative problem-solving between the coach and client. In a psychologically safe space, clients feel comfortable being vulnerable, taking calculated risks and expressing their authentic selves.

All three facets of safety – physical, emotional and psychological – are integral to the efficacy of coaching. They foster an environment that not only promotes meaningful interaction and introspection but also underpins the transformative power of the coaching process.

Coaching Behaviors that Cultivate Trust and Safety

As a coach, engaging with and responding to the client in ways that communicate acceptance, value and acknowledgment is essential. This perception of the client is reflected through recognizing, respecting, appreciating and affirming their uniqueness. The client's distinct identity, perceptions, beliefs, self-expression, talents, insights and ideas are not only welcomed into the coaching conversation but also celebrated as intrinsic to their personal journey, their self-relationships and their interactions with the world.

Along with other markers, trust and safety reflect a coaching mindset steeped in unwavering confidence in the client's capabilities. The coach sees the client as inherently creative, resourceful and whole, honoring the successes they've achieved and the courage and strength they've shown along the way. This recognition goes hand in hand with an understanding of the client's individual and environmental challenges.

The coach's approach is framed and contextualized with a deep acknowledgment of how the client's context – their cultural background, identity, sexual orientation, race and life experiences – has shaped who they are. This understanding is key to recognizing how they perceive and engage with the world, providing invaluable insights into the client's unique journey. Through this lens, the coach empowers the client to navigate their path forward, using their unique strengths and perspectives.

Cultivating trust and safety in coaching conversations is essential to establish a productive and supportive environment: "In this competency, you, as the coach, are being evaluated in terms of your capacity to partner with the client to create a safe, supportive environment that allows the client to share freely."

Competencies Under the Microscope: Behaviorally Anchored Rating Scale (BARS) and Markers

Let's examine the behaviors and markers that indicate both comprehension and deployment of this competency. Since, in ICF, there are three distinct levels – Associate Certified Coach (ACC), Professional Certified Coach (PCC) and Master Certified Coach (MCC) – we will specify the differing requirements at each level to ensure clarity regarding expectations. The examples used in this chapter are merely prompts for you to build your own responses.

CHAPTER 6

Level 1 Aligns with Associate Certified Coach (ACC)

Competency 4: Cultivates Trust and Safety

Definition: Partners with the client to create a safe, supportive environment that allows the client to share freely. Maintains a relationship of mutual respect and trust.

ACC BARS

> A4.1 Coach acknowledges client insights and learning in the moment.
>
> A4.2 Coach explores the client's expression of feelings, perceptions, concerns, beliefs or suggestions.
>
> A4.3 Coach expresses support and concern for the client, which may focus on the client's context, problem or situation, rather than the client holistically.

A4.1 Coach acknowledges client insights and learning in the moment

This particular marker comes to light in distinct ways. The following examples are merely prompts for you to build your own empathic responses.

- "I really appreciate the effort you've put into our session today. Your willingness to open up and explore your thoughts and feelings shows a lot of courage and commitment to your goal."
- "I want to acknowledge the progress you've made since our last session. It's clear that you've been reflecting deeply and applying what we've discussed, and that's making a significant difference in today's session."
- "Up to now, you have challenged yourself and been effective in exploring your insights during this process."
- "I noticed that you expressed a glimmer of learning after a moment of silence."

EXPLORING COMPETENCY 4: CULTIVATES TRUST AND SAFETY

A4.2 Coach explores the client's expression of feelings, perceptions, concerns, beliefs or suggestions

This behavior can be demonstrated in these ways:

- "I have heard your thoughts; might it be an idea to explore your feelings on this topic?"
- "I want to acknowledge you for staying with your emotions, even when you wanted to quit."
- "I believe I just watched you make a dramatic shift. Did you notice this as well?"
- "It is evident to me how committed you are to your goal."
- "The passion that you show toward your independent work is inspiring."
- "As I listen to your behavior changes that you shared, it reveals an impressive level of commitment."
- "I noticed you've put a lot of thought into this decision, and I appreciate your willingness to explore these challenging topics with me."
- "I notice your investment in time and energy toward your goal."
- "Your insights today have been astute; and it's clear you've dedicated time reflecting on these issues."
- "Even though you've encountered obstacles, you've continued to push forward, and that resilience is noteworthy."
- "Comparing where you started to where you are now, I can see substantial growth in your approach, and your hard work."

A4.3 Coach expresses support and concern for the client, which may focus on the client's context, problem or situation, rather than the client holistically

This can be demonstrated in these ways:

- "I am concerned about you being too ambitious regarding your goals. Please make sure that you can achieve them without causing unnecessary stress."
- "What are you afraid might happen if you trust your gut?"

CHAPTER 6

- "I support you in determining what is best for you. Would a SWOT (Strengths/Weaknesses/Opportunities/Threats) analysis work in this situation?"
- "I see that you're facing a challenging situation, and I'm here to support you through it."
- "Are you willing to explore some strategies that could work well in this context to help you move past these obstacles?"
- "It's understandable that this problem is causing you stress. In what part of this issue can I offer support to you?"
- "The concerns you're sharing are important and deserve attention. How can we address these issues in a way that feels manageable for you?"

Table 6.3: Reflective Questions for the Coach

1. Did I show empathy/support for my client?
2. Did I manage my emotions properly?
3. Did I allow the client to express their feelings fully?
4. Could I put my coach bias aside?

Case Study 1: Coach and Client

The client, Aysha, wanted to shed some of the pounds she'd taken on during pregnancy. She felt uncomfortable in her clothes, and wanted a plan to take her to a slimmer version of herself. That seemed clear. As I asked about her desired outcome from our time together, she said emphatically, "I want a plan!" When I asked about her feelings, she replied, "I feel angry, sad and frustrated."

Her coach, Nandi, having battled with weight gain throughout her life, could easily empathize with her. Nandi encouraged Aysha to tell her one "baby step" that Aysha would be willing to take that might move this challenge forward. There was a long pause. Aysha finally looked up and said, "I need to stop snacking." Nandi asked about her favorite snack and Aysha said, "Chips."

Nandi carefully probed further about her vulnerability, about the time of day that she was most vulnerable to a "chip-attack." Aysha admitted there were "two times: in the late afternoon and at night." Nandi explored the feeling at those two times further. Aysha admitted she was often "lonely and self-pitying." Nandi then asked if there was an alternative to snacking on chips. Aysha thought long and hard and said, "I need to get them all out of the house, and declare that I will not buy any more." Nandi checked, "For how long?" Aysha replied, "I don't know." Nandi held the silence, until Aysha finally said, "Two weeks." Nandi checked again: "You sound sure of these two steps, is that true?" Aysha nodded and said, "I will sign an agreement today with you as my witness stating that, as of today, I am stopping my habit of snacking on chips. I will get rid of all the chips in my house, and I promise to refrain from eating chips for the next two weeks. I will sign and date this and give you a copy." Nandi asked what kind of support she needed. Aysha said, "I will text you daily with my updated statement of progress." As her coach Nandi affirmed Aysha's work, "Good work. You have taken the first step toward your goal. I believe that you can and will do this. I am totally here for you and will eagerly look for your daily texts."

Level 2 Aligns with Professional Certified Coach (PCC)

Competency 4: Cultivates Trust and Safety

Definition: Partners with the client to create a safe, supportive environment that allows the client to share freely. Maintains a relationship of mutual respect and trust.

PCC Markers

- 4.1 Coach acknowledges and respects the client's unique talents, insights and work in the coaching process.
- 4.2 Coach shows support, empathy or concern for the client.
- 4.3 Coach acknowledges and supports the client's expression of feelings, perceptions, concerns, beliefs or suggestions.
- 4.4 Coach partners with the client by inviting the client to respond in any way to the coach's contributions and accepts the client's response.

4.1 Coach acknowledges and respects the client's unique talents, insights and work in the coaching process

This particular marker can be demonstrated in these ways:

- If the coach acknowledges and respects the client's context, identity, environment, experiences, values, beliefs, culture, self-expression, perceptions, methodologies, style, use of words and concepts. For example, "I want you to notice the fact that a few moments ago you said you didn't know. However, you just articulated three concrete action steps that you are willing to take to move your process/project forward." Example 2: "I understand that you want me to support you in finding your perfect husband. I also understand that in your culture arranged marriages are the norm. Coaching a person from a different culture and religion is a bit of a stretch for me. However, if you are willing to trust me to support you, then I am willing to stretch into a new situation to support and empower you."

- If the coach understands, recognizes and respects the client's self-concept/identity. For example, "It sounds like you are becoming more aware of how you want to show up in your family, at your job and with your childhood friends. Are you addressing the transition of who you were juxtaposed with who you want to become?" Example 2: "I have heard that you want to be more confident in meetings. I have also heard that when meetings happen a voice in your head insists that you keep quiet. With these different parts of you having a conversation, which part do you want me to support?"

- If the coach does not communicate any judgment of the client's self-concepts verbally or through body language or tone. For example, "When I hear how you reacted to this situation, I am curious as to what you were feeling at the time." Example 2: "I fully understand that your colleague operates differently from you. Do you want to help her develop or do you want to criticize her behavior? I want to help and I need your help; what role do you want me to play?"

- If the coach reflects back in a way that recognizes the client's unique talents and insights, and how they shape the client's work in the coaching process. For example, "Your capacity to lead others is showing up in our coaching conversations when you describe how you want to lead your life with integrity, fairness and caring." Example 2: "You have an ability to multi-task that stands out. Can this ability be transferred to others?"

- If the coach hears and respects the client's frame of reference, thinking or feeling. For example, "It sounds like your thoughts are geared to hold you back, while your feelings are longing to stretch out and take a risk." Example 2: "Your powers of logic and reasoning are well-developed. Is it your intention to develop your emotional intelligence as well?"

- If the coach recognizes and acknowledges the unique challenges faced by the client. For example, "Your parents, it appears, want you to follow in the family tradition of pharmacology; you, on the other hand, want to follow your talents and preferences and go into the new world of artificial intelligence. Do I hear you correctly?" Example 2: "This new career opportunity has been challenging you primarily because you want to please all of your stakeholders. You have put yourself and your family into the choice process and you're looking at what would be best for them versus trying to please everyone, which is very challenging. That indicates a shift in perspective."

- If the coach recognizes or acknowledges the unique challenges the client has overcome in this session or in the overall coaching engagement. For example, "When you arrived today, you were tentative about talking to your boss. However, I noticed a surge of confidence and courage just now when you explained the importance of this issue. I hear your passion!" Example 2: "For the last two sessions you have been clinging to the belief that you cannot have it all. Today, I notice that you are willing to consider letting go of that old belief and possibly explore a life without reasons, regret or remorse. Am I hearing you accurately? Impressive!"

- If the coach recognizes and acknowledges the client's unique talents and insights, and how they contributed to the client's successes or work in the coaching process. For example, "Stepping up and volunteering for this position has put you out there for everyone to see. This is a big step forward given your previous shyness." Example 2: "When we started coaching, you stated that your triggers were an issue in your leadership capacity. With the work that you have done in this area, it seems like your reflections have illuminated the origin of your reactions. This is very effective in our work together."

- If the coach recognizes and acknowledges the client's emerging perceptions, new ideas, insights or realizations. For example, "Did you just notice that burst of insight? I witnessed new enthusiasm and energy that were inspiring!" Example 2: "Did you notice that the judgments you were harboring just shifted into compassion for this colleague? What did you realize that enabled that shift?"

- If the coach encourages the client to explore the client's emerging perceptions, new ideas, insights or realizations. For example, "It looks to me as if you are on a roll; please continue as if nothing could stop you." Example 2: "Congratulations, you have just listed three important leadership qualities that you want to explore in this session. Are you ready to address how they might fit in your overall life?"

- If the coach expresses confidence in the client's capabilities. For example, "If you took charge of this initiative in the past, I could imagine that you could apply those same qualities to this situation that you are facing in the present." Example 2: "I noticed at the beginning of our session, you were holding back; now, I hear your mind and heart working in concert imagining that you could possibly have it all!"

- If the coach recognizes and affirms the client's courage and/or willingness to change. For example, "I am hearing a new-found commitment to take care of your health. This is exciting – what changed for you?" Example 2: "I am hearing a new-found courage that is quite different from the person who I met two months ago. You are tackling challenges that, in the past, would have been unthinkable!"

- If the coach recognizes and acknowledges the client's unique strengths and characteristics that contributed to behavioral changes made by the client. For example, "Are you fully aware of the changes you have made in the last three months? When you first came to me you said that you wanted to stop procrastinating. When I look at you now, I can hardly remember that person; you completely stopped any trace of postponing your tasks. That is a clear transformation!" Example 2: "Two sessions ago, you shared with me that you would lash out at your staff even if they performed adequately. Your negativity drove your staff away from being an intact team. Today, I must acknowledge the behavior changes you've made that demonstrate your leadership and positive role-modeling."

- If the coach recognizes and acknowledges the client's unique strengths and characteristics that have contributed to the client's successes. For example, "Previously you were critical and judgmental of your subordinate. Now you have changed your style and become a leader who empowers; it is evident in your latest promotion that you have become a developer of managers!" Example 2: "You have clearly had a breakthrough with your team that you inherited with your promotion. Congratulations on introducing them to a new standard of excellence and doing it with graciousness and positive feedback!"

4.2 Coach shows support, empathy or concern for the client

This may include assuring or reassuring the client that the coach is there to listen and hold space. Some of the ways this can be demonstrated include the following:

- If the coach is generally supportive, empathetic or caring. For example, "That sounds like a really challenging situation."

- If the coach uses verbal or non-verbal behaviors which demonstrates showing concern, being empathetic or being supportive to the client. For example, "I have experienced something similar, and it was really difficult."

- If the coach treats the client's emotions, thoughts and feelings respectfully, responsibly and with unconditional positive regard. For example, "I get how deeply this has affected you."

- If the coach, directly or indirectly, shows support, empathy or concern for the client. For example, "I admire your perseverance. How does self-care fit into your framework?"

- If the coach uses specific language such as, "What can I do to support you?"

- If the coach makes empathic comments. For example, "I can relate to what you are saying. I had a similar experience in my past." In addition, the coach might hold the space in silence, allowing the client to process the experience internally.

- If the coach demonstrates care or compassion. For example, "I feel the depth of your pain." The coach must also ensure that their tone communicates care, concern and kindness.

- If the coach allows the client to feel their feelings. For example, "Please feel free to fully allow those feelings."

- If the coach shows caring by being sensitive to the client's emotions while not becoming impatient, directive, authoritative or flustered. For example, "Take as much time as you need. I'm here for you."

- If the coach does not try to get the client to "move out of the client's strong feelings" but is okay with strong emotions without getting enmeshed or uncomfortable. For example, "Give yourself permission to feel all of the feelings. This is a safe space where you can release all of your feelings."

- If the coach demonstrates confidence in their ability to work with the client's emotions if they arise in the session. For example, "Did I detect a feeling? Please allow all of your feelings. You can experience everything in here that you couldn't allow out there."

- If, when a client is experiencing strong or difficult emotions, the coach maintains silence to allow client time and space to process their emotions/experience. For example, "Go ahead. I am with you. Let it go."

4.3 Coach acknowledges and supports the client's expression of feelings, perceptions, concerns, beliefs or suggestions

- If the coach affirmatively encourages the client to continue to express themself. For example, "I hear the overwhelm that you are experiencing. Was that everything or is there more?"

- If the coach encourages the client to continue sharing thoughts, feelings, perceptions, concerns, beliefs or suggestions until the client feels they have expressed everything they wanted to express. "Is there more that is on your mind? Are there more feelings that haven't yet been expressed?"

- If the coach allows or encourages the client to fully express their feelings, including anger, anxiety, fear, apprehension, sadness, grief, joy, love and excitement. For example, "I've heard your loss and it is profound. Are there other feelings that may also be present or perhaps hiding behind the loss?"

- If the coach uses specific language. For example, "What more would you like to say about your thoughts? What additional feelings are related to this?"

- If the coach encourages the client to express themselves in ways that are natural and comfortable to them. For example, "Thinking out loud can be helpful?" or "I recall that you like to draw. Would you like to draw those voices that are criticizing you?" or "If you were to dance this expression, what would that dance look like?" or "If you were to write poetry or a letter, what would you say?"

- If the coach is receptive or responsive to what the client has communicated. For example, "Being human has its tests. How do you feel you are doing with your 'life lessons' and the occasional tests to check to see if we have learned the curriculum?"

- If the coach acknowledges the client's expression of thinking or feeling. For example, "I hear your thoughts and they are rational and logical as they should be. What about your feelings: are the emotional realms something that we can explore together?" Or as another example, the client might bring up their divorce and quickly move on to another topic. The coach could notice this and respond: "I noticed something just now. May I share my observation with you?" The client may then respond, "Yes, of course." Having permission to share, the coach might say, "I noticed that when you spoke about your divorce, you cut it short, and I felt as if there is more that you want to say. Please let me know if I am mistaken. I only bring it up because I want to make sure that you feel safe to share all that is important for you to share and know that anything you share is completely confidential. Is there more that you'd like to say about your divorce?"

4.4 Coach partners with the client by inviting the client to respond in any way to the coach's contributions and accepts the client's response

- If the coach shares to build trust, then immediately invites the client to use or not use what the coach has shared however the client sees fit. For example, "I also felt abandonment. It was, of course, different from your experience. If it helps, I can share it. However, I want you to know that this is about you and your situation, and not about me."

- If the coach shares to build trust, then immediately invites the client to agree or disagree with what the coach has shared and accepts the client's agreement or disagreement. For example, "My belief is that we can heal the wounds, loss and trauma that we've experienced. I'm not here to convince you of that, and you may completely disagree. If we were to have that conversation, might it help with your current mindset?" (Note the invitation and the openness to the client's refusal.) The client may then respond with, "No, actually I am okay with continuing with our topic. Thanks for sharing your observation." To which the coach might reply: "Okay, let's do that. So, where would you like to pick up our conversation?"

- If the coach shares to build trust, then invites the client to respond in a way that clearly communicated that the client was free to agree or disagree with what the coach just shared. For example, "I believe that parenting is one of the most difficult jobs in the world, especially with all of the marketing telling our children that they must have the latest gadget to be cool. I'm walking the line between not spoiling the kids and not wanting them to feel left out or bullied because they don't have the latest technology toy. You may disagree, and I would love to hear your perspective. Would you be willing to share how you see it?"

In this competency, assessors are evaluating if the coach "partners" with the client to create a safe, supportive environment that allows the client to share freely. Assessors are also evaluating if the coach maintains a relationship of mutual respect and trust throughout sessions.

Each of these behaviors can be evidenced either directly through verbal language, body language (if relevant) and actions by the coach, or indirectly by observing the coach's way of being. Indirectly, these behaviors can be evidenced through the exchange of language that occurs between a client and their coach, which indicates a comfortable rapport that includes a healthy and functional relationship with each other. The coach would emphasize the importance of providing a safe and non-judgmental space for the client to express themselves fully, share their feelings, beliefs and perspectives. The focus is on fostering trust, promoting self-expression and creating an environment where the client feels comfortable and empowered to explore their thoughts, emotions and options.

Box 6.4: Reflective Questions for the Coach

1. Did I show understanding for my client's emotions?
2. Did I focus on the whole person of my client?
3. Did I invite my client to share about themselves/their identity?
4. Could I identify some talent of my client as they spoke to me?

Case Study 2: Coach and Client

The client wanted to stop smoking. I asked specifically what she wanted from our time together today. She said, "I need to decide on something that is finally going to work. I have failed so many times that I don't believe in myself anymore."

I understood, as her coach, what she meant about failure creating a lack of self-trust. I knew what it meant to make a New Year's resolution and then break it every year. My familiarity made it easy to empathize with her. She then shared all of the attempts she had taken that had failed and left her with a defeatist attitude.

At one point, I asked her to "tell me something you have committed to and followed through on." She became quiet and as she traveled through the video-streaming of her memories, she arrived on an answer: "I stopped biting my nails!" I said, "Great! What did you do to make that happen?" She said, "I decided that it was in my control, and I found a series of things I could do when I felt tempted." I nudged her, "Like what?" She replied, "I started to treat my hands like a precious part of me. I used hand cream, and when possible, I actually got a manicure!" I asked what else. She replied, "I kept manicuring tools handy to use when I felt the urge to bite my cuticles or my need to even off the different lengths. Actually, I made it into a project that I was committed to winning." I congratulated her for her great memory and asked if there was a bridge to take her success with nail biting into her desire to stop smoking.

She was intrigued and liked the challenge. I offered my own way of managing my habits and, after asking for permission, shared a short version with her. I also invited her to share what occurs to her as she listens to me, letting her know that her way could be completely different. She was interested. I said, "For me, building a case against the habit I want to change and growing my self-confidence in my capability helps a lot." She was enthusiastic and said she wanted to experiment with the idea of journaling to see if she had the discipline to go through with it.

I asked her how she felt about her solution and what type of support she wanted going forward. She said, "I will try journaling and every Sunday, I will take a photo of the newest pages and email it to you." I said, "This sounds exciting and I am 100% on your team!" Within three months, she was a smoke-free person and proud of her accomplishment!

Level 3 Aligns with Master Certified Coach (MCC)

Competency 4: Cultivates Trust and Safety

Definition: Partners with the client to create a safe, supportive environment that allows the client to share freely. Maintains a relationship of mutual respect and trust.

Regarding the examples given for the MCC BARS, please take into consideration that in order to meet the requirements for MCC-level coaching, the contextual and relational aspects of the coaching conversation need to be taken into account. These in their wholeness serve as evidence for whether in the given coaching a sufficient depth and variety of dimensions of the client's life, purpose and identity have been fully explored and responded to by the coach.

MCC BARS

> M4.1 Coach engages the client as an equal partner in a collaborative coaching process.
>
> M4.2 Coach exhibits genuine curiosity about the client as a whole person by inviting the client to share more about themself or their identity.
>
> M4.3 Coach provides space for the client to fully express themself and share feelings, beliefs and perspectives without judgment.
>
> M4.4 Coach acknowledges the client and celebrates client progress.

M4.1 Coach engages the client as an equal partner in a collaborative coaching process

This behavior is evident in the following examples:

- "We have discussed your current situation and your future aspirations. For us to be effective today, which one would you like to focus on?"

- "Would brainstorming or a role play help? Which one do you resonate with? Or do you have another way of proceeding?"
- "You have a well-thought-out retirement plan. In what way can I add value to ensure your success?"

M4.2 Coach exhibits genuine curiosity about the client as a whole person by inviting the client to share more about themself or their identity

When an MCC displays genuine curiosity about the client as a whole person, it can deeply enhance the coaching relationship and facilitate the client's self-discovery and growth. Here are some statements and questions that a coach might use to encourage the client to share more about themself or their identity, thus moving them forward:

- "The insight you shared about being an introvert was illuminating. What other preferences will provide me with a richer view of who you are?"
- "You seem to be very devoted to your job. What are the ways in which you take care of yourself in your free time?"
- "I notice that you are focused on taking care of others. What would you like to share with me about how you see yourself in this new role so I can best support you?"
- "I'm really struck by the depth of what you're sharing about your feelings and beliefs. It's important to honor these insights as they are key to understanding your unique perspective and guiding our work together."
- "Hearing you express your concerns and suggestions helps me see the world through your eyes. This is invaluable as it helps us both to align on your goals and the steps we can take to achieve them."
- "It's powerful to witness you delve into your perceptions and beliefs with such honesty. I encourage you to continue exploring these feelings as they will lead us to deeper insights and more meaningful progress."
- "Your experiences are incredibly rich and help me see your process in your growth. I would love to hear more about the moments that have defined you, both personally and professionally."

CHAPTER 6

- "It sounds like there are some powerful values and beliefs that guide you. I invite you to delve deeper into how these have influenced your life choices and the vision you have for your future."

M4.3 Coach provides space for the client to fully express themself and share feelings, beliefs and perspectives without judgment

Master Certified Coaches (MCC) create a non-judgmental space for clients to express themselves fully. Here are some examples of effective statements a coach might use:

- "Your feelings are important and deserve to be recognized."
- "You have acknowledged your beliefs and you have created new ones that honor your new reality."
- "I notice that you are embracing a new way of being that reflects the 'new you'."
- "I want you to feel free to express all of your thoughts and feelings here. This is a space where your perspectives are valued without any judgment."
- "It's important for you to share what's truly on your mind and in your heart. I'm here to listen and understand your beliefs and feelings, so please feel encouraged to share them in their entirety."
- "Your experiences and emotions are valid and hold important insights. I invite you to share your innermost beliefs and perspectives."

M4.4 Coach acknowledges the client and celebrates client progress

This may be demonstrated in the following ways:

- "I want to acknowledge you for your courage in taking on this challenge."
- "Your progress is inspiring and I celebrate your growth."
- "Congratulations on transcending your concerns and committing to your professional development!"
- "I've noticed how you've developed a keen sense of self-awareness throughout our sessions. The way you identified your core

values and aligned them with your career choices is a significant milestone. It's inspiring to see how this awareness is shaping your decisions."

- "Your dedication to transitioning into a new role and the fact that you've not only adapted but thrived, shows your commitment."
- "The breakthrough you experienced in our session redefines what success means to you, and was a profound step forward. It's an honor to witness your journey and the transformation you're undergoing."

Box 6.5: Reflective Questions for the Coach

1. Did I provide enough space – while showing curiosity – for my client to express themself?
2. Did I encourage my client to fully express themself?
3. Could I pick up the underlying emotions?
4. Could I identify new learning/awareness of my client along the session?

Growing MCC

A coach who achieves their Master Certified Coach (MCC) accreditation recognizes this is not an end point. They will continue honoring Competency 2: Embodies a Coaching Mindset by maintaining their self-reflective practice and ongoing learning and development. The path of mastery is a never-ending, fulfilling journey with continuous attention on how Competency 4 is best fulfilled, how trust is built and how the safety of the client is also in the focus, as this leads towards greater transformational presence in work and life.

Case Study 3: Coach and Client

In a coaching session, a client revealed her goal: "to feel safe when communicating with her antagonistic sister." I asked what she meant by "safe communication with her sister." She shared that every time she spoke with her sister, she felt stressed, anxiety-ridden and attacked.

I asked her about a possible takeaway to which she replied, "I want to have a functional, safe relationship with my sister, with action points on how to engage." I asked about trust with her sister. Her keyword response was "disappointment," "anger" and "anxiety."

I asked how she wanted to show up the next time she would see her sister. Her response was clear: "powerful and confident." As she spoke, her demeanor shifted. There were tears as she blurted out the words, "This is what happened when my mother died two years ago from cancer." I offered an extended listening silence. At that moment, she had an intense flashback that revealed the incomplete mourning for her mother's passing.

"Your tears are a powerful expression of your ongoing loss. I'm here to support you. What might be the outcome of acknowledging this grief with your sister?" Her response was enlightening. She said, "By allowing the love and loss that we both shared for our mother, that could bring us closer together."

Affirming the client's feelings provided empathetic support; gently inviting the client toward self-discovery along with strategies for safer communication with her sister opened the door for deeper revelations. Allowing the client to explore her deep personal feelings in a safe environment, trusting that somewhere within her lay the keys to opening the doors to her current dilemma with her sister, enabled revelation to occur in that magical moment.

How "Trust and Safety" Serves the Client

Fostering trust and safety not only in coaching but in all relationships can have a profound impact on individuals and the world as a whole. When people feel safe and supported, they are more willing to take risks, explore new possibilities and work together towards positive change. Here's how creating more safety in relationships, including coaching, can contribute to a better world:

1. **Encouraging authenticity:** When individuals feel safe, they are more likely to express their true selves and share their authentic thoughts, emotions and experiences. This fosters genuine connections and enables deeper understanding between people.

2. **Breaking barriers:** Safety in relationships helps break down barriers, such as fear, judgment and biases. It creates an inclusive space where diverse perspectives are respected, leading to increased empathy, collaboration and acceptance.

3. **Empowering growth:** Safety encourages individuals to step outside their comfort zones and embrace personal growth and development. In a trusting environment, people feel supported in exploring new ideas, taking on challenges and expanding their potential.

4. **Building resilience:** Safety allows individuals to take risks and make mistakes without fear of severe consequences. This cultivates resilience, as people feel more comfortable learning from failures and bouncing back from setbacks, ultimately leading to personal and collective growth.

5. **Enhancing communication:** Trust and safety promote open and effective communication. People are more likely to express their thoughts, needs and concerns honestly and openly, leading to better understanding, problem-solving and conflict resolution.

6. **Nurturing collaboration:** Safe relationships foster a collaborative mindset, encouraging individuals to work together towards common goals. Trust enables people to rely on each other's strengths, share resources and create synergistic outcomes.

7. **Cultivating well-being:** Safety contributes to overall well-being. When individuals feel safe and supported, it positively impacts their mental, emotional and even physical health. This, in turn, extends to the broader community and promotes a culture of well-being that enables people to thrive not just survive.

Incorporating Trust and Safety into Daily Life

By incorporating safety as a foundational element in coaching and relationships, we can help individuals create positive change in their lives. As trust and safety become pervasive in all interactions, we have the potential to transform the world into a more compassionate, empathetic and inclusive place. Coaching, with its focus on empowerment and transformation, plays a valuable role in fostering this shift towards a better future.

CHAPTER 6

How "Trust and Safety" Serves the Coach

When the climate is safe, the coach can take risks based on what they observe, hear and intuit. This also includes self-trust. If you, as the coach, believe that you can trust yourself, you will be more likely to take risks and offer the client an observation or an intuition that might be "wrong." It is those inner whispers that the coach feels and hears to which they respond, "Oh no, not that question!" It is often that exact question or observation that will alter the session from being transitional or transactional into a profound transformational session.

This marks one of the distinct differences between the three certification levels. At ACC level, the coach will focus on the topic, situation or circumstance – or as we at ICF like to call it, "the what." At PCC level, the coach can also focus on the situation; however, there is the addition of inviting the client to focus on themself, their inner thoughts and feelings, or "the who." At MCC level, the focus is mainly on the inner world of the client. The coach invites the client to look within at their inner dialog and to allow their feelings to bubble up to the surface.

Remember, the embodiment of trust and safety involves consistent actions over time that demonstrate reliability, integrity, empathy, respect and a commitment to the well-being of others. Anyone, regardless of their role or status, can embody trust and safety in their interactions with others.

As a coach, you need to pay close attention to whatever it takes for you to embody "trust and safety." Trust and safety start within yourself. By creating a safe space for self-reflection coupled with the desire for personal growth and transformation, you can then extend that trust and safety to others. Through your own actions and qualities, you become a role model for fostering trust and safety in coaching and in all of your relationships. Finally, once you have owned these capabilities and qualities, make them the bedrock of your coaching practice. You have the opportunity to provide feedback to those who sincerely want to be of service. Develop your capabilities to the best of your ability and then pass the torch to those who have been called to the coaching profession.

Your Evolution as a Great Coach

You are on your way to becoming a great coach. As you navigate your way through these behaviors and markers, you are growing exponentially. To conclude this competency in an effective manner, we have provided ten questions to keep you on track with your inner world and your coaching practice, evolving in your professional development with each coaching session that you conduct. These are deep-dive reflective questions to ask yourself after each coaching session.

Reflective Questions

1. Do I create a safe environment for myself?
2. Do I take the time necessary to address my concerns, triggers and issues?
3. Do I trust my intuition, my gut, my inner knowing?
4. Do I allow all of my feelings?
5. Do I give myself permission to process my feelings in a safe space?
6. Do I reflect on my past experiences to share with clients when appropriate?
7. Do I seek out a coach when the depth of the situation exceeds my capacity?
8. Do I believe that I can truly have my life be the way I truly want?
9. Do I believe that I can go for my dreams?
10. Do I walk my talk, and live life as an example of the coaching process?

Conclusion

In this chapter we have explored under the microscope Competency 4: Cultivates Trust and Safety. When you have established an environment of trust and safety, then you can focus on becoming fully present. Each competency is effectively built on the previous one. The next chapter is focused on Competency 5: Maintains Presence.

CHAPTER 7

Exploring Competency 5: Maintains Presence

Svea van der Hoorn and Cindy Muthukarapan
with contributions from Philippe R. Declercq

Introduction

In this chapter we will firstly explore the meaning of competency. Then we will explore how this shows up at each of the credentialing levels: ACC, PCC and MCC. We offer ways in which you can have a relationship with your learning and growth as a coach and the quality of coaching you offer clients, at the different credential levels. In keeping with other chapters, we explore the core competency by drawing on the ACC BARS, PCC Markers and MCC BARS that are part of the ICF quality framework for individual coaching.

Core Competency 5: Maintains Presence signals that the ICF assumes all coaches will already show up with presence in their coaching conversations with clients. What the credentialed coach is asked to attend to is maintaining presence. Therefore, in this chapter we will focus on how to maintain presence, and in particular how coaches can manage their accountability for maintaining presence, without reducing the client's sense of autonomy as a partner in their coaching experience. We will illuminate and illustrate the capability of how coaches go about noticing the quality of their presence, and the variety of ways in which they make adjustments moment to moment to ensure that they maintain their presence. We will also look at how mentor coaching for credentialing purposes and coaching supervision can provide learning and growth environments for coaches in their quest to maintain presence.

But first, what is this thing that the ICF calls "presence?" And then, how do we maintain presence?

As you read the tables below, notice what comes to mind about presence and maintaining presence. Then review and expand your thoughts by engaging with the descriptions, examples, reflection questions and practice activities drawn from the practice insights of the ICF assessors.

Table 7.1: ICF Definition of Maintains Presence

Definition: Is fully conscious and present with the client, employing a style that is open, flexible and grounded.

Table 7.2: Competency 5: Maintains Presence – Descriptors

5.1 Remains focused, observant, empathetic and responsive to the client.

5.2 Demonstrates curiosity during the coaching process.

5.3 Manages one's emotions to stay present with the client.

5.4 Demonstrates confidence in working with strong client emotions during the coaching process.

5.5 Is comfortable working in a space of not knowing.

5.6 Creates or allows space for silence, pause or reflection.

Definitions

Words make worlds. While the words used in the ICF credentialing framework are mostly words that we encounter in everyday life, they have particular meanings in the world of coaching.

We start by inviting you to explore what meanings these words evoke for you as a person. What do they evoke for you in your role as a coach? Is there similarity or difference between the meanings they evoke for you as a person and for you as a coach? If there are differences, do the differences create harmony or discordance? Here is how we think of these words in relation to becoming an ICF-credentialed coach.

CHAPTER 7

What Do We Mean When We Say "Fully Conscious" and "Present with the Client?"

While many coaching approaches and models draw on psychology for theories about change, not all coaches do. Whether you do or not, coaches all aspire to be fully conscious and present with their clients. For all coaches this is about being fully aware of and responsive to oneself, the other, the interactions between self and other, and the contexts that are relevant to the coaching conversation. To maintain presence, coaches engage all their senses, for example, listening with more than their ears – with eyes, with heart, with energy field and more.

For coaches offering psychologically informed coaching, the coaching conversation may include referring to the "unconscious" and drawing distinctions between the conscious and the unconscious. These concepts have become so familiar to the general population that they are often regarded by clients and coaches as facts rather than theoretical constructs. However, coaches who do not draw on psychology – for example, coaches whose coaching is informed by communication theory, by anthropology or by learning theories – are more likely to hold themselves accountable to bring full awareness, capability, noticing capacity and more.

Reflection Questions

1. Clients hire a human coach because they want to be in the presence of a human coach. How can you support yourself to bring your humanity to each coaching conversation in a way that is experienced by your client as you being fully aware and present with them?

2. How can you make sure not to appear distracted or uninterested in what the client is saying?

What Do We Mean by the Word "Open?"

When we think about being open, it implies the opposite of being closed. What does the ICF-credentialed coach hold openness for, and what do they hold a more closed stance towards?

We propose that coaches hold an accountability to maintain a presence of being open in a variety of ways, including, but not limited to, being open minded, open hearted, open spirited, open to diversity and open to variations in theories of change. Instead of imposing a theory of how change happens or needs to happen, the coach who maintains presence will have a conversation with the client about how the client believes change happens based on their past experiences, their knowledge and their values. This is a conversation which the coach will also have with sponsors/buyers of coaching. The results and benefits that sponsors and buyers of coaching expect are connected to their theories of change and hence their confidence in what the coach proposes in terms of the coaching contract – duration, frequency, approach and methods, tools and techniques. While not all coaches offer chemistry sessions, all ICF-credentialed coaches do engage with clients and/or sponsors to agree on the contractual and other arrangements before coaching commences. This is in alignment with standards 1 and 2 of the ICF Code of Ethics (2019). You can read more about this on the ICF global website (https://coachingfederation.org/ethics/code-of-ethics).

Reflection Questions

1. What do your clients and sponsors expect you to hold an openness for, given their expectations about the benefits of coaching? If you are not yet actively coaching, consider the clients and sponsors you would like, or intend, to engage with.
2. How can you minimize making assumptions or judgments about the client and the client's experiences?

What Do We Mean When We Use the Word "Flexible?"

When to be like a willow tree, able to bend in the wind, and when to stand tall and steady like an oak tree? Entertaining this question is already a sign of a coach who maintains presence. This coach has a framework, boundaries and usual methods, but also is alive when customizing these to be sensitive to context and to individual preferences and circumstances, as necessary and appropriate.

The ICF-credentialed coach does not allow this flexibility to result in compromising quality of coaching, nor to stepping out of alignment with the ICF Code of Ethics and ICF core competency framework. They are able to engage in respectful, constructive conversations with clients and sponsors and other stakeholders in which people express the flexibilities they would welcome from the coach and the coaching contract. The maintaining presence coach does not come across as rigid, but rather as demonstrating a flexibility that is about being respectfully steady and quietly confident in creating an environment that is conducive to cultivating client growth (Core Competency 8).

Reflection Questions

1. How can you be flexible without losing alignment with the ICF professional standards and Code of Ethics? What qualities, capabilities and skills can you draw on in yourself? What might you need/want to further develop?
2. How can you pace yourself so that you don't rush through the session without allowing the client enough time to explore?
3. How can you adjust the coaching approach to meet the individual needs of each client?
4. How can you change and adapt the coaching in relation to the client's progress?

What Do We Mean When We Use the Word "Grounded?"

Coaching is filled with many abstract concepts and hence words which can lead to coaching conversations where the everyday world of the client is disconnected from their coaching conversations. For example, compare "I need to spend less time second-guessing my decisions and have the courage to move forward to action once I've made my decision" with "I suffer from imposter syndrome which leads to a lot of self-doubt which makes me procrastinate." We are seeing a rising trend for people to seek stability by labeling and categorizing, drawing information – and sometimes disinformation – from the vast array of advice and self-help resources available to anyone who has a smart phone and access to the internet. The more we talk during coaching conversations in labels and categories, the more we are at risk of losing a person's uniqueness, the particularity of their everyday life, both of which are rich in possibilities for change. Coaches who maintain presence have respect for both the world of principles and abstractions, and the world of the practical and everyday.

Reflection Questions

1. How can you invite your clients to draw on both the world of principles and the abstract and the world of the practical and everyday?
2. How can you self-correct if you hear yourself using jargon, technical terms or humor that the client does not understand or respond well to?

What Do We Mean by the Word "Curiosity?"

Linked to being open is the idea of the coach bringing a curiosity to their work with clients. However, when done in a mindless way, this "be curious" can manifest as being like a tourist in the client's life, wandering about taking photos of whatever catches one's attention and interest. This is not an appropriate way of being curious for a coach who is committed to maintaining presence.

When assessors hear a coach say "I'm curious…" at the beginning of an utterance, they may hold their breath for what comes next. Utterances like "I'm curious to hear what you make of what you are facing" or "I'm curious about where you would like us to focus our session" are quite different from "I'm curious to hear more about why that is happening" or "I'm curious to know what makes you say that." What do you notice about the differences in how a client might experience these ways of coaches using the "I'm curious" words?

The coach who maintains presence is able to regulate their curiosity sufficiently to keep it focused and working in relation to what is significant for the client and has the potential to contribute to the client making progress towards what they want from the session, and what they want for themselves in their life.

Reflection Questions

1. What stood out for you as you were reading about how curiosity shows up when coaches maintain presence? How might you make use of this in your coaching?

CHAPTER 7

> 2. How do you keep yourself alert to not expressing personal opinions or beliefs that could influence the client's sense of autonomy, confidence and self-reliance?
>
> 3. How can you monitor when your curiosity may be experienced as inappropriate, disrespectful or showing signs of bias or prejudice?
>
> 4. How can you quickly adjust when a client indicates that you are coming across as minimizing or dismissive of their vulnerabilities or challenges?

What Do We Mean by the Word "Responsive?"

Coaching is not a question-and-answer language game. This may come as a surprise, as many foundational coaching education courses focus on teaching coaching questions. Mentor coaches and coaching supervisors are regularly asked "What would be the right question to ask when a client says X?" The ICF definition of coaching alerts us to be partners. To be a partner requires responsiveness. However, this responsiveness by a coach who is maintaining presence is guided by the coach's awareness in the moment of the purpose of coaching – learning and growth, by what they are learning about the who/person of the client, and by what the client is hoping for from the coaching. The conversation is co-created by coach and client, moment to moment drawing on what they are sharing with one another, always with an eye to making progress towards the client's desired outcome. Assessors notice a lack of responsiveness when so-called "right" questions are offered by the coach at moments and/or in ways that are not a response to what the client is communicating, but rather driven by a list of standard questions, or by a coaching model or technique. At times this disconnect is amplified when clients say "Pardon, can you repeat that? I didn't get your question." Or when the client simply stops in the conversation, there is a longer than usual pause, and then the client either starts talking about something that is not a response to what the coach just contributed, or they stare at the coach and say "Um, I lost my train of thought" and wait for the coach to speak.

Reflection Questions

> 1. How will you recognize that you and the client are partnering with you being responsive to the client, rather than moving along a checklist of questions?

EXPLORING COMPETENCY 5: MAINTAINS PRESENCE

2. How can you make sure you are not engaging in self-promotion or personal anecdotes that distract from the session, even when the client invites these from you?

3. How will you notice if you are talking too much, or responding too quickly after a client has spoken?

4. What will support you in developing the capacity to pay close attention to verbal and non-verbal cues, and utilize both in your responses?

What Do We Mean by the Words "Creates or Allows Space for Silence, Pause or Reflection?"

A coaching conversation is like music. Without pauses between notes, music becomes one long, not very melodious noise. Without pauses for reflection between utterances, a coaching conversation can be uninspiring and fail to spark awareness and generative learning. "How long is long enough?" is something we often get asked in mentor coaching. Generally, at least double however long you usually pause in a social conversation in the language you and the client are speaking. In English it usually takes between about one and three seconds before one of the speakers begins to wonder what is happening and says something like "Did you hear what I said?" or starts speaking again to smooth out the awkward moment. So, six seconds is common in a coaching conversation, and often much more is needed as a client considers the coach's invitation, engages with what the question/observation evokes, generates a response and then speaks. For many coaches, this is the awkward moment to manage – the pause while they wait for the client to respond, rather than jumping in. Being at ease with a variety of pause lengths and learning to be at ease in silence is something all coaches can become skilled at. It is a deceptively simple capability for maintaining presence – simple but not necessarily easy.

Practice Activity: Start paying attention to how you experience a variety of pauses – simply speak and then watch the clock or watch hands ticking away for six seconds, thirteen seconds, twenty-six seconds, and then speak again. Notice what you experience and begin to become at ease with a variety of longer pauses. Notice your hands, your gaze and your facial expression. These all act to provide our clients with listener responses, and we don't want our unregulated

CHAPTER 7

listener responses to disturb a client when they are responding to an evocative invitation.

What Do We Mean by the Words "Manages One's Emotions to Stay Present with the Client?"

We regard emotions as energy in motion, something which can be detected in subtle and not-so-subtle signals like tone of voice, volume, change of pace, facial expressions, hand gestures and changes in gaze pattern. We regard feelings as names or labels that are used to give verbal expression to these energy shifts.

Most coaches would say that they do not allow their emotions to disturb the client's experience in the coaching conversation. However, this does not take into account the very subtle but influential responses that we all display when we are listening actively (Core Competency 6). These subtle signals – for example, the twitch of an eyebrow – and the more detectable signals – for example, minimal encouragers such as "Uh huh" with the co-speech gesture of a nodding head – are what are called listener responses. In this last example, you will notice that the emotions of the coach that may disturb or detract from staying present with the client may be expressions of empathy and enthusiasm, not only so-called negative emotions.

Staying present with the client is somewhat like binocular vision – can you hold the focus by attending to what you are experiencing in relation to your emotions while also staying attuned to what you are noticing about the client's emotions? This requires discernment and self-regulation – how much to express and share, how much to mask, how much to let go of in the moment?

Reflection Questions

1. How can you support yourself as a coach to self-regulate your emotions so that you stay present with your client without becoming a blank slate or inauthentic?
2. How do you take care of yourself in the moment during sessions if you experience strong emotions? How do you take care of yourself immediately after a session where this has happened?

What Do We Mean by the Words "Space of Not Knowing?"

Adopting a stance of "not knowing" is something that usually unsettles ACC aspirant coaches, perplexes PCC aspirant coaches and becomes an at-ease space for MCC aspirant credentialed coaches. It is quite a paradox and is often expressed in a question like "But why would someone pay me for coaching if I know nothing?" This is a reasonable misunderstanding and requires some reflection on what a coach can or should "know" and for what purpose? Core Competency 1: Demonstrates Ethical Practice and Core Competency 3: Establishes and Maintains Agreements offer insight into what coaches should know about. What does the client desire as an outcome from coaching (CC3)? What is included and excluded from the coaching conversation (CC1)? Most vivid among what coaches are NOT invited to know is what will be best for the client, what the client should do or how the client should go about learning and growing. In coaching education this can be one of the most challenging but also exhilarating developments. Participants begin to dwell in the not-knowing space, and discover that their capability lies more in communicating effectively and co-creating a relationship in which the client's learning and growth can flourish.

One of the areas in which we as coaches confront our ability to maintain presence is when we are in conversations characterized by surprises, for example, in the diversity, equity, inclusion and belonging space. The coach who maintains presence does not head to an internet search engine to find information about how XYZ people do ABC. Rather, they draw on their ability to be in the not-knowing space respectfully, with integrity, and to invite the client to be who they are in their fullness and preferences, hopes and fears. They conduct themselves as a coach who can be relied upon to notice, to make the effort to be appropriately responsive and to be humble when, in the moment, they step out of presence with the client.

Competencies Under the Microscope: Behaviorally Anchored Rating Scale (BARS) and Markers

Having explored some of the worlds that the words of Core Competency 5: Maintains Presence invite us into, the chapter will now explore Core Competency 5 via the details of the ACC BARS, the PCC Markers and the MCC BARS. Grab your notebook and extract the nuggets from the assessors' practice insights that can inform and inspire you as you grow your capability in maintaining presence.

You are welcome to read all the sections on how this core competency manifests in ACC, PCC and MCC coaching. You may prefer to go straight to the section which is relevant to the credential level that you aspire to or perhaps already hold. We hope that what is provided will be as useful for those engaged in the credentialing process as for those seeking to refresh and maintain their credential's capability appropriately. We all become sloppy, we all drift as we improvise and we can benefit from coming back home every so often to shed what does not serve our clients or the quality of our coaching.

You will notice that the definition remains the same regardless of the credential, but how the definition manifests in the being and doing of the credentialed coach varies depending on the credential they hold. If you do work across all three sections, pay attention to what is similar across ACC, PCC and MCC, and what is particular.

Level 1 Aligns with Associate Certified Coach (ACC)

Competency 5: Maintains Presence

Definition: Is fully conscious and present with the client, employing a style that is open, flexible and grounded.

ACC BARS

- A5.1 Coach is curious throughout the session.
- A5.2 Coach acknowledges situations that the client presents.
- A5.3 Coach allows the client to direct the conversation at least some of the time.

A5.1 Coach is curious throughout the session

This ACC BAR focuses on something that is also important in the MCC

BARS, namely, the ability to maintain a behavior across the session, rather than it appearing and disappearing. In this case, the behavior in question is curiosity and the coach begins to discover what curiosity expressed by a coach in a coaching conversation offers a client, as opposed to the inquisitiveness displayed in social conversations. Here are some examples:

- "You mentioned feeling stuck. What does being 'stuck' look like for you?"
- "What values are most important to you in this situation?"
- "Can you tell me about a time when you felt really motivated?"
- "What have you learned about yourself through this experience?"
- "How has your thinking changed since we started working together?"

A5.2 Coach acknowledges situations that the client presents

The focus in this ACC BAR is on acknowledgement, which contributes to Competency 4: Cultivates Trust and Safety. For example:

- "Can you kindly elaborate on the situation you're facing?"
- "I understand this might be challenging for you. How do you feel about the current circumstances you're experiencing?"
- "It sounds like there are some complexities here. What do you think are the key elements or challenges of this situation?"
- "I acknowledge your efforts. How have you tried to handle or approach this situation so far?"
- "What alternative perspectives have crossed your mind in dealing with this situation?"
- "I'm here to support you. What resources or assistance do you think you might need to navigate through this situation effectively?"
- "How do you envision this situation evolving or resolving, ideally?"
- "I sense this might be emotional. Are there any particular emotions or concerns that are standing out for you regarding this situation?"

CHAPTER 7

A5.3 Coach allows the client to direct the conversation at least some of the time

This ACC BAR invites the coach to begin to develop their ability to partner with a client in co-creating, rather than being the one who is in charge of, the coaching process. It reminds the coach to offer the client choice, and then to be responsive to the choices the client makes rather than sticking rigidly to a model or a map. For example:

- "What activities make you lose track of time?"
- "What would you like to focus on today?"
- "What's on your mind that you'd like to explore further?"
- "How can I support you in this conversation?"
- "Which areas haven't we explored yet that you think are important?"
- "Between these options, what would you like us to explore?"
- "What do you need to consider to make this decision?"

Table 7.3: Reflective Questions for the Coach

1. Which of these ACC BARS are already detectable in your coaching?
2. For which of these ACC BARS do you need to design some deliberate practice opportunities for yourself, so that you can better serve your clients?
3. Select a few questions that appeal to you to add to your repertoire. Consider: when would it be appropriate to offer these to clients?

Level 2 Aligns with Professional Certified Coach (PCC)

Competency 5: Maintains Presence

Definition: Is fully conscious and present with the client, employing a style that is open, flexible and grounded.

PCC Markers

5.1 Coach acts in response to the whole person of the client (the who).

5.2 Coach acts in response to what the client wants to accomplish throughout this session (the what).

5.3 Coach partners with the client by supporting the client to choose what happens in this session.

5.4 Coach demonstrates curiosity to learn more about the client.

5.5 Coach allows for silence, pause or reflection.

5.1 Coach acts in response to the whole person of the client (the who)

This marker is one that sets ACC apart from PCC. The PCC coach needs to develop the discipline to hear the content but not be attached to understanding the story, clarifying details of the story or responding to the content, unless they do so in a way that invites the client to become more engaged. For example:

- "As your coach I will be learning about you, your life and what is important to you as we work together. What would you like to tell me about yourself that you'd like me to bear in mind as we begin our work together?"

- "I notice that you provided a number of examples of situations where you say you are 'playing small.' If you were playing with your full you, how would you show up in those situations?"

- "What are you becoming aware of as you hear yourself say how you long for a more joyful life?"

- "Clearly all of that is NOT the kind of leader you wish to be known as. How would you like to be as a leader?"

- "What does this say about the person/parent/friend/manager you are proud to be?"

- "How do your core beliefs influence your decision-making in this area?"

- "What emotions are you experiencing right now as we talk about this?"

- "What gives you the most fulfillment and sense of purpose?"
- "As you describe your feelings about this issue, what additional emotions are surfacing? What might these feelings be signaling to you?"
- "What activities or moments make you feel most alive? How could these moments inform us about your deeper purpose or calling?"
- "Reflect on a time when you felt you made a meaningful impact. What qualities did you embody in that moment that you would like to bring forward more often?"
- "When you imagine the legacy you wish to leave, what do you most want to be remembered for?

5.2 Coach acts in response to what the client wants to accomplish throughout this session (the what)

This marker again focuses attention on being responsive to the client's desired outcome or learning-and-growth agenda, and adds the discipline of "throughout the session." Some allowance is made at ACC credential level for losing focus or introducing elements of the coach's agenda, usually well-intentioned and driven by the coach's mental model of how people change. For example:

- "I hear you are feeling overwhelmed with all these urgent projects. Would you want to explore ways to handle this overwhelm during our session?"
- "You're contemplating alignment between your job and your values and wondering what is informing your decision. How do these values shape your view of the job offer?"
- "You say 'Everything is just too much for me right now.' When you say 'everything,' what specific situations come to mind?"
- "What direction do you feel we should take in exploring this further?"
- "What aspect of this topic do you think we need to dive deeper into?"
- "What insights have you gained so far, and where would you like to go next with them?"

5.3 Coach partners with the client by supporting the client to choose what happens in this session

For many coaches this is a particularly challenging marker. They have read textbooks, attended classes and even been confronted by clients that encourage them to hold to the mantra "the client is the expert in the content; the coach is the expert in the process." Part of the PCC credentialing journey is to extend trusting the client to be able to make choices about *how* they would like to be coached, and not just about *what* they want to be coached on. This is easier said than done. For example:

- The client has been speaking in a metaphor about being adrift in a sea with sharks in the water. They drew a small island in the distance and the conversation has been focused on this. Suddenly the client says there is a second island with people waving. The coach responds "Now that there are two islands, which would you like us to focus our exploration on?"
- "You mentioned three aspects you would like to make progress with. Would you like to cover all three today?"
- "What have you not yet had a chance to say that you would like to add?"

5.4 Coach demonstrates curiosity to learn more about the client

This marker prioritizes curiosity about the client and proposes that this curiosity has the purpose of letting the coach learn more about the client so as to partner more responsively.

- "It sounds like you're searching for a new direction. Can you tell me more about what the new direction looks like for you?"
- "I hear your frustration with procrastination, would you want to explore what might be contributing to your procrastination?"
- "How might this new insight influence how you show up in these progress conversations with your team?"
- "Reflecting on your communication style, what approach do you feel works best with your partner?"

5.5 Coach allows for silence, pause or reflection

In PCC coaching, the coach is inviting the client to generate awareness about themselves (the who) and not just about the situation (the what). Many clients need longer than the time we allow in social conversations to respond. PCC coaches are able to remain fully conscious and present with the client, rather than jumping in with a clarifying statement or a further question. The PCC coach is also sensitive to when remaining silent after a client appears to have stopped speaking will create space and opportunity for the client to go beyond their first response and continue, using the silence as a reflective space in which even more awareness is evoked.

- "Please feel free to say if you would like a moment to gather your thoughts."
- "I see you are making some notes. Let me know when you are ready for us to continue talking."
- "What thoughts are coming up for you during this silence?"
- "As we're moving forward in our session, can we pause for a moment. Reflecting on our conversation today, what are some learnings or insights you've gained about yourself that you find significant?"

Table 7.4: Reflective Questions for the Coach

1. Which of the PCC Markers are already part of your repertoire and coaching style?
2. How can you expand your competence to demonstrate the PCC Markers that are not yet part of your repertoire and regular coaching style?
3. Using the provided questions, generate some more for each marker that will expand your coaching repertoire while also letting you be the coach you want to be.

Level 3 Aligns with Master Certified Coach (MCC)

Competency 5: Maintains Presence

Definition: Is fully conscious and present with the client, employing a style that is open, flexible and grounded.

Regarding the examples given for the MCC BARS, please take into consideration that in order to meet the requirements for MCC-level coaching, the contextual and relational aspects of the coaching conversation need to be taken into account. These in their wholeness serve as evidence for whether in the given coaching a sufficient depth and variety of dimensions of the client's life, purpose and identity have been fully explored and responded to by the coach.

MCC BARS

> M5.1 Coach responds to the client in a manner that keeps the conversation flowing, with the client leading the way.
>
> M5.2 Coach remains curious and attentive to the client, exploring what the client needs throughout the session.
>
> M5.3 Coach engages in the coaching conversation with ease and fluidity.
>
> M5.4 Coach leverages silence to support the client and the client's growth.

M5.1 Coach responds to the client in a manner that keeps the conversation flowing, with the client leading the way

This one of the MCC BARS illuminates the paradoxical nature of MCC coaching. How does the coach keep the conversation flowing while also opening the space for the client to lead the way? Part of the clue lies in "coach responds." Rather than initiating, the MCC coach is responsive and engaged in co-creating a conversation rather than focusing on asking questions. You will notice that the examples below contain more than questions, including observations and linking statements to what the client offered. For example:

- "I hear you expressing gratitude that your values around raising your children are grounded in generational values. Is there any new value addition you want to make that honors your current situation?"
- "I notice a smile as you talk about your new way of being. It sounds like you are noticing changes that please you – what are some of these changes?"
- "Given what we've talked about, what area would you like to explore further right now?"
- "As you shared the immediate challenges you're facing, are there aspects of this issue that feel unexplored to you?"
- "You mentioned feeling overwhelmed/stuck. What's behind that feeling? What thoughts accompany it?"
- "You've mentioned that this decision is critical for you. What makes this critical for you?"
- "As we discuss your next steps, what do you perceive as the main barriers preventing you from reaching [your desired outcome]?"

M5.2 Coach remains curious and attentive to the client, exploring what the client needs throughout the session

The MCC coach is aware of the importance of there needing to be a flow and a sense of coherence across a coaching conversation, rather than it being like a sequence of parts. The MCC coach is fully attached to serving the client's needs, allowing coaching models, tools, techniques and even the core competency framework to be held lightly in support of being engaged and responsive with the client in a co-creating conversation, focused on the client's learning and growth. For example:

- "It sounds like at the time you were trying to be equitable with the amount of time you spent with each of your direct reports, and I hear that there's still a part of you that's wondering, could you have spent more time training her."

- "As you reflect on and voice your internal dialogues, what questions are you asking yourself right now?"
- "What part of you have you discovered through this challenge? How are you experiencing this new part of you?"
- "What are you learning about yourself through this process?"

M5.3 Coach engages in the coaching conversation with ease and fluidity

Listening to an MCC recording can be rather intimidating for ACC and PCC credential holders. "You make it sound so easy." "You make it sound so natural." "How do you know what to pick up on from what the client says and what to ignore, especially when they say so much?" These are common questions when coaches come together for demo coaching or peer coaching events.

One myth is that MCC coaches speak with a fluidity, as if they are reeling off a script they have learned beforehand. The MCC coach has fluidity in maintaining presence. This should not be confused with speaking fluently. Often an MCC coach will be heard to pause, to reconsider, to self-correct, which may at times even make it sound to the unfamiliar ear as if the MCC coach is not particularly competent. However, to the ear of a co-creating listener, the fluidity and ease lies in maintaining presence, being grounded whilst not knowing. For some, this is spoken about as "trusting the process." For others this is referred to as the humility that comes with expertise and mastery – another paradox. For example:

- "I am noticing the trust you're placing in this conversation. How can I support you best as we explore this together?"
- "I am curious about how this issue is impacting you. Would you like to share more about the impacts?"
- "I hear strong emotions in your voice as you talk about this. What emotions are coming up for you as you share?"
- "I am noticing how significant this issue is for you. Is there anything deeper emerging as you share?"
- "I am curious about the strengths you have that might help you navigate through this. Can you identify any?"

- "I hear a desire for change when you talk about this issue. As you talk about it, what change can you envision?"
- "I am noticing a new depth in what we're exploring. What's emerging as new for you?"

M5.4 Coach leverages silence to support the client and the client's growth

Whereas the ACC coach often feels pressure to make sure they speak as soon as the client stops speaking, the PCC coach utilizes pauses and silences deliberately to offer space for reflection. The MCC "leverages" silence, which involves maintaining presence by being at ease with waiting, to allow the client to lead rather than the coach being attached to asking powerful questions continuously. For example:

- "I am hearing you reference a time when you experienced something similar. What did you learn from that experience that could support you now?"
- "What options do you see for moving forward from here?"
- "Which of your values are being touched upon in this situation?"
- "How do your beliefs about yourself influence your perception of this challenge?"
- "What would change if you viewed this situation through a different lens?"
- "What is the strongest emotion you're feeling right now? Why do you think that is?"
- "How do your emotions guide your decisions in this situation?"
- "Can you identify where in your body you're feeling these emotions?"
- "And as you pay attention to yourself, what emotions are you noticing in yourself right now?"

Table 7.5: Reflective Questions for the Coach

1. Which of these MCC BARS are already part of your repertoire and enhance the masterfulness of your coaching style?
2. Which of these MCC BARS do you wish to focus on in order to be masterful with your clients rather than doing masterful?
3. Review a recording of your coaching, noting each and every time you detect examples of the MCC BARS. Pay particular attention to what emerges in the next few utterances between you and the client. What does maintaining presence contribute to the quality of the coaching conversation? What might you like to develop and grow?

Growing MCC

When you have done what it takes to be awarded an MCC credential, the learning and growth do not stop there. In fact, the MCC coach would be wise to be even more committed to quality assurance, as many ACC and PCC coaches look to them as role models. So what kinds of reflection questions and activities can support the MCC coach in enhancing and maintaining their presence?

Table 7.6: Reflective Questions for the Coach

1. How do I stay informed and adaptable to new coaching methods or theories? What steps can I take to integrate new learning into my practice?
2. How effectively am I maintaining focus on the present moment during sessions? What mindfulness practices could I incorporate to improve?
3. How does continuous learning shape my effectiveness as a coach? What areas of coaching am I curious to explore further?
4. How often do I seek feedback on my coaching practice? What have I learned from these sessions that helped me grow professionally?

CHAPTER 7

Case Study

The client, who we will refer to as "Sarah," is experiencing significant emotional stress due to a conflict with her sister, who we will refer to as "Anna." The tension has escalated over unresolved issues related to their family business. Sarah reports feeling stressed and often has knots in her stomach when thinking about the conflict, affecting both her personal well-being and her professional performance. As you read the case study, where do you notice examples of the coach maintaining presence?

Coach: I can see this situation with your sister is really taking a toll on you. Let's take a deep breath together and allow ourselves to be fully present in this moment. [*The coach allows for a pause, during which the client takes in a deep breath.*] What's the most pressing feeling you're experiencing right now?

Client: [*Breathes a long breath out and then says,*] I just feel so anxious all the time. Every time I think about talking to Anna, my stomach just turns into knots. It's like I'm bracing for a storm that never ends.

Coach: I hear you Sarah, those knots… what do you think they're trying to tell you about this conflict?

Client: Maybe… that I'm scared? [*Pauses.*] Scared of losing the bond with my sister over our business disagreements.

Coach: I can sense the fear in you as you speak about this… How might understanding this fear change how you approach your conversations with Anna?

Client: [*Pauses to reflect.*] "I guess I've been so focused on winning the argument that I've not really considered how much I'm losing in the process. [*Sighs and looks down.*]

Coach: [*In a quieter voice and at a slower pace.*] It's powerful that you're recognizing that. [Long silence.]

Client: Yes, that's the first time I've let myself realize this.

> **Coach:** How does it feel to consider the possibility of approaching Anna with this new perspective?
>
> **Client:** It feels lighter, somehow. Like maybe there's a way to communicate where I don't have to always be on the defensive.

These questions not only evoke deeper reflection but also empower Sarah to explore her thoughts and emotions more thoughtfully, enhancing her ability to understand herself and how she manages her relationship with her sister more effectively. Let's continue...

> **Coach:** Sarah, you've shared some powerful insights today about shifting from winning to understanding in your interactions with Anna. As you think about these changes, what are you discovering about yourself in this process?
>
> **Client:** [*Takes a moment to reflect.*] I'm realizing that I've been holding onto being right so tightly that it's been costing me something much more valuable – my relationship with my sister. I'm seeing now that I'm stronger than I thought, strong enough to be vulnerable with her.
>
> **Coach:** What would it look like if you approached Anna, feeling stronger to be vulnerable with her?
>
> **Client:** I think it would look like both of us are actually listening, not just waiting to speak. Maybe I need to be the one to start that change.
>
> **Coach:** That's a courageous step. How do you imagine you can go about initiating this new way of interacting with her?

The client here began to outline how she imagined herself implementing what she was taking from the session. The client left the session feeling empowered to change her communication style with her sister, reducing her anxiety and refocusing on rebuilding their relationship rather than winning an argument. The coach's ability to maintain presence allowed her to guide Sarah through deep emotional insights and facilitated a plan that Sarah felt confident to implement.

This case study highlights the importance of a coach's presence in navigating complex emotional issues. By being fully present, open and flexible, the coach provided the support and space necessary for the client to explore her feelings deeply, leading to significant personal insights and a client-centric approach to resolving her conflict with her sister.

How "Maintains Presence" Serves the Client

As you read these benefits for the client when a coach maintains presence, reflect on which you are already good at, and which you would like to improve so as to offer your clients impeccable coaching experiences.

1. **Creates a safe and supportive environment:** When a coach maintains presence, it helps in establishing a safe and trusting environment. Clients often need to discuss personal and sometimes sensitive issues. Knowing they are in a safe space where the coach is completely attentive and non-judgmental encourages clients to open up and share more freely, facilitating deeper self-exploration.

2. **Ensures individual attention:** Being fully conscious and present means that the coach's focus is entirely on the client, without distractions. This undivided attention enhances the client's confidence in the coaching process and in their own abilities to resolve their issues.

3. **Facilitates genuine discovery and insight:** The flexibility and openness of the coach encourage clients to explore various aspects of their lives that they might not have considered before. This can lead to new insights, learnings and progress, and to client-desired outcomes.

4. **Promotes in-the-moment responsiveness:** A present and grounded coach can quickly adapt their coaching style and techniques based on the client's immediate responses. This responsiveness ensures that the coaching sessions are client-centric and evolve with the client autonomy in the process.

5. **Accurate observations:** Being fully conscious allows the coach to better notice, observe and respond to the nuances in the client's communication, such as tone, pace and non-verbal cues, leading to a deeper understanding of the client's needs.

6. **Cultivates trust:** The consistency and calmness of a grounded coach help cultivate trust. Clients are more likely to open up and delve into deeper, sometimes difficult, issues.

7. **Encourages exploration:** An open coach fosters an environment where clients feel free to explore a wide range of topics. This openness can lead to greater self-discovery, insights and learnings.
8. **Goes beyond the surface:** Curiosity helps in partnering with the clients to delve deeper into issues, moving beyond the obvious to explore underlying patterns, habits, values and beliefs, amongst other things.

How "Maintains Presence" Serves the Coach

When a coach "maintains presence," they become free to focus on learning about the who of the client and their situation, with less attention and energy being used to self-regulate. The coach becomes more human and less performance conscious. Core Competency 5: Maintains Presence interplays with Core Competency 2: Embodies a Coaching Mindset. Together they allow the coach to show up in service of the client and the coaching process, and to engage in multifaceted partnering. Here are some particular ways in which maintaining presence serves the coach in serving the client:

1. **Facilitates deep listening:** Being fully conscious and present means that the coach is not only hearing what is said but is also attentive to how it's said, the non-verbal cues and the emotions behind the words. This deep level of listening helps the coach to understand the client's perspective thoroughly, leading to more insightful responses and guidance.
2. **Cultivates trust and safety:** The ability to remain grounded and confident provides a stable and reassuring presence that can help in building trust. Clients are more likely to feel secure and open up when they sense that their coach is both competent and calm, even in the face of challenging discussions or emotional revelations.
3. **Facilitates client-centered coaching:** Staying conscious of the client and maintaining curiosity help ensure that the coaching remains client-centered. This approach focuses on the client's needs, goals and personal growth, rather than the coach's agenda. It enables the coach to tailor their approach based on real-time sharing and evolving insights about the client.

4. **Promotes client confidence and autonomy:** A coach who embodies confidence can instill the same in their clients. By being present and demonstrating confidence in the client's abilities, coaches can empower their clients to take ownership of their growth, progress and overall achievements.
5. **Deepens understanding:** By remaining fully conscious of the client, a coach ensures they are fully attuned and aware of all aspects of the client's communication. This includes not only words but also non-verbal cues such as tone, facial expressions and body language.
6. **Increases adaptability:** Being present allows coaches to be more adaptable. By being in the moment, coaches can more effectively respond to the client.
7. **Increases the effectiveness of the coaching process:** Overall, this competency directly contributes to the effectiveness of the coaching process. It ensures that the coach is actively engaged, responsive and wholly dedicated to the client's agenda, facilitating a more transformational coaching experience.

Core Competency 5: Maintains Presence is also key for Core Competency 1: Demonstrates Ethical Practice. When the coach maintains presence well, they are more likely to manage bias and blind spots, thus making it more likely they will do good and not do harm (Standard 24, ICF Code of Ethics, 2019; https://coachingfederation.org/ethics/code-of-ethics).

Your Evolution as a Great Coach

You are on your way to becoming a great coach. As you navigate your way through these behaviors and markers, at each level you continue to grow and develop. A key part of this process is being conscious of your areas for development and becoming more self-aware and more situationally aware. This awareness can help us better evaluate the impact of our work and the next areas for our development.

It's worth noting that development is not a linear journey. We sometimes regress due to lack of practice, or we develop bad habits or poor practices. Being mindful of our need to continue to review, to reflect and to challenge ourselves will reduce these risks and help us continue our journey of continuous improvement.

Reflective Questions

1. What was I feeling during the session, and how did I manage my emotions to stay present with the client?
2. How did my physical and mental state affect my coaching presence today?
3. In what moments did I find my attention wandering, and what brought it back?
4. How did I adapt my coaching style in response to the client's needs? Was I flexible enough?
5. What assumptions did I make about the client, and how did these assumptions affect the session?
6. How effectively did I listen to the client, and what could I do better next time?
7. What strengths did I demonstrate that contributed to a strong coaching presence?
8. Were there any moments when I felt over-involved or too detached, and what triggered those feelings?
9. How do I notice my emotional state impacting my coaching sessions? What strategies can I use to center myself before and during sessions?
10. When did I feel overwhelmed or distracted during a session? What brought me back to the moment?

Conclusion

In this chapter we have explored under the microscope Competency 5: Maintains Presence. We hope that you will be noticing how each competency contributes to the overall landscape of coaching that an ICF-credentialed coach is equipped to offer clients. Being able to maintain presence contributes to the quality of your coaching as a whole.

CHAPTER 8

Exploring Competency 6: Listens Actively

Tracy Tresidder, Osama Al-Mosa and Johan van Bavel

Introduction

In the domain of coaching, communicating effectively is paramount to creating transformative client experiences and therefore growth in awareness. Among the foundational skills, active listening stands as a powerful catalyst for building safety, trust, understanding and growth. In this chapter, we explore Core Competency 6: Listens Actively.

Active listening is often referred to as the cornerstone of communication and transcends mere hearing. It encompasses an empathic and person-centered approach to understanding others, allowing coaches to tune into their clients' words, emotions and belief systems. At its core, active listening is a dynamic process that requires both attention and intention. By engaging in this attentive practice, coaches not only establish a profound level of trust and rapport but also gain valuable insights that serve as a springboard for profound coaching interventions.

In this chapter you will discover why active listening is indispensable, benefiting both clients and coaches alike. We'll explore the meaning and examine each aspect of the competency, reviewing how this shows up at each level: ACC, PCC and MCC. A practical checklist will be presented which will aid the coach in self-assessment. We will uncover how active listening serves clients by creating a safe space for exploration, awareness and growth. We will also look beyond the coaching relationship to see how active listening enriches daily interactions and personal relationships. With reflective questions to guide continual growth, this chapter encourages coaches to embrace active listening as a transformative force, propelling their coaching journey to new heights.

Table 8.1: Competency 6: The ICF Definition of Listening Actively

Definition: Focuses on what the client is and is not saying to fully understand what is being communicated in the context of the client systems and to support client self-expression.

Table 8.2: Competency 6: Listens Actively

6.1 Considers the client's context, identity, environment, experiences, values and beliefs to enhance understanding of what the client is communicating.

6.2 Reflects or summarizes what the client communicated to ensure clarity and understanding.

6.3 Recognizes and inquires when there is more to what the client is communicating.

6.4 Notices, acknowledges and explores the client's emotions, energy shifts, non-verbal cues or other behaviors.

6.5 Integrates the client's words, tone of voice and body language to determine the full meaning of what is being communicated.

6.6 Notices trends in the client's behaviors and emotions across sessions to discern themes and patterns.

Definitions

In using the word "listens," we refer to the act of paying attention to understand, to be understood and to comprehend what's being said (and not being said), whilst being present in a very attentive way. "Actively" is about the intentional and the conscious effort we exert to be engaged with our clients in a responsive way. When combining the words, "listen actively" moves the process from receiving auditory information through hearing into a focused approach that requires attention, interest and participation.

Otto Scharmer (2016) identifies four levels of listening, the deepest of which is the generative level, that involves listening from a place of openness and receptivity to emerging possibilities. Individuals suspend their own agendas and mental models, creating space for new insights, ideas and innovations to emerge. The four levels reflect a progression from narrow-mindedness and judgment to deep empathy and generative possibilities.

The competency "Listens Actively" employs our mental and emotional capabilities, exerted firstly by coaches' continuous attention to the client's words, tone, energy and non-verbal cues. Secondly by the coach's empathic ability to put themselves in the client's shoes, suspending judgment and demonstrating genuine care and concern. Thirdly, by picking up the non-verbal cues and receiving them with openness and curiosity. Fourthly, by reflection and clarification to ensure accurate comprehension, and fifthly by providing appropriate understanding and validation which might involve verbal affirmations, empathetic statements, or offering relevant insights or observations.

To truly listen actively, coaches must cultivate a state of being that allows them to absorb not only the client's words but also their emotions and unspoken cues. This state involves several key attributes. Firstly, a good listener in coaching must be fully present, setting aside distractions, suspending personal judgments and dedicating undivided attention to the client. For instance, imagine a coaching session where a client is sharing their challenges at work, including feelings of overwhelm and self-doubt. A coach who is fully present listens attentively, attuned to the client's emotions, providing ample room for the client's complete expression, ultimately facilitating insightful clarity.

Moreover, effective listening in coaching involves being keenly attuned to emotions. Clients frequently convey critical insights not only through their words but also through their emotional expressions. A skilled coach can discern shifts in tone, body language or energy, leveraging these cues to pose pertinent and thought-provoking questions. For instance, if a client becomes emotional while discussing a work-related challenge, an emotionally attuned coach might inquire about the trigger behind those feelings, instigating a deeper exploration of the client's emotional responses and the underlying beliefs and values that underpin them.

Furthermore, adept coaching listeners must embrace the potency of silence, affording clients the necessary time to formulate their thoughts. In the quiet, the client might stumble upon profound insights about their situation. Lastly, effective coaching listeners excel in identifying patterns, recurring themes, limiting beliefs, assumptions and potential opportunities within a client's narrative. We listen to what's not being said! By identifying these patterns, coaches can pose targeted questions that challenge limiting beliefs and open doors to new possibilities for the client.

On top of the above, the impulse to formulate the next question remains a common derailer for the active listening of coaches. To combat this, coaches should prioritize mindfulness and presence. Staying fully in the moment and resisting distractions allows coaches to focus intently on the client's words and emotions. Mindfulness exercises like deep breathing can aid in staying centered. Embracing silence is another crucial strategy. Coaches often feel compelled to fill pauses in conversations, but silence can be profoundly beneficial. Allowing space for clients to reflect and express themselves without interruption can lead to profound insights. Trust that the client will continue when they're ready.

Strategic and very brief note taking is another tool. While staying present is essential, jotting down a key word or emotion can help relieve the pressure of remembering everything. The PIPS model is a useful tool to guide that process, limiting notes to four broad areas: personal information, ideas, plans and suggestions (see Passmore and Sinclair, 2024). These brief notes may serve as valuable references when formulating questions or insights later in the session. However, it's crucial not to become overly consumed with note taking, as it can also be distracting and take away from the coach's presence.

In summary, being a proficient listener in coaching transcends mere auditory reception. It involves creating a receptive state that enables coaches to engage fully with their clients. This state encompasses complete presence, emotional attunement, an appreciation for silence, and a knack for identifying patterns and feeding them back to the client. When coaches embody these qualities, they can navigate coaching conversations with empathy, insight and the ability to foster transformative client experiences and therefore growth in awareness (Bavel, 2023).

Competencies Under the Microscope: Behaviorally Anchored Rating Scale (BARS) and Markers

Let's examine the behaviors and markers that indicate both comprehension and deployment of this competency. Since there are three ICF levels – Associate Certified Coach (ACC), Professional Certified Coach (PCC) and Master Certified Coach (MCC) – we will be specifying the requirements at each level to ensure clarity regarding expectations.

Level 1 Aligns with Associate Certified Coach (ACC)

Competency 6: Listens Actively

"Listens Actively" in Coaching: A Journey through the ACC Level

Definition: Focuses on what the client is and is not saying to fully understand what is being communicated in the context of the client systems and to support client self-expression.

ACC BARS

> A6.1 Coach uses summarizing or paraphrasing to make sure they understood the client correctly.
>
> A6.2 Coach makes observations that support the client in creating new associations.
>
> A6.3 Coach co-creates a shared vision with the client.

At the ACC level, coaches are evaluated on their capacity to listen actively to their clients' needs, respond appropriately to ensure comprehension, and competently integrate the client's communication to support their goals.

At the ACC level we are expecting that the coach will be listening more for WHAT the client is saying in relation to their, the client's, agenda, to ensure clarity of understanding and respond to what the client offers to support the client in achieving their agenda. Listening is more at a surface level and the coach is often more focused on finding the problem and finding solutions to fix it.

A6.1 Coach uses summarizing or paraphrasing to make sure they understood the client correctly

The coach can use summarizing or paraphrasing techniques to ensure they understand the client's communication. This may take the form of:

- Rewording or rephrasing what the client said.
- Offering back main points or key takeaways from the client's communication to validate their understanding.
- The coach checking with the client to ensure they have fully understood what the client has said.

Short, succinct summaries can also build trust as they highlight the coach's presence and attention and give room for partnering to take the session jointly to another direction if needed. For example:

- "If I understood correctly, you want to find ways to balance your work demands and personal life more effectively as it seems that the many pressing work inquiries are in conflict with your life responsibilities. How does that sound?"
- "What I hear you saying is that you're passionate about advancing your career and stepping into a leadership role. However, you feel unsure about the path forward and want to overcome certain obstacles. How accurate is that?"

A6.2 Coach makes observations that support the client in creating new associations

The coach can provide observations to support the client in making new associations or perspectives. This may take the form of:

- The coach offering an observation in response to what the client shared.
- The coach seeking the client's consent before sharing an insight.

For example:

- "I noticed that whenever you talk about your personal time, there are different facial expressions and your voice tone changes. It feels like the tendency is to put a lot of pressure on yourself to fulfill your work and personal life responsibilities."
- "I heard you well! And I've noticed that whenever you talked about your creative pursuits, there's a spark in your eyes. May I share an insight that came to mind while listening to you?" After the OK from the client, the coach said, "It seems to me as if your passion for art is a significant source of inspiration for you!"

A6.3 Coach co-creates a shared vision with the client

The coach can include the integration of the client's words or ideas to build shared meaning and understanding between the coach and client. This could certainly relate to the agreement, focus or outcomes, but it could also relate to other elements of the coaching conversation. This may take the form of:

- Engaging in conversational exchanges with the client.
- Inquiry and posing questions to the client.
- Exploring possibilities and ideas.
- Integrating the client's words to construct mutual understanding.

For example:

- "It's clear that sustainability is essential to you. Can you tell me more about what aspects of sustainability resonate with you the most?"
- "I heard you well: it felt like you are envisioning a workplace that offers sustainability and that values collaboration and inclusivity. How do you see yourself contributing to such an organization?"
- "You mentioned wanting to work for a company that aligns with your values. Can you describe the kind of work culture and company mission that you envision?"

Table 8.3: Reflective Questions for the Coach

1. Did you listen for key words?
2. Did you listen more than you spoke?
3. Did you listen from their point of view?
4. Were you more focused on gathering information to formulate the next question?

Level 2 Aligns with Professional Certified Coach (PCC)

Competency 6: Listens Actively

Definition: Focuses on what the client is and is not saying to fully understand what is being communicated in the context of the client systems and to support client self-expression.

The following PCC Markers are behaviors that represent the demonstration of the ICF Core Competency 6 in a coaching conversation at the Professional Certified Coach (PCC) level.

6.1 Coach's questions and observations are customized by using what the coach has learned about who the client is or the client's situation.

6.2 Coach inquires about or explores the words the client uses.

6.3 Coach inquires about or explores the client's emotions.

6.4 Coach explores the client's energy shifts, non-verbal cues or other behaviors.

6.5 Coach inquires about or explores how the client currently perceives themself or their world.

6.6 Coach allows the client to complete speaking without interrupting unless there is a stated coaching purpose to do so.

6.7 Coach succinctly reflects or summarizes what the client communicated to ensure the client's clarity and understanding.

At the PCC level the expectation is that the coach is listening more for who the client is being, as well as what the client is doing. What is the client bringing to the conversation and how is the coach hearing that and structuring questions, comments and observations? The emphasis is less on finding the solution and more on creating awareness.

6.1 Coach's questions and observations are customized by using what the coach has learned about who the client is or the client's situation

This aspect is about the coach incorporating their understanding of their client and their unique situation to be able to tailor their questions and observations. This requires the coach to go beyond generic, one-size-fits-all questions and observations. For example:

- "You mentioned well-being. What's the impact of this situation on your well-being?"
- "During our previous session, you shared that you have outstanding adaptability and resilience in handling challenges. How can you use these areas of strength to enhance your chances to succeed in a different career?"
- "I hear you have several options [A, B, C]. Which one would you like to choose?"
- "Given the insight you have right now, how does that change your perspective on your situation?"
- "With this learning you have now, how would you like to move on in this conversation?"

6.2 Coach inquires about or explores the words the client uses

This is particularly important when the client repeatedly mentions a word or when the word might be abstract or unique, or relates to the session goal. For example:

- "I've heard you use the word 'frustration' two or three times in relation to your colleague. What does frustration mean to you?"
- "What uncomfortable thoughts or feelings come up when you think about delegating?"
- "What I hear you saying is X. How does that feel for you?"

6.3 Coach inquires about or explores the client's emotions

This is not just about noticing; it is also about exploring. Pay attention to the emotions that might be present for the client. Inquire or explore the meaning that it might hold. This marker also includes when tone or pace of speech does not match the content of what they are saying. For example:

- "I'm noticing that there is a lot of emotion coming up for you right now? What are the tears telling you?"
- "It sounds like there is a feeling of overwhelm. What specific tasks or situations trigger this feeling?"
- "What do you feel right now?"

6.4 Coach explores the client's energy shifts, non-verbal cues or other behaviors

This is also about exploring. Energy shifts refer to the client's change in pace of speech, tone, inflection or volume. Non-verbal cues include eye contact, body language or facial expressions. If the coach explores this, it implies that the coach is noticing and acknowledging. For example:

- "Your tone went a little higher and your speech faster – what is coming up for you now?"
- "I noticed a change in your energy just now. What thoughts or emotions might be surfacing for you?"
- "I see you smiling – what's happening for you now?"
- "Your energy is rising. Please tell me about that."
- "I see you doing X a lot of times when we talk about a specific part of your topic. What's going on for you at those moments?"

6.5 Coach inquires about or explores how the client currently perceives themself or their world

The coach is looking for how the client understands and views themself and their world, and what impact those perceptions might have. The questions can uncover the underlying beliefs or assumptions that may be creating the barrier to change. For example:

- "What assumption are you making about that?"
- "What is your perspective, from where you stand right now?"
- "What's your view to your world you live in?"
- "How do you see yourself in your world?"

6.6   Coach allows the client to complete speaking without interrupting unless there is a stated coaching purpose to do so

The coach needs to create enough space or pause, between when the client stops speaking and when the coach starts responding, to avoid interruption. This silence provides the space for clients to process their thoughts. They also need to listen attentively using minimal sounds of encouragement (such as "aha," "yep," "wow," "mmm," etc.).

If the client is repeating their story or using very long descriptive stories, there may be a coaching purpose to interrupting. Ideally, the client is speaking 80% of the time and the coach is speaking less than 20% of the time. For example:

- "May I stop you here? As you share those details, what is happening for you?"

When the coach is listening to the client, they should aim to allow sufficient time for them to think, process and reflect before they speak. The coach should try to avoid rushing in with another question or observation. Instead, they should be patient and let the client be in their moment. It's most often here where new insights emerge. The result is a coaching conversation which feels relaxed and comfortable, and the client is in control.

6.7 Coach succinctly reflects or summarizes what the client communicated to ensure the client's clarity and understanding

This is a two-part marker. The first part is not a regurgitation of what the client has said but rather the coach offering their understanding – for example, "You mentioned you couldn't possibly go for it, when you spoke about that promotion." The second part of the marker is not the coach needing the clarity and understanding, but rather the client understanding their own sense making – for example, "What makes you sure you couldn't go for it?"

The coach reflects back a summary to support the client in seeing their own thinking. For example:

- "What sense are you making of this now, having said that out loud?"
- "Sounds like a little bit of disappointment. I'd like to check in before we move on."
- "I hear you saying X. Is this correct?"
- "Let's check if we are still on the same page: my listening is that X. Do we still have the same understanding?"
- "If you would summarize what we are talking about in this session, what would you say?"

Reflect on Your Coaching Practice Wherever You Are in Your Coach Development

Table 8.4: Reflective Questions for the Coach

1. Are you listening not just to the words but for the beliefs, assumptions and values?
2. Are you listening for only problems or weaknesses rather than possibilities?
3. Are you listening through your own perceptions and models of thinking and learning rather than the client's?
4. Are you being present to your client by removing distractions, and noticing your own bias or fear of silence?

Level 3 Aligns with Master Certified Coach (MCC)

Competency 6: Listens Actively

Definition: Focuses on what the client is and is not saying to fully understand what is being communicated in the context of the client systems and to support client self-expression.

CHAPTER 8

Regarding the examples given for the MCC BARS, please take into consideration that in order to meet the requirements for MCC-level coaching, the contextual and relational aspects of the coaching conversation need to be taken into account. These in their wholeness serve as evidence for whether in the given coaching a sufficient depth and variety of dimensions of the client's life, purpose and identity have been fully explored and responded to by the coach.

MCC BARS

> M6.1 Coach responds to the client with an invitation into a deeper exploration of client thinking and behaviors.
>
> M6.2 Coach's responses to the client demonstrate an understanding of the client's emotions, energy, or learning and growth, in alignment with the client's agenda.
>
> M6.3 Coach reflects what the client communicates in relation to the context of the whole person.

Coaching at an MCC level is distinguished by the coach's fluid and artful approach to the coaching conversation. Coaching is more focused on WHO the client is being and supporting the client to identify beliefs and assumptions behind opinions and actions, fears and conflicting values. This level of coaching is known as awareness-focused coaching. At the MCC level, the listening shifts to listening as a learner not a knower – listening to unlock and not to solve. The coach is reaching into the client's perspective to open and expand the number of possibilities from that bigger space. An MCC-level coach hears the totality of the client's greatness and gifts as well as limiting beliefs and patterns beyond the client's situation or immediate goals. The coach is listening cumulatively from session to session.

Finally, and not least important, is that an MCC coach primarily listens to themself. An MCC coach is highly aware of who they are and is capable of listening to themself while attending to the client. You might like to consider the following questions:

1. What is the impact of the client's communication on me as a coach?

2. What triggers me and impacts my ability to listen?
3. Am I aware of how my body responds to the coaching dynamics?
4. How do I harness my responses and how can I offer them to the client?
5. How can I regulate my emotions and avoid projecting them onto the client?

M6.1 Coach responds to the client with an invitation into a deeper exploration of client thinking and behaviors

The coach is using the client's contribution, insights and sharing to deepen the learning. The coach is in tune holistically with the client and able to invite the client into deeper exploration of their thinking, perceptions, beliefs or behaviors to create a supportive and insightful coaching environment where the client feels understood, challenged and empowered to make meaningful progress towards their goals. For example:

- "What you are saying is you're carrying a heavy burden of responsibilities both at work and home, and it's causing a lot of stress in your life. I'm curious about what uncomfortable thoughts or feelings come up when you think about managing your responsibilities."
- "What would be most at risk for you if you didn't meet those targets?"

To dive deeper, the coach needs to explore how the client is affected by, and how they make sense of, this problem. Master coaches should aim to support their clients in exploring their own thinking and their sense making. So, the question can be repeated again, after the client responds to the client's answer to the first question. For example, "If performance reviews were coming up and you didn't meet those targets, what's the hardest part about that for you?"

As the coach explores at this deeper level, the client becomes more aware of their meaning making – for example, they can see that they are linking their sense of being a good person with having a good performance review. For some this insight can be a transformational insight.

CHAPTER 8

Before clients are ready to become aware of future possibilities and new behaviors, they need to be aware of where they are in the present moment to move forward. As coaches, we do not specifically explore the past; rather, the client needs to be aware of how the past impacts them in the present.

M6.2 Coach's responses to the client demonstrate an understanding of the client's emotions, energy, or learning and growth, in alignment with the client's agenda

Assimilating the essential behaviors of this competency elevates one to a heightened level of coaching mastery. This advanced skill requires a nuanced comprehension of the client's evolving perspectives. As the coach mirrors the client's unfolding insights, a profound resonance emerges. This is achieved by skillfully reflecting the client's entrenched beliefs, acknowledging their perspective while gently prompting a shift in thinking. The coach's response transcends mere mirroring; it becomes a catalyst for exploration. Similarly, the coach can achieve this by responding dynamically to the client's real-time learning, showcasing not just acknowledgment but also an acute awareness of the client's learning journey. This proficiency guides the client's evolving insights towards practical strategies for growth. The following example explore the transformative impact where the coach's responses show these behaviors clearly.

The coach can share observations, acknowledging strengths, ideas, emotions, values and so forth, and then explore how these might be in service of the desired coaching outcomes. For example:

- "I can really hear the shift in your voice when you speak about stepping into that new role. What's coming up for you now?"

- "What you're saying is that you can now see that you are relying on this external validation as your sense of value in relation to your clients. And this appears to be keeping you stuck in relation to your outcome for the session. What are you more aware of now?"

- "My intuition tells me that there are thoughts in your mind which you cannot yet find the words to express. How does this sound to you when I say it like this"

M6.3 Coach reflects what the client communicates in relation to the context of the whole person

This behavioral rating scale involves deeply understanding and working with the client's communication across various dimensions of their life. It entails integrating and exploring what the client communicates, considering multiple aspects such as psychological, emotional, social, cultural, professional and personal dimensions. The coach maintains a client-centric approach, fostering self-awareness and growth by delving into the interconnectedness of different areas of the client's life. This highlights the coach's ability to engage with clients in a profound and holistic manner, facilitating meaningful conversations that lead to positive change and development.

The coach will consider the client's context, identity, environment and so on – that is, the whole person – and then share observations that connect the client to the future they are trying to create. For example:

- "I'm hearing several threads from what you have spoken about so far. What is most important to you out of what you just shared?"

- "You have mentioned that integrity is a key value and a strength of yours. I'm curious as to how that may be connected with your current situation?"

- "I notice that when we discuss your career aspirations, your voice becomes more animated, and your body language becomes more open. However, when we shift the conversation towards your personal relationships, I sense a subtle shift in your energy, and you seem to hesitate or become quieter. Can you help me understand what might be behind these differences in your reactions?"

Growing MCC

As a Master Certified Coach (MCC), continuous learning is vital for mastery. The MCC will continue to refine their skills, including their skills in "Listens Actively." The MCC will remain adaptable and continue to expand their understanding to include various dimensions like socio-economic context and faith, creating an inclusive space for all their clients to grow. Additional training, such as advanced coaching programs or certifications, and ongoing supervision are essential for enhancing mastery. Supervision offers a structured environment for reflection, feedback and insights from experienced mentors or peers, enabling MCCs to refine their skills, navigate complex dynamics and stay updated with best practices (Passmore and Sinclair, 2024), as does ongoing training. Together, these practices show a continued commitment to development.

Table 8.5: Reflective Questions for the Coach

1. Are you listening to fix or to unlock?
2. How are you helping the client see their thinking?
3. Are you sensing what your client is experiencing as you listen?
4. Are you using silence to allow your client to form new thoughts and perspectives?
5. Are you listening for patterns, themes, limiting beliefs, assumptions, possibilities?
6. Are you listening and exploring facial expression, body language, pace and tone?
7. Are you listening as a learner in regard to the client's abilities, energy, values and how they grow and create?
8. Are you suspending assumptions and biases about meaning and just being curious with the client about what they are saying or not saying?
9. Do you listen to the energy in your own body?
10. Do you listen to your intuition?

Case Study 1

A business advisor sought coaching due to an ultimatum she received: become more collaborative or risk missing out on a promotion. As her coach delved into what "being more collaborative" meant to the client and what felt jeopardized for her if she didn't get promoted, the client expressed her concerns:

> "Everyone knows what 'missing out on a promotion' implies. It's essentially a warning to shape up or ship out. There's only so much

time to dawdle around here… Once you're tagged as inadequate in something, it's incredibly hard to shake off that label. And lacking collaboration essentially means that either your team, peers or, heaven forbid, your superiors or clients, don't favor you. So, what's on the line if I don't rectify this immediately? I'll be shown the door."

The coach listened and responded with: "What would that mean to you?" Renata responded:

"What do you mean, what would that mean? I'd be fired. I thought I had the intellect to thrive here, but apparently, being smart isn't sufficient. I've never faced failure before, so I need to address whatever it takes to fix this. I must be perceived as more collaborative, which I guess translates to compromising on my quality standards, dedicating more time to developing others and refraining from voicing disagreement. If people don't like you in this environment, it's a deal-breaker."

The coach listened and reflected. She identified Renata's assumptions and helped her examine them critically. The coach responded with: "It seems like you may be telling yourself these things, that appear to be true to you at the moment, that:

- Negative feedback = issue to be resolved
- No promotion this year = termination
- Inability to succeed here = failure
- Collaboration = universal likability."

By dissecting these assumptions, the client began to realize that they were constructs of her reality, influenced partly by experience but not universally true. This revelation empowered her to ask herself different questions:

1. What options do I have in response to this feedback?
2. What insights can I gain from this?

The client also made significant shifts in her language patterns, no longer conflating "collaboration" with being liked by others. Instead, she began viewing collaboration in terms of its impact on work quality rather than solely on others' perceptions of her. She also engaged in practices to increase her tolerance for uncertainty, recognizing her tendency to seek certainty in situations.

As the client worked further with her coach, she confronted the assumed constraints she had placed on herself over the years. These constraints included beliefs such as:

- I must accept my boss's feedback even if I disagree.
- I must take action to address any feedback received.
- I cannot take time off when there's an issue to resolve.

By questioning the validity of these constraints and experimenting with alternatives, the client began to dismantle them. She shifted from viewing them as absolute truths to recognizing them as constructs that had guided her behavior but were open to revision.

In conclusion, the client's journey illustrates how identifying and challenging linguistic habit patterns can lead to personal growth and development. By moving assumptions from the realm of unquestioned truths to objects of examination, clients can construct new realities better suited to their evolving contexts. This process embodies the essence of development and fosters adaptive responses to challenges (Coughlin, 2019).

How "Listens Actively" Serves the Client

The ICF competency "Listens Actively" stands as an important pillar in the coaching relationship, offering an array of benefits that serve the client's growth, self-discovery and progress. This competency is not just about hearing; it's about helping clients in meaningful ways that create a safe space for clients to be heard, understood and empowered, leading to transformative outcomes.

Here's how this practical skill can serve clients:

1. **Safety, trust and connection:** Active listening builds trust. Clients feel respected and understood, allowing them to share openly without fear. This connection is the basis of productive coaching conversations. It allows the client to open up more authentically, sharing their thoughts, feelings and challenges without fear of judgment.

2. **Deep self-discovery:** Active listening serves as a catalyst for thoughtful self-discovery. The act of being heard and understood

often prompts clients to reflect on and articulate their thoughts more clearly, which can lead to heightened self-awareness and insights. This enables clients to gain clarity about their goals, values and aspirations, and helps them to "see their thinking," ultimately guiding them towards purposeful actions.

3. **Independent problem-solving:** Active listening facilitates the client's ability to solve their own challenges. This process allows clients time and space to process their emotions and thoughts, often leading them to their own solutions. It allows the clients to tap into their own inner wisdom, boosting their confidence in decision-making.

4. **Seeing from new perspectives:** The coach helps the client explore multiple viewpoints and consider different angles to their situation. This allows the client to shift from limited thinking to more expansive possibilities, which encourages a growth mindset and allows clients to be more adaptable to difficulties.

How "Listens Actively" Serves the Coach

Listening actively, recognized as a crucial skill, serves coaches in numerous profound ways, enhancing their effectiveness and impact within the coaching relationship. At its core, this skill establishes a context of safety, trust and support. Coaches who practice "Listens Actively" create an environment where clients feel safe sharing their deepest thoughts, emotions, body language and aspirations. This dedicated attention fosters openness and encourages clients to express themselves freely, ultimately contributing to a more fruitful coaching journey and results.

Beyond surface-level conversations, "Listens Actively" enables coaches to tap into the deeper currents of their clients' emotions and concerns. By discerning underlying meanings, coaches can offer responses and explorations that directly address the heart of the client's challenges, leading to more meaningful progress and transformation.

Through this practice, coaches can develop deep empathy for their clients. By immersing themselves in the client's perspective, coaches cultivate a strong client–coach relationship based on mutual understanding. This empathy-driven foundation enriches coaching

CHAPTER 8

interactions, ensuring that guidance resonates authentically and effectively with the client's unique circumstances.

"Listens Actively" also sharpens coaches' communication skills. By focusing on active listening techniques such as summarization and paraphrasing, coaches enhance their comprehension and minimize misunderstandings. This skillful exchange facilitates clearer communication and amplifies coaching's positive influence.

The tailored interventions resulting from active listening are another asset. Coaches, equipped with a deep understanding of the client's needs gained through listening actively, can craft interventions specifically aligned with the client's situation. This customized approach greatly increases the relevance and success of coaching strategies, guiding clients more precisely toward their desired outcomes.

Trust, a cornerstone of any coaching relationship, thrives through "Listens Actively." By being client-centered and showing genuine interest and respect, coaches foster an environment where clients feel comfortable sharing even their most sensitive concerns. This environment of trust encourages open dialogue and builds a nurturing and productive coaching journey.

"Listens Actively" can unlock insights and create greater awareness. Active listening supports and encourages the clients to "see their thinking" and explore their feelings more deeply, which can lead to a new level of awareness, which is essential for personal growth and development.

In essence, the competency "Listens Actively" transforms the coaching process from a simple conversation into a powerful and transformative experience. By actively engaging deep listening followed by reflective inquiry, clients are empowered to challenge assumptions, explore new ideas and uncover insights that were previously unknown.

An MCC coach has active listening embedded in their system. The coach not only understands this competency but embodies it in their entire DNA. Active listening is closely connected to asking effective questions. The coach who listens to what the client is not saying is simultaneously skilled at posing thought-provoking questions.

In conclusion, "Listens Actively" serves as a fundamental skill that enhances the coaching process, enriching interactions and fostering growth for both coaches and clients.

Your Evolution as a Great Coach

You are on your way to becoming a brilliant coach. As you navigate your way through these behaviors and markers, you are continuing to grow. To conclude this competency, we have provided ten questions for you to use as part of your reflective practice. By reflecting on your practice, and specifically by using a reflective journal to do so, you will enhance the value of your coaching hours, learning and developing with each coaching session that you conduct.

In the final part of this chapter, we have provided some deep-dive reflective questions to ask yourself after each coaching session.

Reflective Questions

1. How did my active listening contribute to the client's self-awareness?
2. Did I notice any non-verbal cues or subtleties in the client's communication that may have gone unnoticed without listening actively?
3. How effectively did I use silence as a tool to allow the client to think deeply and generate insights?
4. What strategies did I employ to help the client navigate complex or emotionally charged topics during our conversation?
5. How did I foster a sense of trust and rapport through my active listening techniques?
6. Did I guide the client towards exploring underlying beliefs, assumptions or blind spots through skillful questioning and reflection?
7. In what ways did I help the client gain clarity and perspective on their challenges or goals through active listening?

8. How can I notice when I am triggered by something the client brings and then bring myself back to presence and listening actively?

9. How can I become more comfortable with the silence?

10. How can I further refine my active listening skills to better support the client's growth and development in future sessions?

Conclusion

In this chapter we explored Competency 6: Listens Actively. We explored this competency across ACC, PCC and MCC levels, highlighting its evolution. Active listening goes beyond mere hearing, allowing coaches to deeply connect with clients. It benefits clients by fostering exploration, trust and growth. It also aids coaches, enhancing their effectiveness and intervention customization. Trust and clarity thrive, and hidden insights surface, making coaching transformative. The next chapter is focused on Competency 7: Evokes Awareness. When you have established the skills of listening actively, then you can focus on facilitating the client's insight and learning. Each competency is effectively built on the previous one.

CHAPTER 9

Exploring Competency 7: Evokes Awareness

Karen Foy, Leda Turai, Elena Espinal and Ram S. Ramanathan

Introduction

In essence, coaching is primarily and ultimately not about finding ready-made solutions; instead, it's about sparking the client's thinking process and nurturing their creativity to construct something entirely new. This creation might manifest as a new insight, a new realization, a new or different solution, a novel approach to living or even an entirely different perspective. When we can contribute to this as coaches, we are evoking awareness.

If, during or at the conclusion of a session, the client cannot articulate a fresh insight, new-found knowledge or a heightened understanding of their situation or themselves, this signifies that the coach has not effectively triggered awareness. Any question or intervention used by the coach is assessed in the context of its impact on the client and connected to their expressed desired outcome, a key difference between coaching and a supportive chat.

It is crucial to note that, in an evaluation of performance, every question or technique employed by the coach is evaluated by the assessors based on its impact on the client. Consequently, this competency is intrinsically linked to the preceding competencies. The coach's ability to align closely with the client in order to clarify their genuine exploratory intentions and takeaways from the session is paramount. The more adeptly this alignment is established, the clearer it becomes which aspects have yet to be delved into by the client. Moreover, a coach who remains fully present and inquisitive is better positioned to discern the subtle verbal and non-verbal cues that point to what genuinely requires probing, exploration or acknowledgment as the client navigates their path towards their desired objectives.

As you read the examples, be aware that these are only intended to offer an idea of how each aspect of evoking awareness might sound in practice; they are not a list of "powerful questions." There is no such thing. As you read about this competency, we hope the message is clear: the most powerful question is generated from what the client says; it is a response and does not come from a pre-prepared list. We hope this will support your development to ensure you are working in partnership with your clients to have a profound impact on them and their life.

In this chapter we aim to explore the meaning of the competency in more depth and consider how it can be developed in coaching through the levels of ACC, PCC and MCC, giving examples of how it might be demonstrated. We will also explore the concept of Growing MCC in the context of evoking awareness, as we are never finished with our learning. As in previous chapters, we have used the ICF BARS and Markers to explore the competency.

Table 9.1: Competency 7: The ICF Definition of Evoking Awareness

> **Definition:** Facilitates client insight and learning by using tools and techniques such as powerful questioning, silence, metaphor and analogy.

Coaching is a creative, partnered journey between a client and coach to evoke awareness in the client to expand the possibilities, choices and ways of being on their journey to a desired outcome. Since no active "action" takes place in a coaching space and only insights to action are created towards an "agreed" outcome, awareness is the logical end point of the coaching journey. Along this journey, a person can expect to learn more about themselves, their beliefs, feelings, values and motivations that can sustain change beyond one single encounter, challenge or episode.

Table 9.2: Competency 7: Evokes Awareness

7.1 Considers client experience when deciding what might be most useful.

7.2 Challenges the client as a way to evoke awareness or insight.

7.3 Asks questions about the client, such as their way of thinking, values, needs, wants and beliefs.

7.4 Asks questions that help the client explore beyond current thinking.

7.5 Invites the client to share more about their experience in the moment.

7.6 Notices what is working to enhance client progress.

7.7 Adjusts the coaching approach in response to the client's needs.

7.8 Helps the client identify factors that influence current and future patterns of behavior, thinking or emotion.

7.9 Invites the client to generate ideas about how they can move forward and what they are willing or able to do.

7.10 Supports the client in reframing perspectives.

7.11 Shares observations, insights and feelings, without attachment, that have the potential to create new learning for the client.

Evoking awareness is built on the foundation of the earlier competencies and is the foundation for facilitating growth and learning in the client to make sustainable change. As you commit to your development as a coach, you will gradually develop your ability to evoke awareness with more ease, moving from curiosity about the client for your own needs to engaging the client in curiosity about themselves.

Definitions

Awareness is a fundamental cognitive ability that involves being conscious and perceptive of oneself, one's surroundings and the ongoing experiences and events in which one is involved. It encompasses a range of dimensions, including sensory perception, self-awareness, emotional intelligence and mindfulness. Awareness allows individuals to gather information, process it and make sense of their internal and external world. It involves being attuned to thoughts, feelings, sensations and the impact of one's actions on oneself and others. Cultivating awareness can lead to greater self-understanding, empathy and the ability to navigate and respond effectively to various situations.

Awareness plays a crucial role in coaching; it is a necessary call for analysing different points of view and behaviors. One of the most exciting contributions of coaching is to put into practice the game of observing the same situation from different points of view or perspectives, which leads us to realize that "being right" is a waste of time and that, in these conversations, we can broaden our way of observing and be more conscious when choosing the future we want to build. In addition to what we mentioned above, it allows us to discover our behavioral patterns and triggers, our biases and prejudices, and the possibility of generating, in response, a way of acting that was unusual until that moment.

From the definition of coaching, we would like to emphasize a couple of specific words: "thought-provoking" and "creative." In essence, coaching is primarily and ultimately not about finding ready-made solutions; instead, it's about sparking the client's thinking process and nurturing their creativity to construct something entirely new. This creation might manifest as a new insight, a new realization, a new or different solution, a novel approach to living or even an entirely different perspective.

Thus, the initial step in any transformative process involves becoming aware and conscious of something. The ICF breaks down this "something" into two overarching and interconnected categories: the "what" and the "who." These encompass a wide spectrum of facets. The "what" may encompass the client's situation, a challenge, an obstacle, an external circumstance, a goal, an aspiration or a dream. The awareness about the "what" could relate to the past, present and future, all aimed at acquiring essential insights and propelling forward toward a desired future. At times, clients may wish to delve into inquiries related to the "who," such as transforming a constraining belief into an empowering one. In such cases the "what" is the topic the client wants to focus on, and it will be interwoven with "who" they are.

If, during or at the conclusion of the session, the client cannot articulate a fresh insight, new-found knowledge or a heightened understanding of their situation or themselves, this signifies that the coach has not effectively triggered awareness. It's crucial to note that every question or technique employed by the coach is evaluated based on its impact on the client. Consequently, this competency is intrinsically linked to the preceding competencies. The coach's ability to align closely with the client in order to clarify their genuine exploratory intentions and takeaways from the session is paramount. The more adeptly this alignment is established, the clearer it becomes which aspects have yet to be delved into by the client. Moreover, a coach who remains fully present and inquisitive is better positioned to discern the subtle verbal and non-verbal cues that point to what genuinely requires probing, exploration or acknowledgment, as the client navigates their path towards their desired objectives.

Alongside the "what" and the "who," this competency encourages coaches to consider "how" they can facilitate insight. The tools and techniques referred to in the competency description remind the coach to draw on their creativity to evoke awareness. Powerful questions are just one of a range of approaches to heighten awareness and allow fresh thinking to emerge. Whether using questions, metaphor, silence, sharing observations or specific tools or techniques, the key is that the chosen tool is employed thoughtfully in order to be most useful to the client in the moment.

Awareness can be cognitive, emotional and sensory, individually and together. Awareness arises by exploring the needs, wants, beliefs, values and assumptions of the client's way of thinking about themselves in their current reality and invitation to share present-moment experiences. The coach partners with the client in a challenging exploration, without attachment, to go beyond current thinking by reframing the client's perspective to align generatively with the desired outcome. The coach is always aware and focused on what would be most useful to the client, noticing the client's progress appreciatively, sharing what they sense to create new learning, to generate ideas on what the client is able and willing to move forward with and be accountable to themselves for.

There is an implicit underpinning belief in this competency that awareness precedes change. The simplicity of that assertion masks the depth of learning, practice and self-exploration required for a coach to truly partner with their client to explore with them, and evoke their own exploration, to uncover the creative and resourceful source within them. Our aim here is to explore and to share our thoughts and experiences of how this competency develops through our development as coaches from Level 1 to Level 3 and beyond.

Competencies Under the Microscope: Behaviorally Anchored Rating Scale (BARS) and Markers

As mentioned above, this competency is defined as the capacity to facilitate client insight and learning by using tools and techniques such as powerful questioning, silence, metaphor and analogy. The skills required for this, evaluated by ICF assessors, encompass the following:

1. The coach's use of inquiry, exploration, silence and other techniques that support the client in achieving new or deeper learning and awareness

2. The coach's ability to explore with and evoke exploration by the client of the emotional and substantive content of the words

3. The coach's ability to explore with and evoke exploration by the client of the underlying beliefs and means of thinking, creating and learning that are occurring for the client

4. The coach's ability to support the client in exploring new or expanded perspectives or ways of thinking

5. The coach's invitation to and integration of the client's intuition, thinking and language as critical tools in the coaching process.

Based on the above, let's examine the behaviors and markers that indicate both comprehension and deployment of this competency. Since, in ICF, there are three distinct levels – Associate Certified Coach (ACC), Professional Certified Coach (PCC) and Master Certified Coach (MCC) – we will specify the differing requirements at each level to ensure clarity regarding expectations. Remember, the example conversations are just that: examples to spark your own awareness to be responsive. Your interventions will come from what you hear from your clients.

Level 1 Aligns with Associate Certified Coach (ACC)

Competency 7: Evokes Awareness

Definition: Facilitates client insight and learning by using tools and techniques such as powerful questioning, silence, metaphor and analogy.

ACC BARS

A7.1 Coach acknowledges the client's new awareness, learning and movement toward the desired outcome.

A7.2 Coach supports the client in viewing the situation from new or different perspectives.

A7.3 Coach inquires about or explores the client's ideas, beliefs, thinking, emotions and behaviors in relation to the desired outcome.

A7.1 Coach acknowledges the client's new awareness, learning and movement toward the desired outcome

Coach interventions might include:

- "I noticed you're smiling. It seems a shift has occurred. Would you like to share your thoughts?"
- "Now you have realized the drive is not really about finding a new job but creating a more balanced life, what does that make possible?"
- "That sounds like you have learnt something about yourself, that you want to be more assertive. How can you use that realization to create the boundaries you were seeking?"
- "What do you avoid doing when you hold the belief that you are not good enough?"
- "Who do you believe could help guide you deeper into this decision?"

A7.2 Coach supports the client in viewing the situation from new or different perspectives

Coach interventions might include:

- "If you believed that you were good enough, how would your behavior be different at work?"
- "Envision yourself in a state of calm and joy. How might facing the current situation differ from this perspective?"
- "Throughout the session, I noticed you were searching for rational and logical explanations. What emotions and intuitions are associated with this new opportunity?"
- "If you adopt an observer's perspective, what do you notice?"

A7.3   Coach inquires about or explores the client's ideas, beliefs, thinking, emotions and behaviors in relation to the desired outcome

Coach interventions might include:

- "What criteria haven't you taken into account when attempting to make a decision about this new promotion?"
- "What impresses you so much in other people whom you see as confident?"
- "How do you believe spontaneity could benefit you, and to what extent?"
- "What do you avoid doing when you hold the belief that you are not good enough?"

Box 9.3: Reflective Questions for the Coach

1. How much did I notice about the client and their thinking?
2. Did I acknowledge their insights?
3. How curious was I about their perspective?
4. In what ways did I support them to expand their perspective without imposing my own views?
5. How did I support the client to turn their insights into movements towards their desired outcome?

Level 2 Aligns with Professional Certified Coach (PCC)

Competency 7: Evokes Awareness

Definition: Facilitates client insight and learning by using tools and techniques such as powerful questioning, silence, metaphor and analogy.

At this second level of development, the inquiries are deeper and focused on the "who" as well as the "what," and there is an emphasis on the type of intervention. The expectation is now that questions are more succinct, clear and focused, and that the coach is using themselves as an instrument in the conversation, employing their own thoughts, feelings and intuitions in service of the client's new insights and choices. These increased skills are reflected in the range of markers for this level.

7.1 Coach asks questions about the client, such as their current way of thinking, feeling, values, needs, wants, beliefs or behavior.

7.2 Coach asks questions to help the client explore beyond the client's current thinking or feeling to new or expanded ways of thinking or feeling about themself (the who).

7.3 Coach asks questions to help the client explore beyond the client's current thinking or feeling to new or expanded ways of thinking or feeling about their situation (the what).

7.4 Coach asks questions to help the client explore beyond current thinking, feeling or behaving toward the outcome the client desires.

7.5 Coach shares – with no attachment – observations, intuitions, comments, thoughts or feelings, and invites the client's exploration through verbal or tonal invitation.

7.6 Coach asks clear, direct, primarily open-ended questions, one at a time, at a pace that allows for thinking, feeling or reflection by the client.

7.7 Coach uses language that is generally clear and concise.

CHAPTER 9

7.8 Coach allows the client to do most of the talking.

7.1 The coach asks questions about the client, such as their current way of thinking, feeling, values, needs, wants, beliefs or behavior

The coach explores deeper, both cognitively and emotionally, into areas the client repeats or stresses with emotional undertones in word, voice and body. This marker is related to their *current* way of thinking, feeling and behaving, and could be an area that may not be in full conscious awareness for the client. As a thinking partner, the coach can bring to light some of the hidden beliefs and assumptions that may be contributing to these patterns of behavior and ways of being. As the coach listens, notices and asks pertinent questions, a more holistic picture can start to emerge for the client so they can start to challenge any limitations in choices they have and can make. For example:

- "What are your emotions and feelings about your problem areas holding you from what you wish to achieve?"
- "What beliefs fuel those emotions?"
- "I understand and appreciate the vulnerability you're in and how you acknowledge your emotions."
- "I observe a shift in your voice tone [or energy, or body language]. Is there something you may wish to share?"
- "What makes you think that achieving what you want always has to be accompanied by joyful and happy moments?"

7.2 Coach asks questions to help the client explore beyond the client's current thinking or feeling to new or expanded ways of thinking or feeling about themself (the who)

This marker is about asking questions to the client in such a way that the client can explore beyond thinking or feeling to a new or expanded way of thinking or feeling about themself. These are the kind of questions which refer to "who" is the person as a whole.

The importance of provoking questions towards new ways of looking at coaching lies in its ability to expand the client's perspective and encourage creative and reflective thinking. Limiting assumptions and beliefs can be challenged through challenging questions, allowing the client to explore different approaches and solutions. Questioning promotes personal and professional growth and helps to find new perspectives and options to achieve the desired goals. For example:

- "If you think about the future you want to create, what are the values that you think you need to invoke to create that future?"
- "This question is for your heart to answer, not your head: if you could truly choose what you want to achieve, what would be the choice that honors your best version of yourself?"
- "How do you think your ability to choose influences your well-being and personal satisfaction?"
- "What is your approach to balancing your personal needs with the expectations of others?"

7.3 Coach asks questions to help the client explore beyond the client's current thinking or feeling to new or expanded ways of thinking or feeling about their situation (the what)

The focal terms here are "beyond the client's current thinking or feeling" and "new or expanded ways of thinking or feeling about their situation." Before we provide examples illustrating what constitutes evidence for showcasing this skill, we wish to reiterate that the evoking awareness competency assessment will be predicated on the impact on the client. Hence, only questions or inquiries that support the client in delving beyond their current thinking or feeling, leading them to experience novel or broader ways of thinking or feeling about facets of their situation (linked to the session goal and/or overall coaching engagement), will be recognized as demonstrating Marker 7.3. For example:

- "As we are playing with this 'daisy' metaphor and as you are talking to her, looking at her, how is she responding to you?"
- "What touches you most when you hear those words?"
- "In such a quiet, beautiful moment under the blue sky, if we connect those feelings you are talking about with your body again, how do you feel now?"
- "What connection do you see between those seemingly unrelated decisions?"

- "Having connected the dots here, what are all the new opportunities that are opening for you?"

7.4 Coach asks questions to help the client explore beyond current thinking, feeling or behaving toward the outcome the client desires

The first key indicator in the definition of this marker is the concept of exploration beyond the client's current thinking, feeling and behavior, as we have already discussed. The second key concept and distinguishing element of this competency is toward the outcome the client desires. This moves the exploration of possibilities into imagining a desired future, a reminder of the looping back to the imperative for a tangible outcome in establishing the agreement. What might this look and sound like practically? The coach may be encouraging the client to visualize the successful outcome, to embody it and explore the taste of success. They may be employing creative activities, somatic exercises, metaphor, drawing, whatever would be useful and inspire the client based on their way of expressing themselves. From this vantage point, the coach could be encouraging the client to explore all the routes to that goal. Maybe asking about the behaviors that could carry them to that place, what changes in beliefs and thoughts could support that forward movement and what they might stop doing to be set free. For example:

- "So, what would that gracious move to the next stage look like?"
- "As you feel yourself on that solid ground, looking up to the space of dreams, what is the breeze that can carry you there?"
- "As you hold on to the courage you have found, how can you use that to give voice to your needs?"
- "You have explored both avenues. Which one is drawing you forward?"
- "As you visualize yourself in that place and time and look back to today, what do you see as the defining moment?"
- "As you spoke about your commitment to that future, I noticed a shift. What did you notice?"
- "If you were a superwoman or man, what path would you choose to reach the goal you have chosen?"

7.5 Coach shares – with no attachment – observations, intuitions, comments, thoughts or feelings, and invites the client's exploration through verbal or tonal invitation

There are two key phrases in this marker, and we explore them briefly here. Firstly, the "coach shares." Sharing refers to giving, providing or distributing something with others. Sharing is often driven by a sense of generosity, cooperation and communion, allowing individuals to contribute to the well-being or happiness of others or, as in this case, to create new awareness. When a coach shares his/her opinion, thoughts, feeling or intuition, the intention is to support the client's willingness to enter uncharted territory. Learning appears only in the spaces of what we do not see or do not know.

Secondly, this happens, "with no attachment." This phrase takes on crucial weight. "With no attachment" means that the coach not only does not want to be right but also that the client's response to the invitation is not supposed to be important as "yes" or "no," "it is so" or "it is not like this;" rather, its context is more to offer something that may have possible value to the client. That is why a neutral tone of voice is used. In general, permission to share is requested; however, if trust with the client is well established, it is often not necessary to say anything because the client already has the experience of the coach as someone who does not want to impose or has something special as an agenda.

For example:

- "I have an intuition. Can I share it, and you tell me if it works for you?"
- "I feel something, and I offer you to share it, and you tell me what you think. Is that OK?"
- "I perceive that your energy/emotion has changed. I would like to check with you before continuing."
- "Could this be useful for you?"

7.6 Coach asks clear, direct, primarily open-ended questions, one at a time, at a pace that allows for thinking, feeling or reflection by the client

Let's be clear that in coaching the purpose of asking a question is to generate thinking and reflection so the client can learn more about their situation and themselves. They can start to use that learning to help them progress towards their desired outcome. We might slow down and recognize that quick-fire questions are not the most useful approach. Offering short, clear, open questions offers the client the best opportunity to evoke awareness. "Clear and direct" is usually the first stumbling block for coaches, followed closely by "open ended" and "one at a time," leading to less time for thinking, feeling or reflection. Paradoxically, when coaches ask questions that are unclear, it comes from a wish to be clear. At this level, the coaching conversation has a gentler rhythm than the interview style of the less-experienced coach. For example:

- "What patterns have you observed?"
- "So, you have created the opportunity but not the story?"
- "How does that show up?"
- "How will you know which path to choose?"

7.7 Coach uses language that is generally clear and concise

If a coach's place is to foster self-awareness through direct communication, how can he/she create more space for the client? The coach should occupy a smaller place if the focus is on the client. To do so, you can look for the client not to answer the coach's questions, but to make a deep connection with himself/herself and listen to himself/herself.

This changes the coach's communication accordingly. To do this, clear language is very important. As far as possible, the words must be the same or similar to the ones the client uses. In addition, the marker refers to the fact that the message must be concise.

Long-windedness is a vital enemy of a good coach. Being talkative does not mean that a person is a good coach. The coach would be advised to skip preambles, explanations and backstories, go to the essence, what is essential to communicate, and avoid thinking out loud. For example:

- "Can I share with you what I have noticed?"
- "What else can you think of?"
- "Where is this leading to?"
- "What may be the beliefs you have that lead to your feeling or thinking or actions now?"
- "What experiences have you had which are influencing your thinking right now?

7.8 The coach allows the client to do most of the talking

The more experienced the coach, the less they will be heard in the conversation – and when they do speak, it is to encourage the client to fully express themselves. There is no need for sounds of approval or disapproval, these may simply act as distractions for the client. For example:

- "What emotions are coming up for you as you describe your situation?"
- "Have you been feeling this frustration before, and if you have, are you ok to talk about it?"
- "I observe from your body language that there is more in there than what you have said. Are you comfortable sharing more about your feelings?"

Building a relationship through questions can be an effective way to foster learning and understanding between individuals. By asking thought-provoking questions, engaging in meaningful discussions and actively listening to each other's perspectives, coach and client can deepen their understanding and develop a strong learning partnership. This approach promotes critical thinking, empathy and collaboration, leading to mutual growth and knowledge acquisition. The focus of the coach is on creating a thinking partnership that allows the client to fully express themselves at a pace that suits them, with a partner that is fully present, noticing and offering interventions that expand thinking.

Box 9.4: Reflective Questions for the Coach

1. What was the balance of voices in the conversation?
2. What questions did I hold back from asking (and why)?
3. How did I decide on my interventions?

Level 3 Aligns with Master Certified Coach (MCC)

Definition: Facilitates client insight and learning by using tools and techniques such as powerful questioning, silence, metaphor and analogy.

Regarding the examples given for the MCC BARS, please consider that in order to meet the requirements for MCC-level coaching, the contextual and relational aspects of the coaching conversation need to be taken into account. These in their wholeness serve as evidence for whether in the given coaching a sufficient depth and variety of dimensions of the client's life, purpose and identity have been fully explored and responded to by the coach.

Competency 7: Evokes Awareness

> M7.1 Coach partners with the client to explore the client's stories, metaphors and imagery that support growth and learning.
>
> M7.2 Coach stimulates new client insights with minimal, precise questions.
>
> M7.3 Coach asks questions that challenge the client to explore more deeply or go beyond current thinking and feeling.
>
> M7.4 Coach shares with fluidity insights, observations and questions from the client's words and actions, to foster awareness.

At the MCC level, the coach's invitation to the exploration of important issues precedes and is significantly greater than the invitation to a solution.

The coach's way of being is consistently curious, and coaching from a space of not knowing is the most powerful source of questions. Drawing from our extensive experience as coaches and mentor coaches, we have found the ICF's notion that the coach functions as a "learner" within the coach–client dynamic to be valuable. This approach permits the entire conversation to unfurl and develop organically, contingent upon the client's thinking, learning, and creative process.

The following quote from the improvisational violinist Stephen Nachmanovitch describes the atmosphere of MCC coaching: "Faithfulness to the moment and to the present circumstance entails continuous surrender. Perhaps we are surrendering to something delightful, but we still have to give up our expectations and a certain degree of control – give up being safely wrapped in our own story."

During the performance evaluation, assessors are expecting the MCC applicant to ask mostly, if not always, direct, evocative questions that are fully responsive to the client in the moment, to the client's agenda and stated objectives. Assessing the evocative nature of a question is relatively straightforward, as immediate answers from the client are unlikely. The answers will necessitate introspection and self-discovery. Frequent pauses and prolonged moments of silence signify that both the coach and the client have ventured into unexplored territories, where the client's insights have not previously reached. As William Isaac aptly noted, thinking and thoughts are distinct concepts. Most of our thoughts are mere repetitions of pre-existing scenarios. A constructive metric to consider is: has your question encouraged the client to converse or to contemplate?

In alignment with the principles outlined above, it's essential for an MCC applicant to exhibit a capacity for simultaneous presence at various levels. This involves staying immersed in each unfolding moment while concurrently retaining awareness of what has been learned from and about the client throughout the entire session and coaching engagement. These insights will serve as the foundational elements for the coach's subsequent questions and inquiries. Consequently, we observe that the coach regularly and effectively adopts the client's language and learning style to formulate questions, insights or observations.

M7.1 Coach partners with the client to explore the client's stories, metaphors and imagery that support growth and learning

Visual images can be more powerful in reflecting emotion than cognition alone. Stories, metaphors and visualization provide the contextual support for one's emotional content. Often, such imagery brings in directly, or upon exploration, unconscious belief systems, values and needs that limit client thinking and actions. Sometimes, clients may come up with an imagery themselves that the coach can use to explore. Otherwise, the coach can invite the client to suggest an image or what comes to mind. For example:

- "You said that your situation reminded you of a story. Can you expand on it?"
- "What kind of metaphor would relate to what you are going through?"
- "Can you visualize your situation and tell me what's happening in your body?"
- "As I listen to you, I am reminded of a metaphor. Can I share this with you?"

M7.2 Coach stimulates new client insights with minimal, precise questions

It's an unstated golden rule in coaching for the client to do most of the talking. At MCC level the client will be doing 80% or more of the talking. The coach will be listening, observing, acknowledging, inquiring and occasionally sharing (with consent). For example:

- "What is generating this feeling or thinking?"
- "What is the belief that you hold (or need or value) that leads to this conclusion?"
- "Can we see how we can reframe your line of thinking that could work for all?"
- "Can you reflect on what you said just now and see if you can think of an opposite?"

M7.3 Coach asks questions that challenge the client to explore more deeply or to go beyond current thinking and feeling

When the client is disempowered and emotional, they may vent and indulge in long monologues. If the client's thoughts are in a pattern that does not seem to be moving to awareness or towards the desired need they articulated and agreed to, the coach should act to point this out to the client. This may require an interruption. For example:

- "I see that you are emotional and reflective. Is this leading you to awareness in line with what you need?"
- "I notice that you are focused on what the other person is thinking. What's going on within you right now?"
- "You said in the beginning that X. Now, I seem to be hearing something different when you say this."
- "I notice that you are experiencing anger. If you set that anger aside, what would you like to do?"

At the MCC level the coach's way of being is consistently curious, and coaching from a space of not knowing is the most powerful source of questions. Drawing from our extensive experience as coaches and mentor coaches, we have found the ICF's notion that the coach functions as a "learner" within the coach–client dynamic to be valuable. This approach permits the entire conversation to unfurl and develop organically, contingent upon the client's thinking, learning and creative process.

It is expected of MCC applicants to ask mostly, if not always, direct, evocative questions that are fully responsive to the client in the moment, to the client's agenda and stated objectives. Assessing the evocative nature of a question is relatively straightforward, as immediate answers from the client are unlikely. The answers will necessitate introspection and self-discovery. Frequent pauses and prolonged moments of silence signify that both the coach and the client have ventured into unexplored territories, where the client's insights have not previously reached. It's these moments of silence and reflection when insight is gained, not from the mere repetitions of pre-existing thoughts and previously shared stories of events. A constructive metric to consider is: has your question encouraged the client to converse or to contemplate?

- "How might this better serve your growth and desired outcomes?"
- "How might these beliefs shape your future strategies and decisions? Are there any underlying beliefs or assumptions you need to revisit or revise for the future?"

M7.4 The coach fluidly shares insights, observations or questions, derived from the client's words and actions, to foster awareness

The coach's way of talking invites the client to expand their learning and discover, integrate and apply that learning to the present challenges, and to take charge of creating their future. Connection and presence are essential, and to build deeper trust, any observation could be done without the need to prepare the ground for the client to receive the information.

Example observations:

- "I noticed that you are very comfortable with metaphors and analogies." [pausing and waiting]
- "I noticed that every time you mention the name of your colleague, you stop smiling and start fidgeting." [pausing and waiting]
- "What a deep sigh! How does it reflect the real feeling you might be afraid of admitting having in relation to this?"
- "…and I noticed that now you reversed a little bit the order, because before it was who, what and how. And now it sounds like this who is the how."
- "I am paying attention to how you are defining yourself. There were maybe a few hints to defining yourself as a being. You said you're being a child of God, you're being a human, but then many things came through verbs, like you are learning, you're seeking to grow, and it sounded a little bit more like doing. But that's my assumption and I think, my curiosity is more about, what's the difference for you when you are being as opposed to doing?"
- "The way you show up seems to me as I perceive it, shows this grounded place. I see you smiling and breathing deeply, and I see… joy. And I've heard you talking about this grounded place that brings you a lot of contentment…"

- "I tend to notice a discrepancy between what you say and what your body language and tone of voice suggest... What do you notice about yourself?"
- "I notice an interesting pattern of referring to yourself. Sometimes in the middle of the sentence you change the 'I' into 'you.' What does that 'you' point to, when you think about it?"

Examples of intuitions and insights:

- "We have been talking about your values during the last few sessions, and as I listen to you today remembering our past conversations, I get the sense that there might be something more important than these values you keep referring to. How does this resonate with you?"
- "Hmm. I am sensing something here, but I do not have a comprehensive reflection for you, only an intuition, which may or may not be right. When would be the right moment to share it with you? [...] I get this nagging thought that where we are searching for what you wanted, is maybe not the right place. What do you think about this?"
- "What would be your reaction to my intuition, if it said that the key to your decision is exploring not deciding, rather than exploring deciding?"

Box 9.5: Reflective Questions for the Coach

1. How am I helping my client to go deeper in their self-reflections?
2. How am I helping my clients to break away from the previous stories they have told before around this topic?
3. How am I helping my clients to use metaphors which help them to discover new insights for themselves?

Growing MCC

A coach who achieves their Master Certified Coach (MCC) accreditation recognizes this is not a destination. They will continue honoring the competency. The path of mastery is a never-ending fulfilling journey with continuous attention on how Competency 7 offers the capacity to build simultaneous presence at various levels. This involves staying immersed in each unfolding moment while concurrently retaining awareness of what has been learned from and about the client throughout the entire session and coaching engagement.

How "Evoking Awareness" Serves the Client

Awareness is the crucial outcome in a coaching conversation for the client. Awareness lifts the client from their unconscious incompetence level to the conscious incompetence level, allowing them to be aware of their blind spots and limiting beliefs. This is more than half the journey in coaching. Moving from this aware space to learn what would make them competent consciously, and then anchor that as an unconscious competence, can be the follow-up action. This action needs to happen with accountability and perseverance. Awareness opens the closed door of unconscious limiting beliefs and blind spots.

Some shifts that clients experience as they have their "aha" moment include:

1. Discovering what may be most important and useful in their journey
2. Discovering why they think, feel and behave the way they do
3. Moving beyond the way they think and feel now, creating a mind shift
4. Sharing vulnerably and openly what they sense, feel and think
5. Understanding what may be holding them back
6. Realizing what needs to transform to achieve what they want
7. Realizing how they can change the way they think, feel and behave, changing past patterns
8. Generating ideas on how they can learn from their insights to grow.

Awareness serves clients of coaching in several ways:

1. **Self-reflection:** Through the coaching process, clients are encouraged to develop self-awareness and explore their thoughts, feelings, beliefs and behaviors. This increased self-reflection

helps clients gain a deeper understanding of themselves, their values, strengths, limitations and areas for growth.

2. **Clarity of goals, priorities and concerns:** Coaching helps clients become more aware of their true desires, aspirations and goals. By exploring their values, passions and purpose, clients can gain clarity on what they truly want to achieve and align their actions accordingly. Concerns are not goals or commitments. Concerns have to do with what is worth it for life, what moves you in life. This awareness allows them to set meaningful goals and prioritize their efforts.

3. **Identifying limiting beliefs and patterns:** Coaching supports clients in recognizing and challenging limiting beliefs and patterns that may be holding them back. By becoming aware of negative self-talk, self-sabotaging behaviors or unhelpful thought patterns, clients can replace them with more empowering beliefs and behaviors that support their growth and success.

4. **Expanding perspectives:** Coaching helps clients gain new perspectives and alternative ways of thinking. By exploring different viewpoints, considering different approaches and challenging assumptions, clients can expand their thinking and consider fresh possibilities. This awareness broadens their options and encourages creative problem-solving.

5. **Improved decision-making:** Increased self-awareness enables clients to make more informed and conscious decisions. By understanding their values, beliefs and priorities, clients can align their choices with their authentic selves. They become more mindful of their decision-making process, considering the consequences and long-term impact of their actions.

6. **Personal growth and development:** Through coaching, clients gain awareness of their strengths, talents and areas for development. This awareness allows them to focus on personal growth, build upon their strengths and develop strategies to overcome challenges. It empowers them to take proactive steps towards self-improvement and achieving their full potential.

Overall, awareness serves clients of coaching by providing them with deeper self-understanding, clarity of goals, the ability to challenge limiting beliefs, expanded perspectives, improved decision-making and opportunities for personal growth. It supports them in making positive changes, unlocking their potential and achieving their desired outcomes.

CHAPTER 9

How "Evoking Awareness" Serves the Coach

A coach needs to be self-aware to coach. This requires self-coaching to evoke awareness of the way a coach uses the coaching process, supported by supervision. Many learner coaches, especially those who are executives engaged in problem-solving and troubleshooting, tend to offer solutions. As the client speaks, the coach has an inner dialogue processing what the client says, which impels the coach to wait impatiently for the client to finish so that the coach can jump in or interrupt. Awareness is essential for the coach to focus on the client with no inner dialogue, and with a still, non-judgmental mind.

Enhanced awareness serves the coach in a variety of ways:

1. **Self-awareness:** As a coach, being aware of your own thoughts, emotions and biases is crucial. It helps you understand how your own perspectives and experiences might influence your coaching approach, allowing you to manage them effectively and ensure they don't interfere with the coaching process.

2. **Client awareness:** Developing a high level of awareness about your clients is essential. It involves actively listening, observing their non-verbal cues and tuning in to their emotions, needs and aspirations. By being aware of your clients' unique characteristics, you can tailor your coaching approach to their specific circumstances, making the coaching more relevant and impactful.

3. **Contextual awareness:** Understanding the broader context in which your clients operate is vital. This includes recognizing the organizational culture, industry dynamics and societal influences that may impact your clients' goals and challenges. With contextual awareness, you can provide insights and perspectives that align with their environment, enabling them to navigate it more effectively.

4. **Patterns and dynamics:** Developing awareness of recurring patterns and dynamics within your coaching sessions can help you identify underlying issues or themes that may be hindering your clients' progress. By recognizing these patterns, you can address them directly, helping your clients break through barriers and achieve their desired outcomes.

5. **Continuous learning:** Awareness allows coaches to engage in ongoing learning and development. By reflecting on your coaching sessions, seeking feedback from clients and staying curious about new coaching methodologies and research, you can refine your skills and expand your knowledge base, ensuring you provide the best possible support to your clients.

In summary, awareness plays a fundamental role in coaching by helping coaches understand themselves, their clients and the broader context, allowing them to tailor their approach, address underlying issues and continuously improve their coaching practice.

Your Evolution as a Great Coach

Evoking awareness in the client is what makes coaching distinct and different from mentoring, training, consulting, therapy and other outcome-focused interventions. Coaching is founded on the Rogerian belief of client-centricity, the assumption that the client knows best what needs to be done (Rogers, 1957). The coaching process is built around evoking awareness through reframing and other techniques. This awareness in any one situation can be expanded to multiple other interactions. The process trains the coach in reflecting, reviewing and reframing their unconscious limiting beliefs to create conscious competencies, which when anchored become unconsciously competent new mindsets and behavior. The process of evoking awareness ultimately enhances the non-judgmental creativity of the coach in supporting others in their journeys.

Reflective Questions

1. How well did I create awareness of unconscious limiting beliefs and blind spots in the client's mind?
2. How did this awareness of the client's self help the client in creating greater awareness of the client's current reality through the reframing of limiting beliefs?
3. How did this awareness of the client's self and current reality help the client in learning what can be done as action steps?

4. Did I listen to and observe the client's stated and unstated expressions, acknowledge them appreciatively and share what I felt intuitively and non-judgmentally?
5. How well did I create a psychologically safe and trusted space for the client to express themselves freely, with no interruption?
6. How well did I partner with the client, encouraging the client to reflect, feel and think in creatively different ways to evoke awareness?
7. How well did I journey with the client in alignment with the client's desired outcome, supporting the client in new ways of perceiving the situation and themselves?
8. How well did I use tools and techniques to reframe, such as visualization, metaphors and stories to explore and facilitate new client insights?
9. How well did I set the stage with client awareness for the client to help learn and create new ideas to grow and achieve the desired outcome?
10. How could I have done better?

Conclusion

Viewing a coaching conversation from the lens of learning, evoking awareness is central to movement from unconscious incompetence to unconscious competence. The client is limited by unconscious beliefs, which are reframed in an empathetic conversation partnered by the coach, to evoke awareness leading to learning and growth. The next chapter focuses on Competency 8: Facilitates Client Growth.

CHAPTER 10

Exploring Competency 8: Facilitates Client Growth

Meryl Moritz, Dalia Nakar and Keiko Hirano

Introduction

In this chapter we will examine how coaches may partner with their clients to extract every bit of learning possible from the session and then translate that learning into committed next steps. As important, we will consider how celebrating the client's learning and progress contributes to the client's sense of agency. We will go step by step, exploring each aspect of the competency, and review how it shows up at each level: ACC, PCC and MCC. Finally, we will consider how Competency 8: Facilitates Client Growth serves both the client and the coach, and has implications for the greater good.

Table 10.1: Competency 8: The ICF Definition of Facilitates Client Growth

> **Definition:** Partners with the client to transform learning and insight into action. Promotes client autonomy in the coaching process.

From the first encounter the coach has with the client, the coach needs to demonstrate their sensitivity to what is inspiring the client. That is one of the coach's key responsibilities: to draw out actions that emerge from the insights.

Table 10.2: Competency 8: Facilitates Client Growth

8.1 Works with the client to integrate new awareness, insight or learning into their worldview and behaviors.

8.2 Partners with the client to design goals, actions and accountability measures that integrate and expand new learning.

8.3 Acknowledges and supports client autonomy in the design of goals, actions and methods of accountability.

8.4 Supports the client in identifying potential results or learning from identified action steps.

8.5 Invites the client to consider how to move forward, including resources, support and potential barriers.

8.6 Partners with the client to summarize learning and insight within or between sessions.

8.7 Celebrates the client's progress and successes.

8.8 Partners with the client to close the session.

Seasoned coaches often share the principle "Leave the client in action" with newer coaches and coach-aspirants. The core coaching competency "Facilitates Client Growth" embodies this principle.

Ideas and insights tend to vanish unless a committed intention to implement follows – so says the research of numerous change theorists, neuroscientists and adult-learning experts. It is in this spirit that the coach, at whichever stage of their development, needs to embrace the competency of facilitating client growth.

Definitions

What Do We Mean When We Say "Partnership?"

Partnership is key to facilitating client growth. The coach's mindset and capacity to be present as co-explorer, witness, steward and appreciator throughout the conversation are indispensable. Parties in the coaching partnership must alternate between leadership and followership: each commits to learn through their interaction, relying on curiosity and mutual respect to guide them on their path.

What Do We Mean When We Say "Progress/Accountability?"

Progress, or accountability, is whatever the client wants out of the coaching session; both coach and client want to see what progress has been made. Has the gap been closed between where the client's thinking was at the outset of the session and where the client's thinking is near the end of the session? Measures of success defined in the Coaching Agreement and action plans for taking the session work forward provide a means for the coach and the client to review progress. The review process is empowering, conveying the coach's trust in the client and bolstering the client's confidence in his/her/their "self-accountability."

What Do We Mean When We Say "Learning Awareness?"

Learning awareness relates to the energy to act which emerges when the client claims insights and new perspectives gathered in the session. The coach assists the client to identify these learnings and invites the client to articulate how to translate these into actions aligned with the session goal.

What Do We Mean When We Say "Acknowledgement/Celebration?"

Acknowledgement/celebration relates to how the coach acknowledges or celebrates who the client is and the work the client is doing, between and during sessions. Perhaps the client took all committed actions and reported back, even though the actions didn't produce the desired results. Or the client had to overcome a bias or got stuck at the mid-point in the session, yet persevered with courage and candor. Change is difficult and having the coach offer appreciation can contribute to a stronger bond and enhanced motivation.

What Do We Mean When We Say "Closing/Completion?"

Closing/completion is allowing sufficient time and mental bandwidth to bring the session to a productive close, and this is the coach's responsibility. It represents another opportunity to partner with the client, to find out if anything still needs to be said for the client to feel complete. It is the coach's final gift from the session to the client, inviting him/her/them to choose how to end the interaction. A productive closing ensures that nothing is left "on the table" unless the coach and client have identified it as part of the next session's agenda.

CHAPTER 10

Coaching Behaviors that Facilitate Client Growth

Every one of the competencies plays a part in facilitating client growth, starting with the opening conversation when coach and client collaborate to establish the Coaching Agreement. Being patient and fully present, ensuring that the coaching space is an oasis for experimentation and that the client hears from the coach that they can do no wrong are essential if the coach hopes to earn the right to advance from their client. Actively listening beyond words for what matters to the client, and asking questions that invite reflection and new perspectives, can happen in that opening conversation. Reviewing and acknowledging progress keeps motivation high. Everything hinges on the coach's mindset, which is the coach's state as they accompany the client through the coaching process and ensure that the coaching space is safe and encourages reflection.

Prepare to be surprised when ways of being and behaving such as these result in the client asking to end the session a few minutes early so they can begin to take action immediately.

Competencies Under the Microscope: Behavior Anchored Rating Scale (BARS) and Markers

Let's examine the behaviors and markers that indicate both comprehension and deployment of this competency. Since, in ICF, there are three distinct levels – Associate Certified Coach (ACC), Professional Certified Coach (PCC) and Master Certified Coach (MCC) – we will specify the differing requirements at each level to ensure clarity regarding expectations.

Level 1 Aligns with Associate Certified Coach (ACC)

Competency 8: Facilitates Client Growth

> **Definition:** Partners with the client to transform learning and insight into action. Promotes client autonomy in the coaching process.

ACC BARS

A8.1 Coach partners with the client to create or confirm specific action plans.

A8.2 Coach asks questions to support the client in translating awareness into action.

A8.3 Coach supports the client to close the session.

A8.1 Coach partners with the client to create or confirm specific action plans

This particular marker comes to light in the following distinct ways:

- "From what you have learned, how would you like to move forward towards your goal?"
- "What is the best plan to achieve this?"
- "How can I help you design your actions?"
- "Would you like at this point to summarize your actions?"
- "What is your plan for next week so you can progress?"

A8.2 Coach asks questions to support the client in translating awareness into action

This behavior can be demonstrated in these ways:

- "What do you need to keep on going to make the right decisions?"
- "If any issues were to arise in the process, what would they be?"
- "What are your takeaways from today?"
- "How can you move forward with these takeaways?"
- "Let's explore what progress you made today."
- "With your insights, what actions make sense?"

A8.3 Coach supports the client to close the session

This can be demonstrated in these ways:

- "Is there anything else that you would like to talk about?"

- "How shall we bring this session to a close?"
- "We have another ten minutes. What makes you happy now, coming to an end?"
- "We have almost reached the end of session. What would you like to do with the remaining time?"
- "What part, if any, needs to be addressed before we finish our session?"
- "Is there anything left you want to comment on?"

Box 10.3: Reflective Questions for the Coach

1. Did I contribute to the client's growth?
2. What did I learn about facilitating learning?
3. Did I invite the client to choose how the session will be closed?

Case Study 1

Jose is a manager at a company. He is at a crossroads where he must decide whether to stay within the company and advance in his career or start his own business. Coaching sessions are focused on helping him clarify which path to choose.

Initially, Jose expressed feeling limited in his current role. During the sessions, he constantly complained about a colleague, Mary, with whom he was not getting along. Throughout this particular session, Jose said that his valuable time was being wasted. He believed that pursuing a new path would allow him to utilize his abilities and energy more effectively.

Mal, his coach, asked Jose what he valued regarding work: "Jose, what do you want to achieve through your work?" In response, Jose asserted, "I want to accelerate building business. I feel energized when I discover new areas of business opportunities. I enjoy discovering new possibilities and involving many people towards that direction to drive the business forward."

"You looked so confident when you say that," Mal said, acknowledging Jose. "But you seem worn out. What is missing?" "I need more autonomy," Jose replied. "Having to get along with Mary is a distraction. I can't keep my attention on what really matters to me." Observing some irritation inside Jose, Mal said: "You keep mentioning Mary. What does she represent to you?"

"Hmm," said Jose, starting to think. Mal asked, "What strengths does Mary bring, I wonder?"

"When I talk with Mary, she keeps talking about the people instead of business." Jose started to think about Mary's strengths and then admitted, "I gradually lose energy when my expectations of Mary are not met. As I reflect upon this it has become apparent that she may have different capabilities, such as talent development."

Jose continued. "Mary is actually good at recruiting people and developing new talent, so what if she seems to be less interested in building business?" Jose began to understand how Mary utilizes her capability, and he started to see the distinction of their roles.

Mal went back and confirmed Jose's goal from the start of the coaching contract: "You wanted to decide whether you want to leave the current job or stay. With your insights, what actions make sense to you now?"

Jose hesitated a moment and then replied, "I now realize that my loss of energy wasn't due to Mary's poor performance but rather because I wasn't effectively leveraging her capabilities. So, I feel like I can channel the direction of her abilities towards her strengths. And I'm considering entrusting her with talent development so that I can focus on the business development with my team."

Jose seemed to be moving into a learning stage. Following this awareness, Mal pursued the following line of questioning in subsequent coaching sessions to continue drawing out new insights:

- "Have you made any new discoveries?"
- "From what you have learned, how would you like to move forward towards your goal?"
- "Have there been any new initiatives with Mary?"
- "What can you do next week to enhance the discovery?"

Jose volunteered that he was beginning to think more positively about his situation, as demonstrated in these statements:

- "Mary is proposing to deliver a new training that she feels is necessary for our sales team."
- "I've been feeling that the relationship with my team is getting stronger these days. Communication is going really well, and we are giving each other positive feedback."
- "Mary seems to have some ideas about how to utilize human resources more effectively. I'm taking some time with her to talk about this."

Mal acknowledged Jose's work: "Jose, you have started to shift from lamenting the differences between Mary's and your approaches to appreciating the diversity in approaches. It seems this has led to an overall improvement in the relationship, helping Mary enhance her abilities, ultimately boosting her performance and contributing to your bottom line."

"You know?" said Jose, six months after starting the coaching engagement, "with your continuous questioning on what I am learning through this process, I started to perceive difficult situations not as obstacles but as opportunities for new possibilities when I encountered them. As a result, I am able to handle challenges better, my management skills have significantly improved, and my business began to thrive. I have built a better relationship with Mary, and I feel now that I want to continue working with this team. I want to expand the business here."

Level 2 Aligns with Professional Certified Coach (PCC)

Competency 8: Facilitates Client Growth

Definition: Partners with the client to transform learning and insight into action. Promotes client autonomy in the coaching process.

PCC Markers

8.1 Coach invites or allows the client to explore progress toward what the client wanted to accomplish in this session.

8.2 Coach invites the client to state or explore the client's learning in this session about themself (the who).

8.3 Coach invites the client to state or explore the client's learning in this session about their situation (the what).

8.4 Coach invites the client to consider how they will use new learning from this coaching session.

8.5 Coach partners with the client to design post-session thinking, reflection or action.

8.6 Coach partners with the client to consider how to move forward, including resources, support or potential barriers.

8.7 Coach partners with the client to design the best methods of accountability for themself.

8.8 Coach celebrates the client's progress and learning.

8.9 Coach partners with the client on how they want to complete this session.

8.1 Coach invites or allows the client to explore progress toward what the client wanted to accomplish in this session

This particular marker can be demonstrated in these ways:

- "Here we are, midway through our coaching session. What progress have you made toward today's goal?"
- "What still needs to happen for you to achieve your goal in our session?"
- "Thinking back to today's goal, where would you say we are now in relationship to it?"
- "What do you want to acknowledge about your progress today?"
- "What are you aware of now?"

8.2 Coach invites the client to state or explore the client's learning in this session about themself (the who)

Some of the ways this can be demonstrated are:

- "What has happened to you during the session?"
- "What realizations have you had about yourself during our time together?"
- "How did this session contribute to your self-awareness and who you are being?"
- "Who are you now?"
- "What impact has this session had on your view of yourself?"

8.3 Coach invites the client to state or explore the client's learning in this session about their situation (the what)

- "What have you learned about the situation you brought to coaching today?"
- "What insights have you received from exploring your goal?"
- "How do you now see the goal you brought to today's session?"
- "What new awareness have you had about your situation?"
- "What – if anything – has shifted in how you view your situation?"

8.4 Coach invites the client to consider how they will use new learning from this coaching session

- "What do you feel inspired to do with the insights you claimed?"
- "How would you act on the insights you shared with me?"
- "What's important to take action on from this learning?"
- "I invite you to connect with your learning as we formulate post-session actions."
- "Based on the insights you had, what needs your attention going forward?"

8.5 Coach partners with the client to design post-session thinking, reflection or action

- "What is the first step you can take when you leave here?"
- "What will you do to keep your insights alive?"
- "What other actions can you experiment with to progress toward your goal?"
- "What would represent a stretch action for you?"
- "How do your actions align with the discoveries you made about yourself and your situation?"

8.6 Coach partners with the client to consider how to move forward, including resources, support or potential barriers

- "I hear your intention to act: what hurdles do you anticipate as you execute your plan?"
- "As you move into action, what resources do you have to help you?"
- "What additional resources might you need to realize your action plan?"
- "Who can you count on for support as you take your actions?"
- "What might stand in the way of you taking these actions?"

8.7 Coach partners with the client to design the best methods of accountability for themself

- "What is your preferred way to stay on track with actions you plan to take?"
- "What methods have you found that help you follow through on actions?"
- "Imagine yourself, next time we meet, reporting back that you took all your intended actions. What did you do that helped you get to that point?"
- "How will you remain accountable to your plan of action?"
- "What works for you to ensure you take the actions you planned on taking?"

8.8 Coach celebrates the client's progress and learning

- "I am inspired to see you explore new territory today and arrive at new-found insights about yourself and your goal."
- "This exploration today demonstrated your courage and conviction, and the result was an action plan you can feel proud of."
- "It's exciting to see the confidence that came out of you brainstorming options."
- "I noticed your openness and desire to move forward."
- "Who else might you share your progress with and celebrate it?"

8.9 Coach partners with the client on how they want to complete this session

- "How do you want to bring our session to a close?"
- "Are we complete?"
- "As we close our session, what remaining thoughts would you care to share?"
- "We are near the end of our time: what do you need to feel complete?"
- "We still have some topics on the table as we approach the end of the session: what do you want to do as we close out?"

Box 10.4: Reflective Questions for the Coach

1. How did I challenge the client to design actions that really matter?
2. Was I a bystander or an active participant in how my client translated insights into actions?
3. How did I ensure that the client said or did everything needed to feel complete about our session?

Case Study 2

The client, Jun, a young accomplished woman, has risen through the ranks of her company quickly. She came to the session concerned about how she can become more confident and demonstrate more "gravitas" in presentations to important people in her firm and to her external customers. She thought her presentation skills would either hinder her or, if improved, help her attain partner status. At the end of the session, she wanted to walk away with tips and actions she could take that would build a case for her being partner-level material.

With half the time remaining, the coach, Ema, offered: "We're midway through our session, Jun, and I'm wondering how you are thinking about that session goal now: to have tips and actions that will build your case for partner." Jun smiled a little shyly and said, "I notice that my thinking is like that of a junior-level person: very focused on me, what I have to do, and whom I have to impress to get promoted. I need to level-up and see how I can contribute to the firm, in the way I build relationships inside and outside, as well as how I bring in business. I think I want to revise my goal."

Ema responded, "I hear quite a shift in perspective. How would you revise your goal based on this new awareness?" Jun replied, "I want to identify the opportunities to contribute strategically to the firm's success. Since I don't exactly know how to do that, I need to ask people who do know."

Ema observed, "It sounds like you have the beginning of an action plan already – you want to identify opportunities to contribute to the firm's success and you need to ask people who do know how you can do that. So, who are these people you would want to ask?"

Jun was silent for a moment, and then said, "My manager, who really does serve as a mentor, for sure. And his chief of staff, and also the head of strategy. Those are my go-to people anyway." Now, it was Ema's turn to be silent and wait to see if Jun had other ideas. Then Ema asked, "Anyone else come to mind?" Jun couldn't immediately think of anyone, but then added, "I can go to our talent-acquisition head because she has to scout people for senior positions, and she probably looks for evidence in their career of contributing to the firm's bottom line."

Ema then added, "It sounds like you even have some ideas of the kind of questions you can ask, so what's your next step going to be?" Jun eagerly replied, "I'm going to give myself thinking time right after this session to see what questions I know to ask and who I want to approach. Then I want to test my assumption about my presentations and if that's the best way to contribute to the firm's success. I may be aiming too low."

Ema: "What if anything might hinder you from allocating that time to think – and how could you work around that if it happens?" Jun replied, "There's absolutely nothing that can stop me! I'm excited to do this."

To test her commitment to act, Ema pursued the point: "I hear you and yet I also know how busy you are. What will keep you on track with these actions that sound so important to you?"

Jun replied, "Good point! I have an exercise buddy that I work out with. Maybe I can have an action buddy, and I think I know the perfect person: Jill! I'll ask her tonight."

Since it was close to the end of the session, Ema said, "We've covered a lot of ground today, Jun, with you courageously looking at your desire to attain partner status, and what you think may be needed to get you there. What have you learned about yourself as we worked through the revised goal?"

Jun proudly said, "I am actually a pretty confident person. I was thinking tactically like a more junior person, but I do see the bigger picture and this conversation reminded me of that. I've got a new mantra: 'focus on the big picture'."

In closing, Ema remarked, "That's great to hear. I can't wait to find out what transpires when you put your action plan into play. We're at the end of our time – what do you need to say or do to feel complete with this session, Jun?"

Jun replied, assuredly, "Nothing at all. I've got what I came for, and more! Thanks so much!"

Level 3 Aligns with Master Certified Coach (MCC)

Competency 8: Facilitates Client Growth

Definition: Partners with the client to transform learning and insight into action. Promotes client autonomy in the coaching process.

Regarding the examples given for the MCC BARS, please take into consideration that in order to meet the requirements for MCC-level coaching, the contextual and relational aspects of the coaching conversation need to be taken into account. These in their wholeness serve as evidence for whether in the given coaching a sufficient depth and variety of dimensions of the client's life, purpose and identity have been fully explored and responded to by the coach.

MCC BARS

- M8.1 Coach checks in with client and their progress, learnings and insights in natural and spontaneous ways throughout the session.
- M8.2 Coach invites the client to sense and reflect on what they are learning about themselves.
- M8.3 Coach cultivates an environment for the client to intentionally apply their own learning.

M8.1 Coach checks in with client and their progress, learnings and insights in natural and spontaneous ways throughout the session

This behavior is evident in the following examples:

- "As I recall from our last meeting, you learned that you are operating as your best self. How do you envision bringing that learning into this meeting?"
- "What became clearer to you after those new insights you came to last time?"
- "What new learning is going to be most helpful in reaching your goals?"

- "I sense new winds blowing: what's new about you?"
- "What allowed you to change your attitude this week?"
- "How would you apply your learning while keeping this great feeling you have?"

M8.2 Coach invites the client to sense and reflect on what they are learning about themselves

This can be demonstrated in these ways:

- "Please share with me your sense of what you are taking away today."
- "What is your understanding about yourself now?"
- "How might a practice of constant reflection be of service to you?"
- "I notice that you started our conversation today with emotions and high energy from your success during the week."
- "Who will you be after succeeding with your plan?"
- "Can we pause here for a moment to take stock of how far you have come in your thinking since we started the conversation?"

M8.3 Coach cultivates an environment for the client to intentionally apply their own learning

Here are some examples of effective statements a coach might use.

- "As we are reaching the end of the meeting, who are you now?"
- "What inspired you the most from our session today?"
- "Where do you imagine today's learning will take you?"
- "When you think back to the beginning of our session today, what do you feel now about yourself?"
- "What if you close your eyes for a minute and think about the meaningful things you are going to do with this discovery today?"
- "How do you want to execute on your learning?"

EXPLORING COMPETENCY 8: FACILITATES CLIENT GROWTH

Box 10.5: Reflective Questions for the Coach

1. How well did I address the client's well-being and goal equally?
2. Did I bring my whole self to facilitating the client's growth?
3. How has my client's growth contributed to my own growth?

Case Study 3

Donna is a client engagement manager in her organization, which is in the auto industry. She has responsibility for more than fifty car dealerships. Donna is part of a four-person team which includes a marketing manager, a finance manager and a planning and control manager. They work well together.

Donna came to coaching having already set her own goals but subsequently amended these at her CEO's request. The CEO wanted Donna to focus on selling 20,000 cars by the end of the year, which would involve Donna having to really push agencies in a difficult market.

Donna came to the session expressing "frustration and anger." Although she is very confident in her abilities and believes she is the best person for the job, she complained: "But my boss seems to think differently."

The coach, Elinah, acknowledged Donna's feelings: "I hear your frustration. What do you believe will serve you best in this session?" With a loud voice, Donna said: "I know what my qualities are and how good I am at what I do, but I feel I am not appreciated enough by my CEO. She uses my knowledge and actions to succeed in the organization herself and has not promoted me to a more senior position."

Donna wanted to prepare herself and check what she should do so that she could show all her skills and qualities and present them to her boss. Elinah reflected Donna's words back with empathy: "I hear you want to bring out your skills and qualities at that meeting so you can be promoted. I can feel how important this is for you. I also feel your energy and emotions. Can you tell me more about this?"

After Donna's answer, Elinah checked: "What feeling would you like to leave with at the end of our meeting?" Donna was clear: "I want to feel that the CEO has good intentions and will work to promote me."

CHAPTER 10

Elinah asked: "During the meeting, I keep seeing that you know and appreciate the value of your role in the organization. What makes the job of selling cars and being responsible for so many agencies important to you?" Donna thought for a while: "Hmmm. I'm not sure." Elinah reframed the question: "Let me ask it a different way. What is the most significant value you get to express in your work?"

Donna stated: "I am a 'people person'… I know how to motivate sales agents. I am an expert in articulating the value of buying a new car. I also know each and every one of the sales agents. I am an advocate for them and their well-being. So the most significant value for me is to foster excellent relations, and support them."

Elinah: "I am curious: I understand it's all about relationships. Which of your core beliefs or values have contributed most to the development of those relationships over the years?"

Donna quickly responded: "It's fundamentally that I place great importance on being in good standing with all employees, colleagues and clients. That is the hallmark of who I am as a manager, which ultimately leads to excellent results in relationships and in sales performance."

Elinah continued the conversation and pointed out: "When you talked about your hallmark skill, relationship, your whole appearance changed – and there was something else about it that I can't put my finger on."

Donna laughed and said that she was aware of the importance of this in her life and ready to do whatever it took to get the senior position for which she was aiming, so she could have greater impact and influence on the company by being a "people person." Elinah was curious: "How are you going to bring this aspect of who you are into conversation in order to move forward?"

When Donna shrugged her shoulders, Elinah held her to the question: "What does the shrug indicate?"

Donna answered that in front of her manager she felt that she had given up a long time ago and this quality was not reflected in her relationship with her. In conversations with her, she felt that there was communication breakdown, and she was unable to bring her best to the conversation with the CEO.

Elinah continued: "What is the thing that you need to bring out from within yourself in order to be a people person for your CEO?" Donna thought for a while and answered: "Compassion."

Elinah held the silence, and then said, "Mmm. What thoughts can you generate to be with an attitude that will allow compassion to emerge?"

Donna smiled and looked away as if she was looking for words in her brain. After a long period of silence, she said: "I understand now that it is not her. It is me. I am in charge of my attitude and thoughts towards her. I need to understand how I can become a 'people person' with her."

Elinah followed this insight with, "What do you learn about the connection between thoughts and attitude?"

Donna answered: "I believe now that this is my responsibility, to sort out my thoughts before meeting my boss and to enter the meeting when I can be compassionate, understanding that I am not responsible for what she feels, thinks or says but only for what I think and feel."

"How will you prepare yourself for the meeting?" Elinah asked.

Donna: "I believe what works for me is to do a self-dialogue and know that I am good enough… No! No! I am more than that – I am an excellent, successful person regardless of what she thinks of me or does or does not do for me. I will be quite confident that I am authentic and successful, I bring a lot of value to the organization's success and I will take responsibility for who I am and how I feel within the meeting with her."

Elinah: "I acknowledge your insights and what you learned about yourself and your ability to take responsibility for who you are in any meeting or situation. When you think back to the beginning of our session today, how do you feel now about yourself and who you are?"

Donna smiled: "I feel good, something changed. I can see the situation differently and I am satisfied to be responsible for my own attitude."

Elinah closed with an appreciation: "I would like to appreciate your willingness to explore this issue. To what extent do you feel it is possible to end the meeting with this? Or is there something else to investigate?"

"It's perfectly fine to end the meeting now. Thank you," said Donna.

Growing MCC

Coaches who achieve their Master Certified Coach (MCC) recognize this is not a destination. They will continue their journey by developing personally and professionally. We invite you to be a curious traveler and explorer in your own growth in parallel to the way you facilitate your client's growth.

Box 10.6: Reflective Questions for the Coach

1. Am I still journeying?
2. How do I define my responsibility as a holder of the MCC credential?
3. How am I contributing to the coaching profession?

How "Facilitates Client Growth" Serves the Client

"Facilitates Client Growth" is a crucial aspect not only for clients in the context of coaching but also for their relationships with colleagues, family and various stakeholders in the client's environment. This competency exerts a positive influence in driving progress towards the client's goals. Change does not occur by staying in the same safe place; especially in this VUCA world, seeking transformation is no easy task, and the diversity of people involved has increased significantly compared to the past.

Being constantly asked by the coach, "What have you learned?", "How will you apply the learning?" and "What will you do?" significantly influences the client's commitment to enhancing their learning and growth.

Asking this question to oneself not only within each session but throughout the entire coaching engagement leads to the shift of a client's focus from "doing" to "being." Adopting this mindset leads to the client's long-term growth in the following areas:

1. **Prioritizing learning:** Clients will start prioritizing the key elements of their learning as they make progress in achieving their goals. As this practice becomes a habit, clients continue to have the ability to translate learning into action on the way to achieve their goals, even after the end of the coaching engagement.

2. **Increasing self-awareness and insight:** The continuous reflection of "What am I learning from this?", "What impact am I making?" and "What is working well and what is not?" enables clients to broaden their insights and perception, witness their influence and identify areas of needed improvement.

3. **Becoming accountable:** "Accountability" refers to the conscious mindset and attitude of taking proactive responsibility for one's personal/business growth. It goes beyond self-centeredness and requires collaborating with others. Clients driving their own transformation contributes to the continuous development of their collaborators.

4. **Nurturing resources:** By continuously asking "What are the resources necessary to move things forward?", "What support do I need?" and "What would be the barriers?", clients can check on their internal resources as well as gain insight on their necessary external resources. Being aware of the resources throughout the coaching engagement allows the client to utilize them effectively.

5. **Partnering:** The constant dialogue in partnership with the coach has an impact on how clients engage in conversations with others, meaning there is a skill transfer of the coaching dialogue. This will also contribute to the continuous growth of the people interacting with the client.

6. **Committing to results:** In the pursuit of their goals, designing and working towards their achievement is not a singular endeavor. It requires clients to be conscious of their short-term, medium-term and long-term plans, and to strive for specific and measurable objectives. Committing to this process leads to the fulfillment of their broader goals.

7. **Overcoming challenges invites innovation:** Change involves confronting numerous obstacles and challenges. By identifying their resources, support and barriers in the coaching dialogue, clients start to discover new options that differ from their previous approaches. This process of overcoming challenges invites innovation.

8. **Incorporating "Facilitates Client Growth" into daily life:** "Facilitates Client Growth" leads to a continual drive for action. Finding significance in the process of progressing towards goals, we transform our experiences and challenges into opportunities for learning. We uncover new perspectives and hints for approaching situations, develop the necessary skills and foster new relationships, thereby expanding our areas of effectiveness.

Moreover, the commitment to autonomously fostering this process serves as the foundation for building trust and confidence among the stakeholders involved in the coach's journey. By doing so, approaching new endeavors becomes less daunting and challenging. Instead, it becomes a source of energy for creating transformative change through collaborative efforts.

How "Facilitates Client Growth" Serves the Coach

If the coach themselves lacks accountability, exhibits a tendency to blame others or approaches obstacles with a negative mindset, they will be unable to effectively address these issues with the client. In this competency, it is essential for the coach to be a collaborative partner with the client. Therefore, coaches must actively engage in this aspect, as their own commitment to accountability. Sharing their experiences can provide clients with new perspectives and serve as a catalyst for encouraging the clients to move forward.

As the client's level of accountability rises and their ownership of thoughts and actions increases, the coach becomes a powerful partner in co-creating the client's new perspectives and insights. At the ACC level, the coach may still exhibit a tendency to provide some direction or encouragement, as they are unable to fully support the client. At the PCC level, the coach becomes able to elicit the client's spontaneity but may still use guidance or direction, not yet fully embodying a complete partnership. At the MCC level, the coach and client exist as equal partners, each holding their own accountability.

To maintain this state, coaches need to constantly focus on their own growth with accountability. By committing to their own personal development, coaches can gain new insights and knowledge, leading to a more refined partnership. Moreover, coaches can develop a deeper understanding of the client's perspectives, enabling them to engage more effectively.

Coaches must recognize that they are perpetual learners in their relationship with clients. This awareness is crucial. Through continuous learning, coaches can develop higher levels of coaching ability that contribute to the growth and achievement of their clients' growth.

Your Evolution as a Great Coach

This competency, "Facilitates Client Growth," is related to the coach's personal growth as a human being and serves as a valuable opportunity for growth not only for the clients but also for the people who are interacting with the coach outside of the coaching engagement.

To facilitate this, consider reflecting on the questions in the next section.

Reflective Questions

1. How did I contribute to the client's progress?
2. Did I show my commitment to the client's success in how we designed actions?
3. Was I able to be present as a partner and resist the temptation to advise the client on what actions they should take?
4. Was I "attached" to the client's forward movement, experiencing either elation or disappointment – or did I show my full acceptance of the client's choices?
5. Was I courageous in asking the client to generate options and challenging the client to ensure their action plan aligned to their stated goal?
6. What transformation am I going through in this process?
7. What supportive structures do I have in place to process situations where I feel out of my depth?
8. What is my learning and action plan, based on the session I just conducted?

9. How will my client(s) benefit from this learning and action plan?
10. How will my family, friends, co-workers and other "stakeholders" benefit?

Conclusion

As you have now completed the eight competencies, it's worth thinking about why people seek coaching. Coaching is about learning, developing skills and fostering growth. Fundamentally, as John Whitmore (2005) noted, coaching is about developing personal responsibility and greater self-awareness, which enables individuals to become more choiceful.

SECTION 3

Masterful Insights

Section 3 Introduction

In the first section of this book, we invited our experts to share their expertise from the assessment process, competency by competency, BARS by BARS and by Markers. Through exploring these assessment criteria, we hope we have given you, the reader, a deeper understanding of the ICF competencies, what assessors are looking for when assessing submissions and how coaches can bring these aspects alive at each of the three levels of credentialing. Each chapter follows a similar structure to help you the reader.

In Section 3, we wanted to give our MCC coaches free reign. We asked them to share a single "gem" from their years of coaching practice and coach assessment. This chapter provides a less-restricted platform for MCC coaches to self-express. We invite you, the reader, to consider how these insights can contribute to your learning journey. Each has chosen a specific aspect which they believe to be an important ingredient that contributes towards the development of a coach. You may find overlaps in topics but the approach is always unique.

As we have noted throughout this book, mastery is not a recipe. The more one progresses on the developmental journey, the more one needs to apply the competencies with flexibility in response to the individual client, our relationship as a coach with them, their presenting issue and the context or system in which they operate.

We hope this collection of masterful insights will further support your own development journey.

CHAPTER 11

Reflective Practice

Professor Jonathan Passmore

At the heart of learning a practical skill is the ability to reflect, and at the heart of masterful practice is self-awareness. As coaches, we need to cultivate in ourselves the skill of regularly reflecting on what we do, how we do it, how others experience it and how we expect and react to them.

Doing this is easier in the writing than in the doing; and doing it well is even harder. One way to engage in critical reflection is through supervision, but for most coaches such conversations may only happen once a month or once a quarter. Coaches need to cultivate ways to self-reflect and develop insights as part of their daily practice.

In my own practice, I use a simple eight-step self-coaching and self-reflection model which I have called the Henley8, as we use this model on our coach-training programs at Henley Business School. I have summarized the eight questions in Box 11.1 and then unpacked them below.

Box 11.1: The Henley8 Reflective Model

1. What did you notice?
2. How did you respond? (Think about what you felt, thought and did.)
3. What does this say about you?
4. What does this say about you as a coach?
5. What benefits might this offer?
6. What risks might this bring?
7. What did you learn about yourself?
8. What would you do differently next time?

In the Henley8 model, the starting point of the reflection is to notice the events, incidents or statements which trigger you (Passmore and Sinclair, 2024). This is not about judging or critiquing others, but instead observing and reflecting on our responses. The first question is: what did I observe?

Such observations require situational awareness, being fully present and noticing changes in events around us. The observation may be a change in the situation – for example, a fire bell rings during the team meeting. It may be observing a behavior of an individual or, in coaching, the words, phrases or actions of a client.

The second step is to identify our response. The question here to guide this reflection is: what was my response? Your response may have been behavioral, but is likely also to have been cognitive (what was I thinking and why? and also, what was I feeling?). Our thoughts and feelings often drive our behavior, and recognizing the relationship between these is helpful. It is most often our thoughts which start the emotional and behavioral responses.

As we continue the reflection at this stage, it's helpful to explore what is behind these feelings and thoughts. This will be the beliefs, assumptions and values we hold about the world. Being conscious of these, and bringing these core beliefs into our conscious awareness, will help us to challenge unhelpful assumptions and our human biases.

The third and fourth questions involve considering what these behaviors, thoughts, feelings and possibly our beliefs and values say about us as individuals, and what they say about us as a leader or a coach within the context in which we are working. Meanings can vary widely depending on the organizational and national culture, and taking these into account needs to be part of our reflection.

The fifth and sixth questions explore the pros and cons of these beliefs. How do these beliefs or attitudes help or hinder us in our role? Do they make us more effective? Do they contribute to our happiness and well-being? Do they contribute positively to our client and our work as a coach? What do we need to be aware of in terms of how we can build on these positives and what we should guard against?

The seventh and eighth questions focus on what we learn and take away from this reflective exercise. They set the stage for future development.

CHAPTER 11

Reflection without action is meaningless. The purpose of reflection is to understand ourselves and others more deeply and, through this, learn and adapt in the future to enhance our own effectiveness and that of others.

The Henley8 provides a model to guide self-reflection, and can be used as a framework to guide your daily journal writing, as you capture your thoughts. Writing a daily journal provides great value: while we can simply do these reflections in our heads, the journal provides a written record which can help in making choices about what to take to supervision at the end of the month or the quarter. Moreover, as we reflect on the journal, it allows us to observe our development, as well as identify patterns that occur again and again in our work.

CHAPTER 12

Dare to be LAZY

Judit Ábri von Bartheld

Being lazy is not something that we are proud of or openly declare. Yet when you are a coach, being lazy can become an asset. In this context, being LAZY means that you ensure the client does all of the work in a coaching session: it is their issue, their challenge, their pain and ultimately it is their life which has to be worked on, reflected and adjusted as needed. And obviously, the client is the most qualified person to do this. The coach is "just" there to support, to encourage, to hold a mirror, ask open questions once in a while – but most importantly the coach is there to "believe" in the client.

What is LAZY Coaching?

As an ICF coach, you need to refrain from leading the coaching conversation. LAZY coaching is a philosophy: a way of coaching which encourages the coach to place the responsibility for the coaching work with the client.

Practicing in a LAZY style may sound like abdication or a laissez-faire attitude, but in practice it requires from the coach high levels of self-awareness, and sophisticated skills in listening and self-management – being able to sit with ambiguity and not knowing, while freeing clients to explore and discover for themselves what is the right solution for them.

In reality, a LAZY approach is actually hard work. The coach is still listening, empathizing and creating the space for their clients to step forward and take responsibility for their life. The LAZY philosophy is underpinned by a model based on four pillars.

LA³ZY stands for:

L – Listening

A³ – Attention, Awareness, Ambiguity

Z – Zest

Y – You (coaching is all about YOU: the client!)

L – Listening

Experienced coaches communicate through being excellent listeners. Listening requires a firm presence from the coach, who has to work intentionally on excluding the clutter of the environment and stopping their inner voices, which may be eager to jump in with a question to break the flow of the client's dialogue. It takes an effort and the right mindset to remain LAZY.

Listening at different levels is a basic coaching skill. It is a way of showing curiosity for the client as a whole person. It serves as an act of encouragement to the client to keep on sharing and exploring the desired topic further and deeper. Listening with attention and intention helps the client feel safe and respected. Finally, listening is also about being able to hold silence, on purpose, in order to create the fertile ground for new insights.

A³ – Attention, Awareness and Ambiguity

The first "A" in this set is attention. The coach must focus their whole attention on the client. They must manage their wandering mind, giving their full attention to their client.

The second "A" in this set is awareness. Enhancing the client's awareness and encouraging greater personal responsibility are the key aims within coaching. The coach's responsibility is to get out of the way and, through managing the process, to allow the client to accomplish their goal.

This is best achieved through the coach's own heightened self-awareness and through self-management. The highly self-aware coach understands where they need to hold back and give their client the space to think and develop their own insights, and when to intervene with a question which can provoke new thinking.

The third and final "A" in this set is ambiguity. One of the factors driving coaches to speak is a wish to know, and thus to calm their disturbing uncertainty. The experienced coach, however, feels that they are able to embrace the not knowing. They are comfortable with the ambiguity which exists in most client's stories and behaviors.

Z – Zest

Zest is about energy: the energy levels of both coach and client. At the start of each session the coach may like to check their own energy and to maintain awareness of this during the whole session.

It may be helpful also to invite the client to review their own energy level and emotional state at the start of the conversation. These factors can influence both the level of engagement and the outcome of the coaching conversation.

Throughout the session the coach should continue to monitor variations in tone of voice, pace of speech or inflection of the client, and reflect back to the client, developing the client's own self-awareness of their own zest.

Y – You – Coaching Is all about You, the Client

This point may seem obvious, yet it cannot be emphasized enough. The coach can exert too much control on the client, too much influence on their thinking and actions. The LAZY coach leaves their ego outside the coaching room.

The aim is to remain focused exclusively on what the client needs, to enable them to develop greater cognitive and emotional independence.

CHAPTER 12

Co-creation

Using the LAZY model in coaching helps the coach avoid controlling the conversation and, at the same time, aims at partnering with the client to co-create the session. LAZY is both a philosophy and a coaching model that consciously builds on and celebrates the not-knowing status and position of the coach, and empowers the client to take control of the coaching conversation and ultimately to take control of their life.

CHAPTER 13

Questions at the Heart of Coaching

Elena Espinal

Socrates believed that true knowledge comes from recognizing one's own ignorance. Through questioning, he aimed to expose contradictions and limitations in people's beliefs, encouraging critical thinking and self-reflection. Socrates saw questioning as a means to stimulate learning and uncover deeper truths, rather than simply providing answers. By engaging in dialogue and questioning, Socrates aimed to foster intellectual growth and encourage individuals to examine their own ideas and values.

When we use this coaching approach, the coach asks thought-provoking questions to guide the client towards exploring their thoughts and emotions at a deeper level. The aim is to help the client expand their perspectives and discover new insights about themselves. It is a way of learning also described by Reuven Feuerstein and by Ivan Vigotsky – learning mediated by a third party, who, with their questions, assists in observing, relating, comparing and other actions. Furthermore, they always start from the proactivity and responsibility they want to learn, to build more complex learning by these means.

Building a relationship through questions can be an effective way to foster learning and understanding between individuals. By asking thought-provoking questions, engaging in meaningful discussions and actively listening to each other's perspectives, people can deepen their understanding and develop a strong learning partnership. This approach promotes critical thinking, empathy and collaboration, leading to mutual growth and knowledge acquisition.

The importance of provoking questions towards new ways of looking at coaching lies in its ability to expand the client's perspective and encourage creative and reflective thinking. Limiting assumptions and beliefs can be challenged through challenging questions, allowing the client to explore different approaches and solutions. Questioning promotes personal and professional growth and helps to find new perspectives and options to achieve the desired goals.

Asking questions about what matters to the individual, what they are seeking in life and their relationship with what they are seeking creates a space that allows for greater self-knowledge, goal clarity, and alignment between actions and personal desires. In addition, it helps make more conscious decisions and find a greater sense of purpose in life.

Conversations that seek to find new ways of relating to a situation are often valuable, as they encourage adaptation, innovation and growth. It is essential to be open to change and explore different approaches to address challenges.

These moments are characterized by thinking, creating, relating to others or circumstances, learning, feeling, valuing, recognizing the way of looking at the world and choosing who they want to be in the world.

When we use this coaching approach, the coach asks thought-provoking questions to guide the client toward exploring their thoughts and emotions at a deeper level, in different dimensions. The aim is to help the clients expand their perspectives and discover new insights about themselves.

It is essential to take care of the space. The coach should not ask questions that lead to, or for which they expect, a particular answer, or continue with questions that keep the client in the same place where the conversation started – like stirring up the past or keeping them in the old conversation about themself.

If the coach fully accepts their answers without rejecting, judging or devaluing the answers, and if the client communicates that they do not want to change a certain point of view about themselves, that demonstrates that the coach shows respect for the client's choices.

CHAPTER 14

Pause Gives More Time than it Takes

Janet M. Harvey

Be still. Be attentive. Be reflective on practice. Masterful presence only arises through continuous and alert focus. Everything we desire already exists and we recognize it through wonder, the rapt astonishment with something new emerging into our awareness, a spontaneous experience of human wholeness.

No-one can choose the unfolding of our life for us. Yet, the core of our being knows how, even if we don't know it directly. Our mindfulness or contemplative practice reminds us that all things are possible in the stillness of a quiet mind. Brain science supports this experience, as does our engagement with others. Allowing moments of pause infused with full presence always evokes deeper inquiry, surprise and revelation for any domain of life. And for those attached to busyness, expressing there's not enough time in the day, reflect on this idea for a moment: pause gives more time than it takes.

The nature and power of giving attention evoke spontaneous breakthrough experiences. Sometimes it is thinking *preceded* by a bodily and emotional response to a relational field. The first step in strengthening authentic self-presence arises by becoming aware of our inner witness, the part of us that notices what is occurring and the impact on us as it is happening, without losing presence with the other person in the dialogue.

When we are attentive from our wholeness, we may notice judgment and choose artful pause – as simple as a quiet breath – to welcome curiosity that accepts everything and builds on it with wonder on behalf of the other person.

It is our attention with other people, not our input, that produces a sequence of evocative curiosity-based questions – for example, what to achieve, based upon what assumptions, blocked by what beliefs, seeing what belief operates as the most significant obstacle, testing what is valid and what causes a person to choose to hesitate or stand still? As seen from our essential self, what is true stimulates choices, leading them to ask how to achieve the goal organically and naturally.

It is who we are, operating from whole-self presence, that allows us to enjoy the difference, welcome disturbance, and trust that, by inviting others to share learning, thinking and insight, we will most honor the partnership in our conversation to generate something beneficial for both.

Being accomplished, competent and confident as an adult in a professional capacity is seductive and creates blinders and obstacles to continuous development and evolution. Reflection on practice is the antidote to complacency, boredom and doubt, liberating our potential and the power of vulnerability and self-trust for and with everyone in our life. Being reflective on practice is the most empowering resource available for professional development because the answers arrive inside-out as gifts of consciousness and give us the power of choice.

Here are four practical reflection questions to engage with to strengthen artful pause for maintaining our authentic presence.

- What stirs my addiction to a certainty that fuels mistrust of another's wholeness, resourcefulness, capability and creativity?
- What fuels my fear of silence and the discomfort of allowing another's independent thought to emerge?
- What self-trust becomes essential in surrendering to curiosity on behalf of another person without condition?
- What resourcefulness do I possess that reminds me of the privilege and fulfills my responsibility to witness another being express their full potency?

Meditate, journal, walk in nature or do any other activity that allows you to separate from the doing and busyness of life, to engage with internal wisdom. Use voice memos on your phone or some easy way to capture the spontaneous insights that naturally bubble. I use one question a week and cycle through these each month, to maintain a continuous relationship with the evolution of my presence. Being human is a privilege; whole presence is a responsibility.

CHAPTER 15

Walking Home to Self

Karen Foy

My reflections as a coach brought me to this understanding of my approach. In the privileged partnership which is coaching, my only hope is that I can remind the person I am walking alongside, for a short part of their journey, that their home is their own wisdom. How many of us spend our lives aiming to "be better," "do better" or change who we are? As Carl Rogers says: "the curious paradox is that when I accept myself just as I am, then I change." The liberation for both travelers in this is that neither of us needs to "perform" to demonstrate our worth, we just need to be. What a simple but mind-blowing insight for me as a coach: nothing relies on my skill, intelligence, training or any other clever trick.

As coaches, we all need to build our skills by learning the basic coaching competencies first. Just as in Piaget's child development theory a child must master the skills and cognitive appreciation of earlier stages to move through to the next, so as coaches we need to develop the ability to "do" coaching before we can get to a place of "being." We learn the fundamentals, we practice them and gradually build our coaching persona, gathering our credentials, client base and accolades for getting results. Once learnt, there is a time to let go of the theories and techniques, as Carl Jung suggests, and be just another human soul sitting with another human soul.

Richard Rohr, a Franciscan priest, noted the two halves of life, sequential and dependent on each other – but also that not everyone gets to the second half. These two halves of life are nothing to do with age or longevity but more related to our spiritual and psychological growth. The gateway to the second half is preceded by a "fall": "The heartbreaks, disappointments and loves of the first half of life are actually steppingstones to the spiritual joys that the second half has in store for us."

This concept is useful as we learn, develop and grow as coaches, to get to the place where we can lose our need to perform and develop. Our development journey must stretch beyond skills to free us from the first half of coach development trappings of proving our value, so that we may become self-aware and accept that our presence is transformative if we can be in service of the client finding their own wisdom.

Self-reflection and radical self-assessment constitute one route to a "fall," by noticing ourselves reacting to "hooks" in the coaching conversation, defending our worth, failing, getting stuck, both in our coaching and in our ways. At these points of falling where we notice we have stopped growing or we have lost our earlier passion, we are at the place of choice; we can hold on to our persona and training and stay in the first half of our coaching life or we can step into the unknown terrain of the second half.

A first-half decision might be to learn more tricks, get more teaching or mentoring on the competencies or methods and stay attached to the coaching persona we have worked so hard to build in order to "do" coaching better. The move into the second half will require us to shed the protective coaching cloak that gives certainty in goals and processes, and to start the hero's journey where we face our fears, battle the dragons and become willing to sit with the discomfort of not knowing in the service of "being" a coach.

There are no shortcuts, but there are signposts that can help the journey; there are companions to walk us home and to remind us of the value of our quest. To move towards being comfortable to walk with others without the need to prove our worth as coaches means investing in our own journey of self-discovery through investing in our own coaching, supervision and often therapy. No-one can offer us each a unique map of what we should see, but they can point to the places that might be worth looking at. Only when we have explored our own "scary places" and dropped the defenses have we the right to walk alongside others on that journey. As with our coaching, this exploration is not aimed at helping you do anything different but to awaken you to all you are already.

CHAPTER 16

Learning for Transcripts and Recordings

Carly Anderson

As coaches we are in the "human development" business. By embracing a continuous learning mindset, we are constantly evolving ourselves to become the best coach we can be for our clients. In doing this, we are also aligning with ICF Core Competency 2: Embodies a Coaching Mindset, 2.1: Engages in ongoing learning and development as a coach and 2.3: Develops an ongoing reflective practice to enhance one's coaching.

A powerful self-learning tool is to regularly review and reflect on our own coaching. We can periodically ask permission from a coaching client to record some coaching sessions, for the purpose of reflecting on what worked well, what we may have missed and what, as the coach, we could have done differently.

Many online platforms offer embedded transcript tools. Alternatively, you can access one of the many specialist tools available for transcription. A transcript reveals what the client verbally said and how you verbally responded. This order is important, as a coach listens, and is responsive to, what the client says. In this piece our focus is on the transcript. However, if you also record the video content this too will contain rich content for reflection and learning.

Here's one example which demonstrates what can be learned by studying your coaching session transcript.

CHAPTER 16

Listen for what the client says as they arrived at their coaching session, and how the coach responded.

Let's say the coach asked their client as they arrived, "How are you today?" and their client replied, "I feel a bit flustered. A meeting ran late and I'm now late for our coaching session. And this is how my day usually goes." Here are some examples of possible verbal responses the coach might make:

> Response 1: No problem. So what would you like to focus on in our coaching session today?
>
> Response 2: I'm thinking that this might be a good focus for our coaching session today – what do you think?
>
> Response 3: I hear you're feeling flustered. What do you need to say or do in this moment that would help you most?
>
> Response 4: You said you're feeling flustered and I sense some emotions present as well. What more would you like to say about feeling flustered?

The first two of the above possible responses are general in nature. The other examples are customized because they use client words to craft a response.

If the coach reads their transcript, even the first few sentences spoken by the client, you can do what I did above and create alternative responses which could have been spoken instead. In this way you can expand your "listening," and develop your responsiveness for next time, because you have more awareness of the different responses possible other than a generic response.

This same approach can be applied by reading the next paragraph (and the next paragraph, and the next paragraph…) of what the client says, and crafting possible responses the coach might have had instead of what they said.

Using the example from above, if the client uses the word "feel" – as in "I feel a bit flustered" – you can search the transcript for the word "feel" and find how many times the client said "feel," "feels," "feeling." When I do this process with a mentoring client, they are often surprised at how many times the client said "feel" and they instead responded with "thinks." This reveals a mismatch in learning preference and gives the coach an opportunity to learn how to listen and be more present next time to client use of "feel" and respond using "feel" in their response.

The potential learning from your transcript is endless! Here are some other examples:

Observe the client's patterns of speaking: Observe emotional words such as "frustration," "mad" and "upset." An example response might be, "You've said 'frustration,' 'mad' and 'upset' in the past few minutes. What more would you like to share about how you're feeling?"

Notice the metaphors or visual concepts the client uses: A client says, "I'm looking for my next career path, and there's a few pathways I could take, yet none that really interest me to keep going down that path." Example questions in response might include:

- When you look ahead up the path instead of down the path, what do you see?
- What might be a secret pathway you'd like to take?
- What do you see along the different pathways?
- What might be blocking the path ahead?

We may believe we're a good listener – until we review a transcript of our coaching session. The more we become aware of the opportunities we have missed, the more we can then practice what we might have said instead that would have been more responsive and customized to this client – and the better able we will be to be more responsive next time.

CHAPTER 17

Trust and Safety

Michael Pomije

After many years as a Master Certified Coach (MCC), I've come to appreciate the critical importance of trust and safety in any coaching relationship. Trust and safety are not merely components of a strong coaching relationship, they are the foundation that allows clients to delve into profound self-exploration, to discover their core truth, and to take the necessary steps and/or leaps for their personal and professional evolution. This journey is not only about reaching their destination; it is also about embarking on an exploration into the art of personal transformation.

For the coach to truly embody the essence of trust and safety, it is critical to be both a trusting presence and an empathetic guide, illuminating the path for the client. The coach's role involves not only understanding the client's journey but also becoming a beacon of trust and empathy that shines a light on the way forward, empowering the client to navigate their passage through personal growth and self-discovery to their transformation.

I believe that it is absolutely essential to create a nurturing environment where the coach can meet the client exactly where they are, with no expectations, no agenda and no judgments. This engagement in a genuine heart-to-heart connection, honoring the client's feelings, thoughts and aspirations is met with deep empathy and unwavering support. Creating a safe space where clients feel their progress is recognized and valued, bolstering their confidence, courage and motivation, and opening the possibility for true transformation – that is the mission of an MCC. For example, when a client expresses a new-found insight, I might affirm them with, "It's impressive how you've shifted your perspective to see this crisis or challenge as a genuine opportunity!"

Clients must feel secure to explore and address the intricate and subtle facets of their lives. I have frequently been tapped on the internal shoulder to share an intimate and empathic moment with the client. From this short intuitive delivery, the client drops into a deeper level of trust and faith in themselves to overcome a difficult challenge.

Authenticity is the cornerstone of coaching mastery. Mastery requires that we create a space where our clients experience freedom and safety from all negativity so that they can be true to their essential selves, focus on their desired outcomes and evolve into the person they truly aspire to become.

My dedication and commitment lie in shaping the authentic narratives of my clients, capturing pivotal moments that serve as bridges over emotional challenges or blocks, thereby forging a deep and enduring connection rooted in trust and safety.

Every achievement is yet another chapter in life. The coach assists the client in untangling their complex narratives, unraveling self-doubt, confusion and apprehension. Like a skilled artisan, we guide them to weave these threads into a tapestry that aligns with their passions and core values.

CHAPTER 18

The Trap of the "Knower"

Michael Stratford

One of the most profound influences on my coaching is the fundamental premise that the client is unique and not replicated over the entire course of history, over the entire globe. This crucial mindset is perhaps the most important distinguisher between coaching (as we know it) and other personal, professional development methodologies. If a coach honors this, they won't be tempted to offer their advice, strategies or best practices, as is so common among some coaches.

No matter how much a client's situation looks or appears like one the coach has experienced before, it isn't. They haven't lived this client's history or had their experiences, their body, neurology or emotional life. They… are not them. The coach was never in the exact same scenario as the client because their world is different, in many ways both in large and in little. Again, the coach is not the client.

Coaches gravitate toward their experiences and acquired information, and the learned skills that fit them. They assume it's their value. They think transferring those insights benefits the client. That's the trap. The trap of the "knower."

The true value of the coach comes after subtraction: subtraction of their need to feel important, liked or approved of in the interaction; subtraction of their own fears, concerns, worries and needs; subtraction of any attachment to their way, beliefs, system or path to success being the best way.

The coach then shows up to the session to be with the client as a space of loving acceptance and curiosity about the client's difference. There, the client explores their own uniqueness to discover their way forward.

CHAPTER 19

The Polarity between the Science and Art

Osama Al-Mosa

The paradox of art and science is a puzzle for many professionals.

The science of coaching helps us to understand and apply methods to boost our practice. We can best achieve this through continuous learning and research; staying up to date on the latest research in the coaching field and active as a continuous learner by applying these scientific insights to our practice. However, there is a danger in overemphasizing the science of coaching by relying excessively on rigid methodologies. This can suppress creativity and limit the depth and authenticity of the coach–client relationship.

While science may offer a strong foundation, the art of coaching enables this practice to become transformative. By instilling empathy and using active listening skills, we can truly understand our clients; I create a safe and compassionate space for reflection and opportunities for new insights to emerge.

This blending of art with science allows for flexibility in one coaching style: recognizing that each client's journey is unique.

However, overemphasizing the use of art or adopting pseudo-science practices is just as dangerous. For example, the coach may trust their intuition without having fully understood a method or practice, risking harm to a client, for example, who should have been referred to a mental-health professional.

As the popularity of coaching grows, so have the pseudo-science approaches, often with unsubstantiated and grandiose claims. Coaches need to exercise discernment to review the evidence or think critically about the claims made. While it is important to remain open to new ideas, it is equally important to approach them with a healthy dose of skepticism.

By being cautious and discerning, you can safeguard both yourself and your clients from falling into the trap of pseudo-sciences and clichéd methodologies that may undermine the integrity and effectiveness of coaching. Your commitment to the principles of scientific inquiry, critical thinking and evidence-based practice will ensure that your coaching endeavors remain grounded in authenticity, professionalism and ethical conduct.

CHAPTER 20

Make Your Coaching Client Do the Work!

Peter J. Reding

Facilitating clients and making them do the work is at the heart of coaching. This can be hard for many coaches who want to show their expertise and mastery, but in taking on the work we deprive our clients of autonomy and personal responsibility.

In coaching we sometimes experience client expectations which can work against coaching.

Client's expectations:

- I want you to advise me on best practices using your experiences to accelerate my development.
- I want you to tell me how to be ready for my next promotion faster than my peers.
- I am (or my company is) paying you for your expertise, so just tell me.

Pretend-coach's desires:

- I am here to take care of everyone.
- I am uncomfortable seeing them go through this pain.
- I am here to help them create a better life for themselves by using my wisdom and strategies.

Coaching has evolved over decades and works best when we encourage our clients to become self-responsible and both to explore their day-to-day issues as well as to answer their existential questions. Who am I? Why am I here? What is my life purpose?

Coaching questions can be disturbing for many people who have been conditioned by life, culture, gender or race to look to others for the answers. However, we should invite them to consider questions such as:

- What do you want?
- What's important to you?
- What best serves you?
- What steps would work best for you to achieve your life's aspirations?

These questions require the client to decide for themselves, to take a stand and, in many cases, not to abide by the external voices of who they "should" be and how they "should" be living their life.

As the coach:

- Be patient and… *allow your coaching client to do their work!*
- Be understanding and… know your coaching client may be doing this work for the first time in their life.
- Be supportive and… express your comfort with your coaching client to do this work now, or later, or not at all – it's their choice.
- Be reassuring and… have compassion and appreciation that your coaching client is trusting you enough to do their deep and inner work.

CHAPTER 21

Dancing with Polarities

Ram S. Ramanathan

Polarities are like the yin and yang of life. They are opposing forces that are both necessary and interconnected. For example, there is the polarity of work and life, of independence and collaboration, of risk and caution. Polarities can be challenging, but they can also be an opportunity for growth. When we recognize and manage polarities effectively, we can create a more balanced and fulfilling life.

Polarities are essentially dilemmas of contradictory but interrelated available options that make our decision-making difficult. It may be as life threatening as "what dress should I wear for my date?" or something as simple as "what job offer should I take?" The truth is that in every dilemma and polarity the answer perhaps lies outside the dilemma options in a third truth, the fork that does not show up in the roads to be taken.

In coaching as in life, polarities manifest through competing values, needs or perspectives, as pairs of opposing but interrelated elements that exist in a dynamic equilibrium. Unlike problems that have solutions, polarities cannot be resolved; instead, they must be managed and balanced. Failure to recognize and manage polarities can lead to frustration, stagnation and missed opportunities for growth. Let's look at how polarities emerge in various contexts.

Dancing with Polarities

Identify the polarities. What is your meaningful objective? What are the two opposing forces that are at play in deciding?

1. Acknowledge the legitimacy of both polarities. Both polarities have their own strengths and weaknesses. Map the benefits and risks. It is important to recognize that there is no one-size-fits-all solution.
2. Find the third truth. Look for a solution that honors both polarities to the greatest extent possible. The third truth is often a creative synthesis of the two polarities.
3. Be flexible and adaptable. Things don't always go according to plan. Be prepared to adjust your approach as needed.

In the following three paragraphs, I have included two examples of how polarities can be brought to life in our coaching practice with live issues.

Work from Home vs. Work from Office

In the aftermath of the pandemic, many executives have struggled to decide whether or not to return to the office. Working from home offers flexibility and work–life balance but not the collaboration and social interaction of the office. Coaching in polarities helps to evaluate the pros and cons of both options with a set of criteria. Many decided to return to the office on a hybrid basis, two days per week, allowing them to gain the benefits both of working from home and of working from the office.

Risking a Career Change vs. Staying Stable

A senior leader in a multinational was unfulfilled in her current role. She aspired to start her own business in wellness, but was afraid to take the risk. Coaching in polarities helped her to identify her skills, passion and purpose to set long-term goals, and to manage the transition to entrepreneurship. The leader now runs a successful wellness enterprise.

Being Efficient vs. Being Creative

A product manager at a start-up struggled to balance the need to be efficient with the need to be creative. She was under pressure to deliver results quickly, while she was brimming with innovative growth plans. Coaching in polarity helped her to balance her time and energy more effectively with speed and creativity.

I have used polarities to reframe decision dilemmas in systemic team coaching with success, as well as in one-to-one work. Try dancing with polarities in your workspace with your leadership teams!

CHAPTER 22

A Beginner's Mind

Dalia Nakar

"You start everything from the beginning, but you see and experience it through different eyes." This simple phrase is at the heart of mastery: the beginner's mind.

This mindset encourages the experienced, wise coach to set aside their knowledge and to see the client with fresh eyes. This "new sight" allows fresh thinking and a response to each client as the unique human being they are.

It also facilitates the ability to learn and explore other possibilities. To explore new meanings, to understand anew. The coach can work to examine their client's meaning and lead them to an in-depth study of who they are, what is their uniqueness, what is their contribution to their immediate and distant environment.

The ability to carry out such an inquiry is only made possible by a coaches' willingness to surrender and leave aside what they already know about themselves in order to open up to new things that have not yet been enlightened by them.

As a coach, educator, mentor and supervisor, I have the honor of supporting coaches on their journey to becoming excellent coaches. Those who make the fastest progress are those who are curious and who delight in their clients, helping them to develop and reach heights that were previously impossible for them.

If you are reading this book, I assume that you share this desire to learn, explore and understand the profession. As you develop, let me encourage you to hold onto the beginner's mindset and the curiosity for learning, growth and development in yourself.

CHAPTER 23

Graceful Steps to Mastery

Meryl Moritz

"Begin where you are, do what you can gracefully, step out in faith, expect your inner guidance system to help!" So, I encourage the beginner coach (ACC) to accept where they are and focus on learning what it means to be a coach, what it takes to unfold the coaching process with the client and to keep paying attention to the client – not just what the client's goal is, but the whole person.

To the intermediate coach (PCC), I'd say keep building on your technical skills so you hard-wire them into your brain. This in time will allow you to "be with" your client and create a true partnership, working in the present moment. Trust the client's potential and wisdom, trust the coaching process and trust yourself. Offer your insights loosely as a contribution to possible learning, but be ready to gently let them go. With this attitude and practice, you are certain to progress.

To the aspiring master coach (MCC), congratulations on getting to this place in your vertical development! You know what coaching is, how the process unfolds, how to balance attention paid to both the "who" and the "what," and how to leave the client in action. You have the knowledge and skills to conduct coaching engagements with proficiency and confidence and have the courage to ask more of your clients than they ask of themselves. And now, you have to forget all you know! Be ready to step into the unknown space with your client. Dare to drop your predispositions about your performance or your investment in the client's success. Resist being a knower and delight in being a co-learner with each and every client or team, in each and every coaching session. Boldly ask the client, "Is this all?" "Is there more?" "What do we need to uncover to make this new behavior durable and lasting?" Recall your own development journey and the difficulties you encountered so you have patience with the client's adjustment to incremental and then transformative change. Expect a degree of resistance on the part of the client and even from yourself. Name it, use it and work alongside it. You are sure to change with the client as long as you remain receptive and adaptive.

To coaches at any stage of development, get involved with coaching supervision, whether in a group or one-on-one, to deepen your understanding of who you are being and how you are performing your craft. Supervision unlocked some vulnerable part of me and made me more authentic as a coach. My way of coaching radically changed and continues to change, as my blind spots get revealed and solutions to my challenges get illuminated. It is a rare privilege to receive supervision and – in my case – to supervise other coaches as they explore how to grow in new ways.

CHAPTER 24

Learning from Feedback

Sandra L. Stewart

The Independent Review Board (IRB) reviews all formal ethical complaints against ICF coaches from around the world. The ICF's Ethical Conduct Review (ECR) process applies to ICF-certified coaches who, at the time of the complaint, are acting as an ICF professional including as an instructor, mentor, coach or other professional capacity. This means they have used their association with ICF as part of their presentation to the client or colleague. The ECR process is a rigorous ethics review investigation and determination based on the ICF Ethics Code, whereby the complainant must prove negligence according to the standards that address a coach's responsibility to clients, professional practice and society. This process is essential to establish coaching as a self-regulated profession so as to avoid regulation by government bodies that may require licensing and requirements undesirable to the profession. Combined with the core competencies, ICF values, and the accreditation and certification processes, it sustains the standard of coaching that helps all coaching as a trustworthy profession.

So, what spurs people to bring complaints? The IRB has noted that often the driving force behind the complaint is one that is emotional and personal. The complainant may have a sense of wrongdoing or hurt. That feeling will often be paired with the feeling they are not comfortable discussing the issue with the coach.

This suggests an area for all coaches to explore – this is how we listen to and receive feedback from our clients, students, mentees and colleagues. We can ask ourselves – how do I make it easier for my clients to offer feedback? How do I respond when that feedback is critical? Do I have a way to check in with my clients during our engagement to elicit any discomfort? Some ideas on embedding feedback include the following:

1. Embed quality check-ins in your engagement contracts so that clients can anticipate a time when their feedback will be elicited.
2. Employ an automated survey or independent interviewer to solicit feedback over the course of the engagement.
3. Every session is an opportunity to ask the client, "how is this working for you in terms of coaching style?" If you use a lot of challenge in your coaching, point to it and say, "sometimes I wonder if my challenging style is too much or too little? Can you help me calibrate that with you?"
4. Notice and address any discomfort for the client, even if it is transitory, as sometimes clients upon reflection can experience these concerns more acutely.

Additionally, emphasize the value of partnership. Some ways to ensure a transparent partnership include:

1. Establish the value of partnership from the beginning. We must be aware that even though we have the intention to act as partners to our clients, they may well see us as having more power in the relationship. For example, they may perceive us as experts on psychology, business or leadership. Therefore, it is important that we speak to partnership as an underlying value of the relationship in the contracting.
2. Use transparency in your thinking and questions to support partnership. For example, you might say, "I am thinking it might be helpful to go down this line of questioning, but I am not sure that it would be of value to you." And pause. Or you could say, "so what I am about to ask assumes X, but correct me if I am wrong."
3. When contracting with the client, remind them that their role in the partnership is to express their discomfort. This statement in the contract is a strong reminder to the client of what is expected of them in the partnership.

CHAPTER 25

Focusing on Exploration, Partnership and Intentionality

Dr. Damian Goldvarg

As an MCC assessor, for the last twelve years I have spent many hours listening to coach recordings. What this has taught me is to recognize that mastery comes in many forms. It is not a single recipe; it is unique and adaptive, depending on what the client needs at that moment. Mastering is about the ability and confidence to be creative and innovative, while also staying aligned with ICF competencies.

Based on my experience, I consider there to be three key elements that reflect masterful coaching:

- What is the depth of the exploration?
- What is the depth of the partnership?
- What is the depth of the intentionality?

Firstly, the depth of the exploration is about how much you help the client to explore their worldview. Secondly, the depth of the partnership is about how you work in association with the client throughout the session. Thirdly, intentionality is your intervention in your interactions. Let's look at each in turn.

The first one of the three is the depth of exploration. The progression towards becoming a master coach happens through the depth of the conversation. An external observer might see this brought to life by the coach not being satisfied by the surface, or superficial, answer provided by the client in their first response. The coach might ask: "What else?" They may repeat this question several times or hold the silence, encouraging the person to move from conscious, initial thoughts towards thoughts outside their immediate awareness. The coach aims to help the client to keep going deeper and deeper, to explore what is the underlying issue, to get to limiting beliefs, assumptions and values. To get to emotions and fears that may be there. This requires the coach to keep following up on the answer. A useful metaphor here is to see the client journey as an onion, with the invitation to peel away layers, to discover the true power which lies beneath.

The second one is the level of the partnership. The master coach will leave more of the conversation direction with the client, letting go of the control of the session. They may ask, "where would you like to start exploring?" "Where would you like to go now?" "How would you like to end the session?" These questions help to create a truly collaborative experience, where the coach and client co-create the session. Always letting the client lead. The metaphor I like to use here is letting the client drive the car, while the coach is the on-board computer system, helping, facilitating and supporting, but always under the full control of the driver.

The third element is intentionality. Intentionality is about being aware and choosing the interventions. It is about thinking before speaking. It is about the coach being clear, concise and precise in their questions and observations. It is also about embracing silence as a choice. A useful metaphor here is an elite athlete, choosing the pace and way of running a race based on their experience and knowledge, and backed by science.

CHAPTER 26

State

Leda Turai

Stepping into the role of coach transforms our daily state of being. Each role we adopt carries with it distinct and highly specific states, where "state" refers to a blend of mental, psychological and bodily systems. So, what constitutes the ideal state for a coach? More precisely, how can a coach achieve a state that fosters an environment where masterful coaching naturally unfolds?

Several key questions can guide us in understanding this optimal state for coaching: in which state are you profoundly present, attuned to both the explicit and implicit layers of a person's narrative, their emotions, thoughts, values and worldview, as well as to your own intuitive undercurrents? When are you most alert to all relevant details, whether direct or tangential, most relaxed and open to the unfolding magic of the moment, and most creative and confident in navigating the unseen thresholds between what is and what is on the verge of coming into being?

Partnership: Partnership in coaching transcends mere collaboration; it's about intentionally crafting the relationship, the direction of the conversation that deciphers the optimal way to blend the coach and client roles for maximum impact. This partnership isn't limited to the outcome, but extends to the entire coaching process. Masterful coaching avoids assumptions, preferring to explore explicitly and frequently what the client seeks, envisions as outcomes and perceives the process to be. Effective contracting is the groundwork for this co-creation, weaving itself into the session's fabric. By continuously empowering the client to intentionally set and choose the direction of their exploration, coaching reveals its greatest value: fostering a more profound, reflective thinking style in the client.

Process: At its heart, coaching celebrates the emergence of collective intelligence and creativity, with the interplay between coach and client sparking unforeseen creations. Yet, the creative journey is inherently unpredictable. Despite having a vision or direction, the process's actual unfolding is beyond our control, with insights often appearing in the most unexpected moments. Essential to this process are clear contracting, deep curiosity and an openness to the unknown, all while maintaining vigilant attention to the important aspects of the unfolding conversation within and sometimes beyond the intentionally designed frames of the conversation. By allowing the process to flow and simultaneously holding space, we capture critical nuances, encourage the client to recognize and connect them, and navigate the various layers of thought to distil new-found understanding.

Learning and development: Learning demands a unique kind of thinking – one that synthesizes, clarifies and concludes. Amidst deep reflection, clients may not immediately grasp all insights, prompting the coach to facilitate a shift to a meta-level perspective. This reflection introduces new dimensions to the dialogue, and alternating between freeform thinking and focused reflection cultivates a potent mix of divergent and convergent thought processes. Coaching, in my view, integrates first- and second-person action inquiry with narrative, phenomenological and grounded-theory methodologies. These approaches share a commonality: they're driven by curiosity and a high-quality, critical, systemic and philosophical mindset aimed at uncovering the client's world for actionable insights.

Mastery: Thus, masterful coaching is both an art and a "scientific" pursuit, valued for its unique, timely revelations and their practical applications. Art and science each capture only fragments, but their continuous exploration is where true mastery lies.

CHAPTER 27

The Dynamic Process

Keiko Hirano

I believe that deep inside, we all share the fundamental questions "Who are we?" and "Where are we going?" However, we forget to ask ourselves these questions, which makes it challenging to realize our goals and dreams. Coaching is a process that affords us the opportunity to express and bring these goals and dreams to the surface through the coaching dialogue between the client and the coach. That is why coaching is a dynamic experience. With more people utilizing coaching in their personal and organizational environment, I believe this dialogue will bring out diverse possibilities and a realization of many of the things that we want to accomplish.

My encounter with the concept of coaching was in 1997. I learned that there were coach training programs in the US, and I also discovered that these training sessions were conducted via teleconferencing. Experiencing this training from Japan through teleclasses was a whole new experience for me. While it's common now to engage in virtual learning activities, back then, this experience alone was innovative. Entering the field of coaching itself was an encounter with new cultures and learning experiences.

Since starting my journey as a coach, I believe I have taken on multiple roles in the coaching field, including coach, creator of coaching training programs, trainer, mentor, assessor and, most importantly, continuous learner. Throughout these various roles, I have experienced changes in goals, areas of interest and growth stages.

As a beginner, I started my coaching journey with the question "How do you do coaching?" This phase marked my transition from not knowing about coaching to being able to utilize coaching effectively, requiring me to learn several skills and theories.

CHAPTER 27

The next phase for me was about "how can I become a coach at the next level?" or in other words, "how can I improve the quality of my coaching?" It was very beneficial to assess my current level through certification exams and identify specific challenges to reach the next level. Taking proactive measures to achieve these challenges was instrumental in improving my coaching quality.

After having been active as a coach for twenty-five years, I entered a phase of questioning: how to continue being a coach? This phase focused on the way of being a coach, which was more challenging than transitioning from not being a coach to becoming one (from 0 to 1). This is because continuing to be a coach involved not just acquiring skills and knowledge, but also working on the "way of being."

"What principles do we base our dialogue on?", "What is possible for us as coaches?", "What are we co-creating with our coachees?" These questions were very deep and had no single correct answer. The clues to the answers were provided by model pioneer coaches. Meryl, with whom I collaborated on this project, has been an acquaintance for decades and clearly provided one of those answers, serving as a role model for me as a coach. And Dalia, whom I collaborated with for the first time in this project, provided me with a new perspective that I did not have before.

What I want to convey is that continuing to be a coach means adopting a coach's mindset, and what is essential for that is a commitment to an ongoing, never-ending learning journey. In fact, I believe this is the most crucial competency for us to have as we operate in a world that is constantly changing. I hope you approach this ongoing journey with enthusiasm. And as one of the tools for your journey, I would be very happy if this book proves to be helpful.

CHAPTER 28

The Paradox of Asking Powerful Questions in Coaching

Johan van Bavel

In the realm of coaching, the importance of asking powerful questions is frequently emphasized. These questions are considered to be the key to unlocking insights, stimulating growth and fostering change in clients. However, behind this seemingly straightforward approach lies a paradox: powerful questions are not pre-programmed in a coach's arsenal but are dynamically created in interaction with the unique needs, context and perceptions of the client.

The Illusion of universal power: The concept of a "powerful question" implies some sort of universal formula that guarantees impact on every situation and individual. In reality, the effect of a question is heavily dependent on the complex dynamics between coach and client, the stage of the coaching process, the context of the conversation, and the client's personal history and beliefs.

Resonance – the heart of effective questions: The true hallmark of a powerful question is not the question itself, but the extent to which it resonates with the client. Resonance occurs when a question aligns with the emotional, intellectual, reference framework and spiritual depths of the client, engendering a sense of urgency, engagement, self-reflection, awareness, learning and growth.

The art of adaptation: An effective coach understands that there is no one-size-fits-all approach to asking questions. Instead, mastery in questioning requires a deep understanding of the client and the ability to be flexible in formulating questions based on ongoing feedback and responses from the client.

The importance of active listening: In addition to asking questions, listening is an essential component of effective coaching. By actively listening to the words, non-verbal cues, energy, emotions and silences of the client, a coach can pick up subtle signals that may lead to asking more relevant and resonant questions. Questions that have an effect on the client in that particular situation or not.

The path to authentic change: Rather than focusing on finding the "perfect" question, a coach should focus on cultivating a relationship of trust, respect and openness with the client. By collaborating on exploring personal values, beliefs and goals, coach and client can create fertile ground for authentic growth and transformation.

Conclusion: The paradox of asking powerful questions in coaching reveals the depth and subtlety of the coaching process. While there is no universal recipe for formulating powerful questions, the true power of coaching lies in the ability to create resonance between coach and client. By listening, adapting and cultivating authentic connections, coaches can have a meaningful impact on the lives of their clients and contribute to sustainable change and growth.

CHAPTER 29

The Power of the Pause

Teri-E Belf

Since 1974 I have studied *The Kybalion* (Three Initiates, 1908), a study of the Hermetic philosophy of Ancient Egypt and Greece. I was fascinated by the use and power of silence. As coaches, we can use this ancient wisdom to greatly increase our coaching mastery.

When I began coaching, I spoke too much. When I spoke, I listened to myself. I liked control and being in charge. Not a coaching model. When I focused on the client, I ignored myself and I wore blinders to other intelligence.

Because I value the underlying coaching principle that clients have their own answers, there had to be a way to help them find these answers. Silence? Are we paid to remain silent? Are we supposed to say nothing? Listening requires silence. I erroneously assumed silent space had "nothing" to offer. Early on, I felt unethical: "You are being paid to sit here and do *nothing*?" However, curiosity in combination with "not knowing" sourced a space for clients to solve their problems.

I had been oblivious to the third party in a coaching partnership: you, your client *and* the space in between and around both of you… and beyond.

In Ancient Greece, the third partner existed in the space of "Dunamis." It is the space of creative emergence where all 15 billion possibilities exist in any one moment, according to neuroscience. It is space! Dunamis meant power, the power of creative potentiality, a humongous, grandiose, spectacular, mysterious space for our coaching curiosity to explore and download. We are more effective when we recognize it and masterfully use its gift.

CHAPTER 29

Unless this wisdom is applied, all is for naught. As ancient wisdom says, "The possession of knowledge, unless expressed in action or manifestation is a vain and foolish thing. Knowledge is intended for use."

How is this "knowledge" of Dunamis essential to coaching mastery? How could I use this in coaching? My experiment began with being quiet, gingerly entering the "not-knowing space." Inner chatter screamed: "My client must think I am stupid because I am not speaking." I was present with myself, not in the space of Dunamis. I had to practice silence and receptivity to my inner/outer self, my client's inner/outer self *within* the space of Dunamis.

I began by applying this to questioning. Imagine pausing before you ask a question, being in curious silence… waiting until something is a possibility of value. Be patient and remember everything that happens has value, and that you and your client are the detectives to explore what that value might be. Wait for sprinkles of wisdom to pop up without expectation. Many times, as I was about to speak, the client said it before me. Had I spoken, they reported afterwards, they would not have taken the responsibility to do the work themselves. This has a sustainable coaching benefit because when clients answer their own questions, it embeds in *their* memory in the neocortex, solidifying ownership and accountability.

When something emerges, check the client is ready to receive it and not involved in their internal processing, then share the question. If it is an evocative question, the client pauses for reflection. We might say the question is *sandwiched in silence*. Silence before the question emerges; silence after it is spoken.

No longer will you squirm to find the right question. You will experience the "power in the pause" in Dunamis. Honestly, at times I still have the urge to interrupt the silence and say something; however, we are better coaches when we partner with Dunamis.

CHAPTER 30

The Magical Journey to the Center of the Self

Chérie Carter-Scott

In a world where we learn to become outer-centered, accommodating the values, opinions and principles of others, we diminish, discount and discredit our own innate knowing. This is the reason why so many people respond with the words "I don't know" when asked what they want. They have been "trained" to defer to another to avoid disapproval, criticism and humiliation. This approach has restricted creativity and left the majority of people floundering with essential life questions like: What should I want? What should I do? What should be important to me? What should my values be? What should I do with my life? Who should I partner with? Where should I live? What should I do to support myself? And finally, Who am I?

"Outer-centered shoulds" are not intentionally diminishing, they have evolved from a culture in search of the expert, authority or all-knowing guru who can and will tell the others what they "should" decide. The know-and-tell helpers believe they are doing a service to those who are clueless about what they want. They have built a life based on knowing what is best for others and their conviction is so dominating that it eclipses the subtle whispers of the innocent spirit. The fundamental difference in the new coaching paradigm is that we believe that all people have their answers inside themselves, and they also possess the power to make those answers become reality. We are not here to help unaware people receive direction, but rather to find the key that unlocks the truth to their essence, their spiritual DNA.

When you discover that you have a "calling" to help people, then you will start considering various options. There are many ways to offer support to another: consulting, mentoring, therapy, ministry, medicine, social services, education – the list goes on and on. When you discover coaching and you connect with the power that it offers, you have officially "come home."

Coaching enables you to be your best self and then to empower your client to be their best vision of themselves. Coaching is the purest way that you can focus 100% of your energy on another, helping them discover and connect to their authentic self, uncover their truth and then take action. The experience is so much more than problem-solving. It is so much more than coming up with logical, reasonable and rational answers to a challenge. It is in the connected "creative void" when coach and client come together to invite the concealed truth to bubble up to the surface unlocking their deepest desires, secret yearnings and ultimately their life purpose.

Welcome home! You have found a way to be true to yourself while simultaneously helping others make choices about what is important to them. You have found a non-judgmental, non-intrusive way to support others to become more aware, to embrace their learning and transform into who they ideally want to be. You have discovered a way to empower others on their journey to fully become their essential selves.

Living life as a coach is the surest way to continue to live in the coaching mindset, and *not know* what is best for others. Reflecting on our circumstances, learning from everything that happens to us and choosing to take the road of respect, deep listening, empowerment and inner truth is what will keep us all pure in this journey to the center of the self!

CHAPTER 31

Synchronizing Presence through the Three Selves

Dr. Paul Jeong

In the structured domain of coaching, presence is a nuanced and potent force, reminiscent of the silent power found in a calm, profound ocean. Presence is not a static condition; it is an active dynamic of awareness, understanding and connection. This dynamic is systematically coordinated by the interaction of "three selves": the Background Self, the Memory Self and the Experiential Self.

The Background Self serves as a consistent, reliable beacon, providing guidance with its steady, serene illumination. This entity is a silent observer, representing pure consciousness, impartially observing life's unfolding scenarios without judgment or attachment. When coaches engage with their Background Self, they establish themselves in a space characterized by stability and clarity. This engagement facilitates the maintenance of a grounded, open and adaptable presence, empowering coaches to remain focused, observant and responsive, thereby providing empathetic support to clients without judgment.

The Memory Self functions as a constructor of narratives, subtly shaping our identity while being influenced by past experiences, memories and learned behaviors. This entity quietly narrates our history, influencing our present perceptions and reactions. Understanding the Memory Self, both our own and those of our clients, is crucial. It enables navigation through the complex maze of past fears and joys, providing valuable insights into the narratives that shape our lives and responses to the present.

The Experiential Self is actively engaged with the present moment, experiencing emotions, perceiving sensations and interacting with the environment in real time. This entity is the pulse of the present, vibrating with life's rhythm. Engaging with the Experiential Self involves immersing oneself in life, approaching each moment with curiosity, openness and a readiness to explore and co-create.

Maintaining presence in coaching is a dynamic process involving the three selves. It requires full consciousness and presence, emotion management, and openness and responsiveness to clients. It also involves demonstrating confidence when facing strong emotions, being comfortable with uncertainty and providing space for silence, pauses and reflection.

When coaches skillfully navigate through their three selves, they not only maintain presence but embody it, exuding it in every interaction, session and moment. The interaction of the three selves is a dance of presence, awareness and engagement, necessitating practice, awareness and attunement. This interaction is where the true efficacy of coaching is realized.

CHAPTER 32

Letting Go in Three Steps

Karen Burke

Many coaches have found that one of the most challenging parts of achieving their ICF credentials, particularly at the MCC level, was to capture recordings that represented their true coaching skills. They express frustration and curiosity, asking: "why is it difficult to showcase my excellent coaching, in a recorded format for the performance evaluation?" This step is necessary to attain an ICF credential.

As a coach, it is natural to seek growth by diving into books, learning from mentor coaches and practicing with clients. All are valuable steps towards greater coaching mastery. However, there is another powerful tool you can add to your tool belt: "improv." Integrating improv techniques into your practice can rapidly enhance your coaching mastery and confidence.

Improv cultivates curiosity, spontaneity and presence, which are invaluable to coaching. When applied to coaching, these skills help you respond adeptly to prompts from your clients as you trust your instincts. This diminishes performance anxiety and allows you to authentically demonstrate your coaching edge, increasing the likelihood of success in generating a recording for your performance evaluation. Additionally, improv teaches active listening, empathetic presence and the art of building upon what's presented, skills that further enhance your coaching mastery.

Given our brain's tendency to focus energy on anticipated outcomes, including both positive and challenging scenarios, the prospect of sharing and assessing recordings for certification can summon the performance-anxiety monster. This anxiety can be exacerbated when operating outside one's comfort zone, making it difficult to showcase one's best coaching self. Additionally, this discomfort can inadvertently transfer to the coaching space through mirror neurons, impacting both the coach and the client. As a result, the recorded session may fall short of demonstrating the coach's true capabilities due to the shared sense of unease.

Incorporating improv techniques into your coaching practice can significantly enhance your mastery. Here are three steps to get started:

1. **Step outside your comfort zone:** Begin by enrolling in an improv class, whether online or in person, to learn the fundamentals. Many classes offer flexibility to fit into your schedule. Embrace the opportunity to stretch yourself, make new connections and explore new techniques.

2. **Trust the process:** As you engage in improv exercises, trust the tools provided and allow yourself to let go. (This can be hard for many of us!) Practice being fully present in the moment, knowing that this presence will enable you to respond authentically to whatever arises. Embrace the experience and let it guide you.

3. **Integrate somatic insights:** Bring the somatic awareness gained from improv into your coaching practice. Embrace deep listening, letting go of preconceived notions and saying "yes" to the moment with whatever is arising with your client. If you incorporate these skills into any recorded coaching session, it will allow for greater spontaneity and authenticity.

By following these steps, you'll enhance your curiosity, exploration and resilience, reducing the impact of the performance-anxiety monster. Notice the transformation in your coaching approach and the positive feedback from your clients as you apply these new-found skills in your partnership work and demonstrate greater coaching mastery.

CHAPTER 33

Shifting from Transactional to Transformational

Tracy Tresidder

In the dynamic landscape of coaching, the distinctions between novice, intermediate and masterful coaches lie not merely in skill, but in philosophy. While novice or intermediate coaches may excel at identifying surface-level issues and offering quick fixes, masterful coaches embark on a journey of transformation with their clients. This journey involves a shift from transactional coaching, which focuses on addressing apparent, immediate problems, to transformational coaching, which delves deep into the core of the client's being to unearth the underlying motivations, beliefs and assumptions that shape their actions and inhibit lasting change.

Masterful coaches embody several key distinctions that catalyze profound shifts in both themselves and their clients, facilitating a transformational journey of self-discovery and growth.

The following are a number of distinctions that will support a coach's growth towards more masterful coaching.

What vs. who: Transactional coaching often fixates on the "what" – the observable behaviors or actions. However, transformational coaching transcends the surface to explore the "who" – the essence of the client's being. It entails a deeper understanding of sense-making and meaning-making, unravelling the intricacies of motivations and aspirations. By shifting the focus from external behaviors to internal motivations, masterful coaches guide their clients towards a deeper understanding of themselves, paving the way for authentic growth and transformation.

Problem vs. person: At the core of novice coaching lies a focus on problems and solutions; yet transformational coaching transcends this narrow lens by delving into the person behind the problem. It prompts critical thinking, fostering an expansive perspective that transcends short-lived fixes and cultivates enduring change. Rather than simply addressing symptoms, masterful coaches seek to understand the root causes of their clients' challenges, empowering them to navigate life's complexities with wisdom and resilience.

Subject vs. object: The journey towards higher stages of adult development necessitates a profound shift from subject to object. Subjective notions, such as self-concepts and ingrained beliefs, often hinder growth by confining individuals to fixed perspectives. Transformational coaching facilitates detachment, enabling clients to view their beliefs and emotions objectively. By recognizing that they are not defined by their subjective experiences, clients gain agency to navigate their inner landscape with clarity and resilience. Masterful coaches guide this process of self-discovery, helping clients unlock their full potential and embrace new possibilities.

Solution focus vs. awareness focus: While solution-focused approaches may offer temporary relief, they often overlook the underlying patterns that perpetuate the problem. In contrast, transformational coaching adopts an awareness-focused stance, illuminating the beliefs and fears that underpin actions. By fostering self-awareness and introspection, coaches empower clients to navigate their challenges with new-found clarity and confidence. Rather than imposing solutions from the outside, masterful coaches facilitate a journey of self-discovery, guiding clients towards insights that catalyze profound transformation.

In essence, the journey from transactional to transformational coaching represents a profound evolution in the coach–client dynamic. It transcends mere problem-solving, offering a holistic approach that fosters self-discovery and growth. By embracing these key distinctions, masterful coaches empower their clients to navigate life's complexities with wisdom, resilience and authenticity. Through deep listening, empathetic guidance and a commitment to growth, masterful coaches become catalysts for profound transformation, guiding their clients towards a life of purpose, fulfillment and authenticity.

CHAPTER 34

Client Readiness

Kaveh Mir

Coaching can be compared to a theatrical performance, with the coach on the stage with the client. Analogous to a musician adjusting their instrument, the coach must adapt and align themselves with their client. Understanding the client's coachability is part of this alignment process.

In coaching, we often refer to the person we coach as a "client" or "coachee." However, such labelling may inadvertently suggest that all clients are alike and possess equivalent coachability. This could lead us to neglect to adapt our approach depending on a client's receptiveness. To counter this issue and fine-tune our coaching style, it may be helpful to consider how coaching clients may vary in their readiness to engage in coaching.

One method for doing this uses a two-by-two matrix. The X-axis denotes how a client can trust their coach and the overall process involved in coaching. The Y-axis indicates how effectively they can express their goals for each session.

They trust the coach and the coaching process (i.e. they are ready for coaching) and can articulate or reflect on a goal – top right on the two-by-two.

Using this dimension, the coach can utilize their time during sessions to pose questions that encourage self-reflection, as these clients are more skilled at such exercises. The more relevant activities here are captured in Competency 8: Facilitates Client Growth.

Diagram 34.1: Readiness Assessment

```
                    Ready for Coaching
                           ▲
            ┌──────────────┼──────────────┐
            │  Competency  │  Competency  │
            │      3       │      8       │
            │              │              │
            ├──────────────┼──────────────┤
Not Clear on the ◄─────────┼─────────► Clear on the Goal
   Goal     │              │              │
            │  Competency  │  Competency  │
            │    3 & 4     │      4       │
            └──────────────┼──────────────┘
                           ▼
                  Not Ready for Coaching
```

Dos

Ensure tasks are centered around enhancing skills directly linked to the session's goal. Repeatedly check in to gauge how the client perceives their advancement.

Don'ts

Dedicating an extended period to establish a goal is unnecessary for this individual with a well-defined session goal.

They trust the coach and the coaching process (i.e. they are ready for coaching) but cannot articulate or reflect on a goal – top left on the two-by-two.

Using this dimension, the coach should focus more on the agreement and listen to the activity with curiosity and invitation to explore, spending more time on Competency 3: Establishes and Maintains Agreements.

Dos

Stress the necessity of profound understanding and self-perception before delving into outlining objectives. Engage in activities centered around identifying values and strengths before setting goals or allocating resources.

Don'ts

Aiming for a session goal without a clear vision often results in superficial objectives, leading to declining engagement over time.

The client does not trust the coach and the coaching process (i.e. they are not ready for coaching) but can articulate or reflect on a goal – bottom right on the two-by-two.

Clients in this category are not ready for coaching yet. This might be due to a lack of trust in the coach or (more likely) the coaching process. The coach should consider paying more attention to focus more on building the coach–client relationship and an understanding of, and trust in, the coaching process (Competency 4: Cultivates Trust and Safety).

Dos

Showcase profound curiosity by participating in open-ended queries, reflections and summarizing expressions. Choose activities supported by scientific evidence and ensure sessions are focused and straightforward.

Don'ts

This individual possesses immense clarity; however, they may take considerable time to become comfortable in the coaching relationship and might perceive themselves as overly exposed to complicated or powerful questions at the very start of the session.

CHAPTER 34

They do not trust the coach and the coaching process (i.e. they are not ready for coaching) and cannot articulate or reflect on a goal – bottom left on the two-by-two.

For some coaches, this segment represents the most challenging clients to be coached. The advice is not to rush into a deep coaching conversation, but instead pay attention to competencies 3 and 4.

Dos

Proceed gradually, dedicating additional time to establishing a strong coaching partnership and fostering mutual understanding and trust. Clarify the concept of coaching and its numerous advantages.

Don'ts

Avoid leaping to set objectives. Without readiness from the client, these are likely to become superficial aims, and participation will decrease. Be careful of presuming that this client comprehends the coaching process.

All the competencies

All eight ICF competencies are essential for all the above segments and would require attention during the coaching session. It is necessary to notice that a client might be in one segment on one topic whilst being in a different segment on a different coaching topic.

CHAPTER 35

Imbalances in Power and Coaching

Lola Chetti

Ethics are the bedrock of the coaching professional career. Clients willingly open their hearts and minds to their coach, trusting that their personal thoughts and feelings will always be safe. This expectation of trust goes beyond what they share within the safety of coaching sessions; clients also have an implicit psychological expectation that within this relationship, they will not be harmed.

Coaching rightly places an immense responsibility on coaches, especially when the relationship with the client is embedded in other relationships within which we may be professionally accountable: payee, sponsor, direct manager and so forth. It can be tempting to feel safe in the notion of a code of ethics, but we all know that ethical behavior is not neatly contained or captured within the four corners of a standard "code of conduct." This is not to say that codes of ethics are not useful guides, but ethical practice is complex and nuanced.

One of the areas that is least spoken about and yet infiltrates every coaching relationship is the dynamics of power in a relationship. Ignoring the fact that a coaching relationship exists within a landscape of existing power differences among individuals, groups, genders, races, cultures and socio-economic groups only serves to exacerbate the impact of these existing power differences.

The ICF Code of Ethics invites the coach to be "aware" and to "manage power or status difference." We often think that the coaching client comes with a need, and so the power rests with the coach. On occasions, this may be true. But on other occasions the reverse may be true, when working with highly successful leaders of large global organizations or charismatic individuals, for example.

Coaching calls for us to ask ourselves, every time, some important questions about our own perceptions of power dynamics in each of our coaching relationships, including:

- Would we experience discomfort in challenging this client, sponsor or stakeholder in this engagement?
- Would we hesitate in raising any specific area of work or life with our coaching client?
- Would we feel comfortable reminding our client, sponsor or stakeholder of ethical boundaries?
- Are there any client experiences which we have difficulty accepting (gender, race, sexual orientation, etc.)?
- Are there perceived power dynamics standing in the way of a relationship based on equity?

There is no ready-made formula to deal with the power dynamics inherent to any coaching relationship, but good practices include creating awareness, seeking guidance and taking action to manage the balance of power.

CHAPTER 36

Managing Our Own Saboteurs

Frances Penafort

When we coach our clients, we sometimes get a feeling that our own saboteurs arise within us. These saboteurs have a serious detrimental impact on us professional coaches. Instead of holding a safe space for our clients, the opposite may be in effect. In this mini chapter, I want to share some possible saboteurs, what triggers them, why they emerge and how we can manage them. By gaining this knowledge and understanding, we can be supported in our continuous journey of learning as a professional coach.

Firstly, let's look at the saboteurs. The term "saboteurs" refers to something that prevents us fulfilling our roles and responsibilities, as a result of our perceptions. Some examples include:

- Situations in which a client is perceived by the coach to have a "lower status" than the coach. If this is the case then the coach may unconsciously think, talk, act or behave condescendingly towards the client. This will be in contrast towards how he should show up as a professional coach, as he would not be serving the client where they are in their current situation.

- Conversely, if there is a perception that the client has a "higher status" than the coach, then the coach may unconsciously think, talk, act or behave with deference towards the client. The coach may patronize his client or the coach may not be willing to challenge the client in areas that need to be challenged. In worst-case scenarios, the coach may see himself as "not good enough." Again, these behaviors will be contra-indicators to successful coaching.

In both these examples, these perceptions act as saboteurs which get triggered when the coach is in the space of the client. The coach can get triggered by the client's choice of words, how the client behaves, their mannerisms, culture, religious beliefs, age, race or professional position, among other factors. When triggered by any of these, the coach can move into a space of judgment. In this space the coach is not able to operate at their full capacity – and this inhibits the creation of psychological safety and a trusting relationship.

Now let's look at how we can manage these saboteurs.

The coach's friend is the maintenance of a high level of self-awareness, to notice in the present moment shifts or changes in their bodily sensations. The body communicates emotional responses before the mind is able to label these – as fear, disgust or anger, for example.

Some of the quickest ways to overcome these perceived saboteurs include:

- Staying aware of what's happening in our body
- Noticing changes or shifts in our bodily sensations
- Slowing down our breathing (this can be done by deliberately taking a deep breath and observing a slowing down within the coach)
- Taking a deliberate pause
- Using visualization of the desired outcome or state.

CHAPTER 37

Coaching Mindset

Ann Fogolin

To embody a coaching mindset means we demonstrate the traits, ideas and concepts of what it means to be a coach. Our actions, demeanor and presence are qualities that go beyond understanding coaching from a conceptual context and demonstrate these behaviors in a manner that's observable. There are so many qualities used to describe what it means to be a coach, such as being client-centered, open minded, flexible, curious, present, intuitive, empathetic, respectful and resilient. All are important.

This competency invites us to do our own work, to build a foundation that supports us in creating the life and practice we desire. The process is one that takes time, energy, patience and compassion for ourselves, as there will be moments along this path that may feel uncomfortable; that's where the greatest learning will take place. Working with our own support system, including a coach, we can be truthful with our experiences, vent our frustrations and allow ourselves to keep learning the lessons that continue to come our way. The hurdles we may need to overcome can be reframed and seen as opportunities to navigate, rather than making them mean something negative.

As coaches, we're very "other" centered. Developing and embodying a coaching mindset invites us to deliberately invest in ourselves, prioritizing how we spend our time and energy. Making the time to feel and embrace "who" we are becoming may feel unnatural, yet it is critical in our development. Reminding ourselves of the importance of these milestones will support us when hitting a rough patch and help us summon the courage to continue to build on this foundation.

Regardless of the credential we may hold, it's imperative we continue our learning and evolving to ensure we are developing and improving.

When we authentically model honesty, integrity and empathy, we build trust and rapport with our coachees. Reflective practice encourages us to examine our own beliefs, biases and assumptions, helping us to become more self-aware.

Experiencing some of the benefits of our efforts might include a shift in priorities and taking better care of ourself: we'll thus have more energy and life will become simpler. At the same time, we may lose friends or colleagues and begin to expect more from others as we're now expecting more from ourself. The best way to enjoy these changes is to understand that we're "walking the talk" in creating this life we say we want, and modeling what that means for our coachees. Modeling healthy habits and effective coping strategies can be useful for our coachees to gain confidence and motivation to perhaps make similar changes in their own lives.

Engaging in reflective practice and ongoing learning demonstrates commitment to self-improvement and growth. While these practices cultivate professional competence, they embody the qualities we wish to instill and thus make an impact on the lives of our coachees.

CHAPTER 38

Using Silence, Pauses and Reflections

Cindy Muthukarapan

Let's start this teaching/learning moment with an excerpt from a conversation between a coach and a client. The conversation explores a significant issue faced by the client. In this conversation, note how the coach skillfully and patiently uses silence as a tool to invite the client to reflect deeply on their feelings and thoughts. Each silence invites the client to dive deeper, uncovering underlying issues and eventually leading to a self-realized insight about their need for a values-aligned workplace. This excerpt demonstrates the power of silence in facilitating meaningful discovery and personal growth in coaching sessions. Note that silence is indicated in square brackets, so that you can get a sense of the reflected, slow, thoughtful pace of the responses of both coach and client.

At the end of the excerpt, I have included a few teaching/mentoring reflective moments for a coach to include in their practice.

> **Coach:** You mentioned feeling overwhelmed and underappreciated about the challenge you are experiencing at work. Can you talk more about that?
>
> **Client:** Yes, it's been really tough. No matter how hard I work, it seems like it's never enough for my boss. I'm always the last to leave, and yet… [*Silence.*] And… I guess I feel like I'm invisible. Like what I do doesn't really matter.
>
> **Coach:** [*Nods, maintaining silence.*]
>
> **Client:** [After a pause] It's just… sometimes I wonder if all the effort is even worth it.

Coach: It sounds like you're questioning the value of your hard work. [*Pauses, allowing the silence to settle.*] What does recognition look like for you in this context?

Client: [*Silence as they reflect.*] I suppose… it's about knowing that my contributions make a difference. That they're seen.

Coach: [*Silence.*]

Client: And that maybe I'm part of something bigger, you know? But I just don't feel that way right now.

Coach: [*After a moment of silence.*] How does it affect you, not feeling part of something bigger?

Client: [*Takes a deep breath, silence allowing them to gather thoughts.*] It's demotivating. I start to question my own abilities and whether I belong in this role or even this career.

Coach: [*Silence.*]

Client: [*Silence.*] Maybe that's what's really been bothering me. Not just the lack of recognition but feeling like I don't belong.

Coach: Where do you feel you belong?

Client: [*Silence, visibly reflecting.*] That's a good question. I've always been passionate about my work, but maybe it's not about the job itself but the environment… the people and the culture.

Coach: [*Silence.*] Mmmm.

Client: I think I need to find a place where my values are aligned with the work and where people recognize and support each other.

As you read the excerpt again you may like to reflect on the following suggestions:

1. Pause after asking a deep or provocative question. Example: "What do you think is at the root of your hesitation to take the next step in your career?" (Pause and wait, allowing the client time to reflect before responding.)

2. Incorporate non-verbal cues to encourage silence. Example: your body language invites the client to continue delving deeper into their thoughts.

3. Ask/invite open-ended questions without rushing for answers. Example: "How does this align with your values?" (Ask the question and then comfortably settle back, signaling that you're giving them time to explore their thoughts without immediate pressure to answer.)

4. Ask for permission to pause. Example: "Can we pause for a moment on that thought?" (This shows respect for the client's pace and signals a deliberate use of silence for reflection.)

5. Reflect on the silence itself.

CHAPTER 39

The Significance of Opening Coaching Sessions

Svea van der Hoorn

Coaches ask "but which recordings should I submit for assessment to pass?" While this deserves a multifaceted response, I offer one essential consideration – how the coach opens the session can be the deal-breaker, both for assessment success and for client satisfaction and benefit. It goes to the heart of what distinguishes ICF-credentialed coaches in an increasingly crowded coaching provider market.

Coaching should be experienced as different from other conversations, such casual conversations, friendship conversations, managerial conversations, and more. These conversations are more like a question-and-answer language game.

The coaching conversation is characterized by partnering with the client for the purpose of cultivating learning and growth. When listening to a recording, I bear the following a question in mind: how well does this recording deliver on the promise that the ICF definition of coaching offers clients, sponsors and other stakeholders? So, what is the ICF promise? The ICF-credentialed coach commits to partner with the client in a thought-provoking and creative process that inspires the client to maximize their personal and professional potential.

How effectively the coach signals that this is a coaching conversation becomes evident in the session opening they offer. Does the coach start with an invitation that is so wide open that it minimally signals that a coaching conversation is beginning? For example: "What do you want to talk about?" or "What would you like to explore?" In both these openings, the "how" is signaled – we will be talking/exploring – but the "what" and the "who" are not explicitly invited. Such openings leave the responsibility with the coach to partner by both acknowledging what the client has offered, and inviting the client to begin to talk about themselves and what they want to see change in their lives. Without this, reaching a Coaching Agreement is unlikely. The recording will meet neither the ethical nor the Core Competency 3 requirements, and will most likely lead to an applicant being asked to re-submit. The coach can prevent this by attending to their choice of opening.

First-session openings that invite the "who" and "what" of the client to engage sound more like these: "What would you like to see happening in your life that you'd like this coaching session to contribute to?", "When you made the appointment, what were your hopes about how coaching can be beneficial/worthwhile for you?", "OK, so your parent/manager thought it was a good idea for you to come to coaching… what do they hope the coaching can offer you?" and "Let's suppose this coaching turns out to be really beneficial to you. What might be signs that you and others might notice?" Subsequent session openings should offer choice, making space for progress talk as well topic clarification. For example, "How would you like to start today… with progress or is there something new?"

Establishing an agreement honors the client's hopes, desires, needs and wants, enabling the coach to be a learning and growth partner.

CHAPTER 40

Humility

Peter Hayward

Humility is often overshadowed by other qualities in coaching, such as powerful questions or even coaching models, yet it remains a cornerstone of truly impactful practice.

As coaches, the journey from Associate Certified Coach or Professional Certified Coach to Master Certified Coach involves deepening not only our skills but our self-awareness and empathy, qualities intrinsically linked to humility.

At its core, humility in coaching is the ability to hold space for the client's story, needs and growth without inserting our own ego or agenda. It's an acknowledgment that, despite our expertise and experience, we are perpetual students.

To me, as a seasoned coach, humility enhances my practice in five ways:

1. **Fostering openness and learning:** Humility invites a learning stance in every interaction. When coaches approach sessions with curiosity and openness, free from the need to prove their competence, they create a safe space for clients to explore and reflect.

2. **Building trust and rapport:** Clients are more likely to feel valued and understood when they sense genuine humility in their coach. This humility manifests as a sincere interest in their thoughts and a respectful acknowledgment of their experiences and expertise.

3. **Encouraging client autonomy:** A humble approach empowers clients, enhancing their autonomy and encouraging them to take ownership of their developmental journey. By asking open-ended questions and allowing clients to arrive at their own insights,

we reinforce their capability in navigating challenges and making decisions.

4. **Enhancing adaptability and responsiveness:** Humility helps coaches remain adaptable. Each client is unique and so a one-size-fits-all approach never works. A humble coach listens deeply and adapts their techniques to better fit the client's individual style and needs rather than rigidly applying predefined methods.

5. **Modeling behavior for clients:** Finally, demonstrating humility can serve as a powerful model for clients, who may see its value and mirror it in their own professional and personal interactions. This modeling can enhance their leadership style, improve their relationships and increase their effectiveness in various roles. Witnessing their coach handling misunderstandings or mistakes with grace and accountability can inspire clients to adopt similar behaviors.

The cultivation of humility is a dynamic and ongoing process. It requires continual self-reflection, an openness to feedback and a genuine commitment to the client. For those on the path to becoming master coaches, embracing humility not only enriches your practice but also profoundly impacts the lives of those you coach.

CHAPTER 41

Bias

João Luiz Pasqual

In the realm of coaching competencies, a pivotal aspect for practical application is the mitigation of biases, a key competency in line with a coach's fundamental duty to remain objective and to offer equitable guidance. Central to enlivening this skill in coaching endeavors is a multifaceted approach.

Coaches are to be encouraged to partake in routine introspection regarding their sessions, embracing the understanding that biases are a part of the cognitive tapestry, thus fostering a keen awareness of their own potential partialities. Pursuing an array of perspectives and welcoming feedback from colleagues serve as catalysts for challenging and broadening a coach's own convictions and techniques.

This pursuit is complemented by the adoption of structured tools intended to cast a light on client progression, steering clear of biases rooted in a coach's individual preferences. These instruments are pivotal for an all-encompassing appraisal of a client's life and accomplishments. Parallel to this, it is critical to emphasize goal setting that is client-driven, assuring that the coaching trajectory is influenced by what the client seeks to achieve.

Balanced feedback is the cornerstone of objective coaching, where coaches should become proficient in identifying and communicating achievements alongside areas needing improvement to circumvent overvaluing results that reflect their personal viewpoints.

Some concrete examples of biases include **confirmation bias**, which may lead a coach to validate a client's achievements in areas that resonate with their own beliefs while overlooking other essential aspects. **Availability bias** can also arise, influencing a coach by the most readily available information, which could result in erroneous interpretations of a client's actions, such as attributing their absence from group activities to a lack of interest rather than possible logistical issues like time-zone differences.

Additionally, **affinity bias** might cause a coach to allocate more attention and resources to a client with whom they share common traits or interests, inadvertently providing less support to clients who might seem less similar.

Regular professional growth, especially centered on the neuroscience behind biases, is essential, enhancing a coach's grasp of how biases develop and equipping them with strategies to mitigate the impact of biases effectively.

By harnessing these interwoven strategies to confront biases, the field of coaching can be significantly refined, ensuring that coaches are able to foster their clients' development in a thorough and equitable manner.

This comprehensive support not only upholds the integrity of the coaching profession but also maximizes the potential for client growth and achievement.

CHAPTER 42

Not Knowing Is Your Greatest Strength

Philippe R. Declercq

The aphorism "ignorance is bliss" takes on a whole new meaning in the realm of coaching. Here, not being privy to all the answers isn't a liability, but a potent catalyst for unlocking a client's true potential.

When a client ventures into uncharted territory, it presents a golden opportunity for us to wield the full spectrum of our coaching toolbox: probing questions, genuine curiosity, the thrill of discovery and the collaborative magic of co-creation.

When a client steps into our domain of expertise, resisting the urge to dispense pre-packaged solutions can be a Herculean task. Despite our best efforts to maintain an objective stance, the siren song of advice and direction can be tempting. Years of experience sharpen our awareness of this trap, yet the danger ever lurks. Our knowledge, a double-edged sword, can subtly color our internal narrative and, by extension, the client relationship.

Here's where the unbridled joy of not knowing enters the picture. It empowers us to unleash a barrage of exploratory questions, innocent and open-ended. We become facilitators, guiding the client on a journey of self-discovery. They delve into their past, forging connections between seemingly disparate experiences. This process fosters a blossoming awareness of their own strengths and capabilities, a treasure trove they then share with us.

In this shared space of exploration, co-creation flourishes. We learn alongside the client, their insights informing the development of potent action steps that are entirely organically derived from their new-found self-awareness.

The power of not knowing in coaching is a true paradigm shift. It's not about feigning ignorance, but about embracing the opportunity to learn alongside the client, fostering a space of empowerment and co-creation.

This shift in thinking has several benefits:

- **Deeper client exploration:** When the coach experiences the joy of not knowing, the client has the freedom to delve deeper into their own experiences and thought processes. This can lead to unexpected insights and breakthroughs.

- **Increased client ownership:** By co-creating solutions, the client feels more invested in the process and more likely to follow through on action steps.

- **Continuous learning for the coach:** "Not knowing" allows the coach to learn from every client interaction, expanding their own experience base and becoming a more effective coach.

Overall, not knowing is a powerful tool in coaching that fosters a more collaborative, empowering and ultimately more successful coaching experience for both the coach and the client.

References

Bavel, J. Van (2023) *Co-Creation: A Practical Guide for Coaching.* Self-published. https://www.intentioncoachingtraining.com

Belf, Teri-E (2002) *Coaching with Spirit: Allowing Success to Emerge.* New York, US: John Wiley & Sons.

Coughlin, C. (2019) *Two Structural Doors – Assumptions about Equals and about Constraints.* https://www.cultivatingleadership.com/author/carolyn

ICF (2019) ICF Core Competencies. Retrieved on 1st March 2024 from: https://coachingfederation.org/credentials-and-standards/core-competencies

ICF (2020) ICF Code of Ethics. Retrieved on 1st March 2024 from: https://coachingfederation.org/ethics/code-of-ethics

ICF (n.d.) Associate Certified Coach (ACC) Credential. Retrieved on 1st March 2024 from: https://coachingfederation.org/credentials-and-standards/credentials-paths/acc-credential

ICF (n.d.) Professional Certified Coach (PCC) Credential. Retrieved on 1st March 2024 from: https://coachingfederation.org/credentials-and-standards/credentials-paths/pcc-credential

ICF (n.d.) Master Certified Coach (PCC) Credential. Retrieved on 1st March 2024 from: https://coachingfederation.org/credentials-and-standards/credentials-paths/mcc-credential

ICF (n.d.) PCC Markers. Retrieved on 20th April 2024 from: https://coachingfederation.org/credentials-and-standards/performance-evaluations/pcc-markers

Passmore, J. (2021) How can I refer clients to another helping professional? In *Succeeding as a Coach: Insights from the Experts* (pp. 82–84). Shoreham-by-Sea, UK: Pavilion Publishing.

Passmore, J., and Sinclair, T. (2024) *Becoming a Coach: The Essential ICF Guide* (2nd edition). Worthing, UK: Pavilion Books.

Passmore, J., Widdowson, L., Barbour, P., and Kanalidouk, K. (2024) *Becoming a Team Coach: The Essential ICF Guide.* Cham, Switzerland: Springer.

Pedrick, C. (2020) *Simplifying Coaching: How to Have More Transformational Conversations by Doing Less.* Maidenhead, UK: OUP.

Reynolds, M. (2020) *Coach the Person not the Problem: A Guide to Using Reflective Inquiry*. San Francisco, US: Berrett-Koehler.

Rogers, C. R. (1957) The necessary and sufficient conditions of therapeutic personality change. *Journal of Consulting Psychology*, 21(2): 95–103. https://doi.org/10.1037/h0045357

Scharmer, C. O. (2016) *Theory U: Leading from the Emerging Future* (2nd edition). A BK business book. San Francisco, US: Berrett-Koehler.

Three Initiates (1908) *The Kybalion: The Hermetic Philosophy of Ancient Egypt and Greece*. Chicago, US: The Yogi Publication Society.

Whitmore, J. (2005) Coaching for Performance. London: Nicholas Brealey.

SECTION 4

Appendices

APPENDIX 1

Useful Links

ICF Core Competencies:

> https://coachingfederation.org/credentials-and-standards/core-competencies

Download link:

> https://coachingfederation.org/app/uploads/2021/07/Updated-ICF-Core-Competencies_English_Brand-Updated.pdf

ICF Code of Ethics:

> https://coachingfederation.org/ethics/code-of-ethics

Download link:

> https://coachingfederation.org/app/uploads/2021/01/ICF-Code-of-Ethics-1.pdf

Minimum Skills Requirements:

> https://coachingfederation.org/credentials-and-standards/performance-evaluations/minimum-skills-requirements

PCC Markers download link:

> https://coachingfederation.org/app/uploads/2021/06/Updated-ICF-PCC-Markers_English_Brand-Updated_Final.pdf

APPENDIX 2

Minimum Skills Requirements for ACC Credential

ICF believes that it has an obligation to support its member coaches in the growth of their skill set. Every Master Certified Coach (MCC) started as a beginner. They progressed through an intermediate level of skill and became masterful, where the hallmark is deep evidence of the coach's role as learner about the client. ICF's three levels of credentials reflect the continuum of growth and learning along the coaching journey.

This document has been created to support coaches as they prepare for the Associate Certified Coach (ACC) credential performance evaluation. We also hope that this document will assist mentor coaches and supervisors in supporting these coaches, and coaching education and training providers in undertaking accreditation of their programs. The aim is to support coaches in successfully completing the ACC performance evaluation and in continuing to develop their skill set as coaches, in alignment with the updated ICF core competencies, 2019 (https://coachingfederation.org/credentials-and-standards/core-competencies).

For those seeking a credential, this document will provide an understanding of what assessors evaluate in relation to each ICF core competency. It will offer the minimum level of skill necessary to successfully demonstrate an ACC level of competency, and also help you understand what non-coaching behaviors might prevent successful completion of the ACC performance evaluation. This document can help each individual coach answer the following queries:

1. What does it mean to be an ACC coach?
2. What do ICF assessors listen for when they are evaluating an ACC coach?

3. As I progress on my coaching journey, what are my strengths and what are the skill-set areas that I need to grow to pass the ACC performance evaluation?

Finally, ICF strongly believes that clients receive real and substantive value from ACC coaches. That value rests always in the coach's attention to the client and what the client wishes to accomplish, as well as the coach's complete support of the client's agenda. We honor each and every coach on their journey and look forward to supporting your path of growth as a coach and your credentialing path within ICF.

1. Demonstrates Ethical Practice

Definition: Understands and consistently applies coaching ethics and standards of coaching.

1. Demonstrates personal integrity and honesty in interactions with clients, sponsors and relevant stakeholders
2. Is sensitive to clients' identity, environment, experiences, values and beliefs
3. Uses language appropriate and respectful to clients, sponsors and relevant stakeholders
4. Abides by the ICF Code of Ethics and upholds the Core Values
5. Maintains confidentiality with client information per stakeholder agreements and pertinent laws
6. Maintains the distinctions between coaching, consulting, psychotherapy and other support professions
7. Refers clients to other support professionals, as appropriate

Important Note: Familiarity with the ICF Code of Ethics and its application is required for all levels of coaching and the standard for demonstrating a strong ethical understanding of coaching is similar for an ICF credential at any level – Associate Certified Coach (ACC), Professional Certified Coach (PCC) or Master Certified Coach (MCC).

An applicant must demonstrate alignment with the ICF Code of Ethics in the performance evaluation. An applicant who commits a clear violation of the ICF Code of Ethics within a performance evaluation recording would not pass this competency and would be denied a credential.

An applicant must also remain consistently in the role of coach within the performance evaluation. This includes demonstrating a knowledge of the coaching conversation that is focused on inquiry and exploration, and a focus based on present and future issues. An applicant would not pass this competency if they focused primarily on telling the client what to do or how to do it (consulting mode) or if the conversation were based primarily in the past, particularly the emotional past (therapeutic mode).

If an applicant is not clear on basic foundation exploration and evoking skills that underlie the ICF definition of coaching, that lack of clarity in skill use will be reflected in skill level demonstrated in some of the other competencies listed below. For example, if a coach almost exclusively gives advice or indicates that a particular answer chosen by the coach is what the client should do, trust and safety, presence, active listening, evoking awareness and facilitating client growth will not be present and a credential at any level would be denied.

2. Embodies a Coaching Mindset

Definition: Develops and maintains a mindset that is open, curious, flexible and client-centered.

1. Acknowledges that clients are responsible for their own choices
2. Engages in ongoing learning and development as a coach
3. Develops an ongoing reflective practice to enhance one's coaching
4. Remains aware of and open to the influence of context and culture on self and others
5. Uses awareness of self and one's intuition to benefit clients
6. Develops and maintains the ability to regulate one's emotions
7. Mentally and emotionally prepares for sessions
8. Seeks help from outside sources when necessary

APPENDIX 2

Competency 2: Embodies a Coaching Mindset serves as a foundational competency for coach practitioners, focused primarily on the "being" of the coach. The related behaviors are typically demonstrated across a coach's practice, more so than in any specific coaching session. This competency area is therefore more difficult to consistently assess within the performance evaluation process. As a result, there are no behavioral or skill statements in this competency area that are used for assessment purposes. Rather, an applicant's knowledge of and ability to apply Competency 2: Embodies a Coaching Mindset are more directly evaluated in the ICF credentialing written exam.

3. Establishes and Maintains Agreements

Definition: Partners with the client and relevant stakeholders to create clear agreements about the coaching relationship, process, plans and goals. Establishes agreements for the overall coaching engagement as well as those for each coaching session.

1. Explains what coaching is and is not and describes the process to the client and relevant stakeholders
2. Reaches agreement about what is and is not appropriate in the relationship, what is and is not being offered, and the responsibilities of the client and relevant stakeholders
3. Reaches agreement about the guidelines and specific parameters of the coaching relationship such as logistics, fees, scheduling, duration, termination, confidentiality and inclusion of others
4. Partners with the client and relevant stakeholders to establish an overall coaching plan and goals
5. Partners with the client to determine client–coach compatibility
6. Partners with the client to identify or reconfirm what they want to accomplish in the session
7. Partners with the client to define what the client believes they need to address or resolve to achieve what they want to accomplish in the session
8. Partners with the client to define or reconfirm measures of success for what the client wants to accomplish in the coaching engagement or individual session

9. Partners with the client to manage the time and focus of the session
10. Continues coaching in the direction of the client's desired outcome unless the client indicates otherwise
11. Partners with the client to end the coaching relationship in a way that honors the experience

Key Skills Evaluated

1. The clarity and depth in creating an agreement for the session
2. The coach's ability to partner and the depth of partnering with the client in the creation of agreement, measures of success, and issues to be addressed
3. The coach's ability to attend to the client's agenda throughout the session

At an ACC level, the minimum standard of skill that must be demonstrated to achieve a passing score for Competency 3: Establishes and Maintains Agreements is that the coach invites the client to identify what the client wants to accomplish in the session and the coach attends to that agenda throughout the coaching, unless the client indicates otherwise.

Specifically, ACC applicants are assessed on the following skills within Competency 3: Establishes and Maintains Agreements as part of the performance evaluation process:

- Coach and client reach an agreement on what the client wants to accomplish in the session
- Coach invites the client to identify their desired coaching outcome
- Coach attends to the agenda set by the client throughout the session, unless the client indicates otherwise
- Coach shows curiosity about the client and how the client relates to what they want to accomplish.

An applicant will not receive a passing score for Establishes and Maintains Agreements on the ACC performance evaluation if the coach chooses the topic for the client or if the coach does not coach around the topic the client has chosen.

APPENDIX 2

4. Cultivates Trust and Safety

Definition: Partners with the client to create a safe, supportive environment that allows the client to share freely. Maintains a relationship of mutual respect and trust.

1. Seeks to understand the client within their context which may include their identity, environment, experiences, values and beliefs
2. Demonstrates respect for the client's identity, perceptions, style and language, and adapts one's coaching to the client
3. Acknowledges and respects the client's unique talents, insights and work in the coaching process
4. Shows support, empathy and concern for the client
5. Acknowledges and supports the client's expression of feelings, perceptions, concerns, beliefs and suggestions
6. Demonstrates openness and transparency as a way to display vulnerability and build trust with the client

Key Skills Evaluated

1. The coach's depth of connection to and support of the client
2. The coach's demonstration of trust in and respect for the client and the client's processes of thinking, creating
3. The coach's willingness to be open, authentic and vulnerable with the client to build mutual trust

At an ACC level, the minimum standard of skill that must be demonstrated to receive a passing score for Competency 4: Cultivates Trust and Safety is that the coach shows genuine concern, support and respect for the client and is attuned to the client's beliefs, perceptions, learning style and personal being at a basic level.

Specifically, ACC applicants are assessed on the following skills within Competency 4: Cultivates Trust and Safety as part of the performance evaluation process:

- Coach acknowledges client insights and learning in the moment
- Coach explores the client's expression of feelings, perceptions, concerns, beliefs or suggestions
- Coach expresses support and concern for the client, which may focus on the client's context, problem or situation, rather than the client holistically.

A coach will not receive a passing score for Cultivates Trust and Safety in the ACC performance evaluation if the coach demonstrates significant interest in the coach's own view of the situation rather than the client's view of the situation; if the coach does not seek information from the client about the client's thinking around the situation, if the coach is unsupportive or disrespectful to the client; or if the coach's attention seems to be on their own performance or demonstration of knowledge about the topic rather than on the client.

5. Maintains Presence

Definition: Is fully conscious and present with the client, employing a style that is open, flexible, grounded and confident.

1. Remains focused, observant, empathetic and responsive to the client
2. Demonstrates curiosity during the coaching process
3. Manages one's emotions to stay present with the client
4. Demonstrates confidence in working with strong client emotions during the coaching process
5. Is comfortable working in a space of not knowing
6. Creates or allows space for silence, pause or reflection

Key Skills Evaluated

1. The coach's depth of focus on and partnership with the client
2. The coach's depth of observation and use of the whole of the client in the coaching process
3. The coach's ability to create space for reflection and remain present to the client through both conversation and silence

APPENDIX 2

At an ACC level, the minimum standard of skill that must be demonstrated to receive a passing score for Competency 5: Maintains Presence is that the coach demonstrates curiosity about the client and the client's agenda and is responsive to the information the client offers throughout the session.

Specifically, ACC applicants are assessed on the following skills within Competency 5: Maintains Presence as part of the performance evaluation process:

- Coach is curious throughout the session
- Coach acknowledges situations that the client presents
- Coach allows the client to direct the conversation at least some of the time.

The ICF notes that Cultivates Trust and Safety and Maintains Presence are quite related competencies. Therefore, a coach will not receive a passing score for Maintains Presence on the ACC performance evaluation if the coach demonstrates significant interest in the coach's own view of the situation rather than exploring the client's view of the situation, does not seek information from the client about the client's thinking around the situation or is unresponsive to that information, the coach consistently directs the conversation, or the attention seems to be on the coach's own performance or demonstration of knowledge about the topic.

6. Listens Actively

Definition: Focuses on what the client is and is not saying to fully understand what is being communicated in the context of the client systems and to support client self-expression.

1. Considers the client's context, identity, environment, experiences, values and beliefs to enhance understanding of what the client is communicating
2. Reflects or summarizes what the client communicated to ensure clarity and understanding
3. Recognizes and inquires when there is more to what the client is communicating

4. Notices, acknowledges and explores the client's emotions, energy shifts, non-verbal cues or other behaviors

5. Integrates the client's words, tone of voice and body language to determine the full meaning of what is being communicated

6. Notices trends in the client's behaviors and emotions across sessions to discern themes and patterns

Key Skills Evaluated

1. The coach's depth of attention to what the client communicates in relation to the client and the client's agenda

2. The coach's ability to hear on multiple levels including both the emotional and substantive content of the words

3. The coach's ability to hear underlying beliefs, thinking, creating and learning that are occurring for the client including recognizing incongruities in language, emotions and actions

4. The coach's ability to hear and integrate the client's language and to invite the client to deeper exploration

At an ACC level, the minimum standard of skill that must be demonstrated to receive a passing score for Competency 6: Listens Actively is that the coach listens to what the client communicates in relation to the client's agenda, responds to what the client offers to ensure clarity of understanding, and integrates what the client has communicated to support the client in achieving their agenda. The coach's behaviors in this competency may include listening to what the client has communicated verbally, as well as what the client may communicate in other ways, such as tone of voice, energy or emotional shifts, or body language.

Specifically, ACC applicants are assessed on the following skills within Competency 6: Listens Actively as part of the performance evaluation process:

- Coach uses summarizing or paraphrasing to make sure they understood the client correctly

- Coach makes observations that support the client in creating new associations

- Coach co-creates a shared vision with the client.

APPENDIX 2

A coach will not receive a passing score for Listens Actively on the ACC performance evaluation if the coach does not demonstrate listening that is focused on and responding to what the client communicates, or the coach's responses are not related to what the client is trying to achieve. The coach will not receive a passing grade on the ACC performance evaluation if the coach appears to be listening for the place where the coach can demonstrate their knowledge about the topic or tell the client what to do about the topic.

7. Evokes Awareness

Definition: Facilitates client insight and learning by using tools and techniques such as powerful questioning, silence, metaphor and analogy.

1. Considers client experience when deciding what might be most useful
2. Challenges the client as a way to evoke awareness or insight
3. Asks questions about the client, such as their way of thinking, values, needs, wants and beliefs
4. Asks questions that help the client explore beyond current thinking
5. Invites the client to share more about their experience in the moment
6. Notices what is working to enhance client progress
7. Adjusts the coaching approach in response to the client's needs
8. Helps the client identify factors that influence current and future patterns of behavior, thinking or emotion
9. Invites the client to generate ideas about how they can move forward and what they are willing or able to do
10. Supports the client in reframing perspectives
11. Shares observations, insights and feelings, without attachment, that have the potential to create new learning for the client

MINIMUM SKILLS REQUIREMENTS FOR ACC CREDENTIAL

Key Skills Evaluated

1. The coach's use of inquiry, exploration, silence and other techniques that support the client in achieving new or deeper learning and awareness

2. The coach's ability to explore with and evoke exploration by the client of the emotional and substantive meaning of the client's words

3. The coach's ability to explore with and evoke exploration by the client of the underlying beliefs and means of thinking, creating and learning that are occurring for the client

4. The coach's ability to support the client in exploring new or expanded perspectives or ways of thinking

5. The coach's invitation to and integration of the client's intuition, thinking and language as critical tools in the coaching process

At an ACC level, the minimum standard of skill that must be demonstrated to receive a passing score for Competency 7: Evokes Awareness is that the coach uses inquiry, exploration, silence and other techniques to support the client in achieving new or deeper learning and awareness.

Specifically, ACC applicants are assessed on the following skills within Competency 7: Evokes Awareness as part of the performance evaluation process:

- Coach inquires about or explores the client's ideas, beliefs, thinking, emotions and behaviors in relation to the desired outcome

- Coach supports the client in viewing the situation from new or different perspectives

- Coach acknowledges the client's new awareness, learning and movement toward the desired outcome.

A coach will not receive a passing score for Evokes Awareness on the ACC performance evaluation if the coach focuses consistently on instructing the client or sharing the coach's own knowledge, ideas or beliefs; if the majority of the coach's questions are leading or contain pre-determined answers by the coach; or if the coach's questions and explorations attend to an agenda or issues not set by the client, but set by the coach.

8. Facilitates Client Growth

Definition: Partners with the client to transform learning and insight into action. Promotes client autonomy in the coaching process.

1. Works with the client to integrate new awareness, insight or learning into their worldview and behaviors
2. Partners with the client to design goals, actions and accountability measures that integrate and expand new learning
3. Acknowledges and supports client autonomy in the design of goals, actions and methods of accountability
4. Supports the client in identifying potential results or learning from identified action steps
5. Invites the client to consider how to move forward, including resources, support and potential barriers
6. Partners with the client to summarize learning and insight within or between sessions
7. Celebrates the client's progress and successes
8. Partners with the client to close the session

Key Skills Evaluated

1. The coach's ability to support the client in exploring their learning about themselves and their situation and the application of that learning toward the client's goals
2. The coach's ability to partner fully with the client in designing actions from their new awareness, which may include thinking, feeling or learning, that support the client in moving toward their stated agenda or goals
3. The coach's ability to support the client in developing measurable achievements that are steps toward the client's stated goals or outcomes

MINIMUM SKILLS REQUIREMENTS FOR ACC CREDENTIAL

4. The coach's ability to partner with the client to explore and acknowledge the client's progress throughout the session

5. The coach's depth of partnership in closing the session

At an ACC level, the minimum standard of skill that must be demonstrated to receive a passing score for Competency 8: Facilitates Client Growth is that the coach supports the client in exploring how to apply the client's learning and awareness to post-session actions that are related to the client's stated agenda and have the potential to move the client forward in their thinking, learning or growth. At this level, the coach may also suggest resources to assist the client in achieving their goals so long as the resources are not forced on the client.

Specifically, ACC applicants are assessed on the following skills within Competency 8: Facilitates Client Growth as part of the performance evaluation process:

- **Coach asks questions to support the client in translating awareness into action**
- **Coach partners with the client to create or confirm specific action plans**
- **Coach supports the client to close the session.**

A coach will not receive a passing score for Facilitates Client Growth on the ACC performance evaluation if the coach insists the client carry out specific actions prescribed by the coach, the coach suggests actions or steps to the client that do not have a clear relationship to the client's stated agenda, the coach does not invite the client to identify or explore how the client's learning can be applied to future actions or activities that support the client's agenda, or if the coach does not support the client to close the session.

APPENDIX 3

ICF PCC Markers

Assessment markers are the indicators that an assessor is trained to listen for to determine which ICF core competencies are evident in a recorded coaching conversation and to what extent. The following markers are behaviors that represent demonstration of the core competencies in a coaching conversation at the Professional Certified Coach (PCC) level. These markers support a performance evaluation process that is fair, consistent, valid, reliable, repeatable and defensible.

The PCC Markers may also support coaches, coach trainers and mentor coaches in identifying areas for growth and skill development in coaching at the PCC level; however, they should always be used in the context of core competency development. The PCC Markers should not be used as a checklist in a formulaic manner for passing the PCC performance evaluation.

Competency 1: Demonstrates Ethical Practice

Familiarity with the ICF Code of Ethics and its application is required for all levels of coaching. Successful PCC candidates will demonstrate coaching that is aligned with the ICF Code of Ethics and will remain consistent in the role of a coach.

Competency 2: Embodies a Coaching Mindset

Embodying a coaching mindset – a mindset that is open, curious, flexible and client-centered – is a process that requires ongoing learning and development, establishing a reflective practice and preparing for sessions. These elements take place over the course of a coach's professional journey and cannot be fully captured in a single moment in time. However, certain elements of this competency may be demonstrated within a coaching conversation. These particular behaviors are articulated and assessed through the following PCC Markers: 4.1, 4.3, 4.4, 5.1, 5.2, 5.3, 5.4, 6.1, 6.5, 7.1 and 7.5.

As with other competency areas, a minimum number of these markers will need to be demonstrated to pass the PCC performance evaluation. All elements of this competency will also be evaluated in the written assessment for ICF credentials.

Competency 3: Establishes and Maintains Agreements

3.1: Coach partners with the client to identify or reconfirm what the client wants to accomplish in this session.

3.2: Coach partners with the client to define or reconfirm measures of success for what the client wants to accomplish in this session.

3.3: Coach inquires about or explores what is important or meaningful to the client about what they want to accomplish in this session.

3.4: Coach partners with the client to define what the client believes they need to address to achieve what they want to accomplish in this session.

Competency 4: Cultivates Trust and Safety

4.1: Coach acknowledges and respects the client's unique talents, insights and work in the coaching process.

4.2: Coach shows support, empathy or concern for the client.

4.3: Coach acknowledges and supports the client's expression of feelings, perceptions, concerns, beliefs or suggestions.

4.4: Coach partners with the client by inviting the client to respond in any way to the coach's contributions and accepts the client's response.

Competency 5: Maintains Presence

5.1: Coach acts in response to the whole person of the client (the who).

5.2: Coach acts in response to what the client wants to accomplish throughout this session (the what).

5.3: Coach partners with the client by supporting the client to choose what happens in this session.

5.4: Coach demonstrates curiosity to learn more about the client.

5.5: Coach allows for silence, pause or reflection.

Competency 6: Listens Actively

6.1: Coach's questions and observations are customized by using what the coach has learned about who the client is or the client's situation.

6.2: Coach inquires about or explores the words the client uses.

6.3: Coach inquires about or explores the client's emotions.

6.4: Coach explores the client's energy shifts, non-verbal cues or other behaviors.

6.5: Coach inquires about or explores how the client currently perceives themself or their world.

6.6: Coach allows the client to complete speaking without interrupting unless there is a stated coaching purpose to do so.

6.7: Coach succinctly reflects or summarizes what the client communicated to ensure the client's clarity and understanding.

Competency 7: Evokes Awareness

7.1: Coach asks questions about the client, such as their current way of thinking, feeling, values, needs, wants, beliefs or behavior.

7.2: Coach asks questions to help the client explore beyond the client's current thinking or feeling to new or expanded ways of thinking or feeling about themself (the who).

7.3: Coach asks questions to help the client explore beyond the client's current thinking or feeling to new or expanded ways of thinking or feeling about their situation (the what).

7.4: Coach asks questions to help the client explore beyond current thinking, feeling or behaving toward the outcome the client desires.

7.5: Coach shares – with no attachment – observations, intuitions, comments, thoughts or feelings, and invites the client's exploration through verbal or tonal invitation.

7.6: Coach asks clear, direct, primarily open-ended questions, one at a time, at a pace that allows for thinking, feeling or reflection by the client.

7.7: Coach uses language that is generally clear and concise.

7.8: Coach allows the client to do most of the talking.

Competency 8: Facilitates Client Growth

8.1: Coach invites or allows the client to explore progress toward what the client wanted to accomplish in this session.

8.2: Coach invites the client to state or explore the client's learning in this session about themself (the who).

8.3: Coach invites the client to state or explore the client's learning in this session about their situation (the what).

8.4: Coach invites the client to consider how they will use new learning from this coaching session.

8.5: Coach partners with the client to design post-session thinking, reflection or action.

8.6: Coach partners with the client to consider how to move forward, including resources, support or potential barriers.

8.7: Coach partners with the client to design the best methods of accountability for themself.

8.8: Coach celebrates the client's progress and learning.

8.9: Coach partners with the client on how they want to complete this session.

APPENDIX 4

Minimum Skills Requirements for MCC Credential

ICF believes that it has an obligation to support its member coaches in the growth of their skill set. Every Master Certified Coach (MCC) started as a beginner. They progressed through an intermediate level of skill and became masterful, where the hallmark is complete evidence of the coach's role as learner about the client. ICF's three levels of credentials reflect the continuum of growth and learning along the coaching journey.

This document has been created to support coaches as they prepare for the MCC credential performance evaluation. We also hope that this document will assist mentor coaches and supervisors in supporting these coaches, and coaching education and training providers in undertaking accreditation of their programs. The aim is to support coaches in successfully completing the MCC performance evaluation and in continuing to develop their skill set as coaches, in alignment with the updated ICF core competencies (2019).

For those seeking a credential, this document will provide an understanding of what assessors evaluate in relation to each ICF core competency. It will offer the minimum level of skill necessary to successfully demonstrate an MCC level of competency, and also help you understand what non-coaching behaviors might prevent successful completion of the MCC performance evaluation. This document can help each individual coach answer the following queries:

1. What does it mean to be an MCC coach?
2. What do ICF assessors listen for when they are evaluating my coaching?
3. As I progress on my coaching journey, what are my strengths and what are the skill-set areas that I need to grow to pass the MCC performance evaluation?

Finally, ICF strongly believes that clients receive real and substantive value from MCC coaches. That value rests always in the coach's complete attention to the client and what the client wishes to accomplish, the complete level of partnership with the client, as well as the coach's complete support of the client's agenda. We honor each and every coach on their journey and look forward to supporting your path of growth as a coach and your credentialing path within ICF.

Overall Behaviors for MCC-level Coaching

Among the hallmarks of MCC-level coaching is the fluidity and artistry with which a coach engages in a coaching conversation. This can manifest in a variety of ways. Most commonly, MCC-level coaching is demonstrated through the depth of skill in a specific coaching behavior or through the integration of multiple competencies simultaneously in a seamlessly blended manner.

The structure of the Minimum Skills Requirements for MCC-level coaching is designed to reflect the unique characteristics of masterful coaching, with behaviors identified for each of the core competency areas, as well as overarching behaviors and skills that reflect MCC-level coaching across the competencies. Both the overall MCC-level coaching behaviors and the competency-specific skills have been identified through research with MCC-credentialed coaches.

At the MCC level of coaching, an applicant should demonstrate trust in the client as a full partner throughout the coaching engagement, supporting the client in directing the focus and approach of the session and exploring the client's learning in a way that supports their continued growth. An applicant should exhibit a genuine interest and curiosity in and support for the client as a whole person – beyond the client's situation or immediate goals – and should support the client in reflecting on their learning and discovery about themselves at a holistic level. The applicant should also demonstrate genuine trust in and respect for the client's choices, perceptions, insights and contributions throughout the coaching, engaging in the coaching as a supporter and active learner and encouraging the client to explore their learning and growth at a deep level.

APPENDIX 4

Specifically, MCC applicants are assessed on the following general coaching behaviors as part of the performance evaluation process:

- Coach invites the client to explore the lens through which the client is observing their current situation
- The coach's comments and questions come from the totality of what they have learned about who the client is and their coaching purpose
- Coach's invitations to the client primarily focus on exploring deeper learning or a path forward.

1. Demonstrates Ethical Practice

Definition: Understands and consistently applies coaching ethics and standards of coaching.

1. Demonstrates personal integrity and honesty in interactions with clients, sponsors and relevant stakeholders
2. Is sensitive to clients' identity, environment, experiences, values and beliefs
3. Uses language appropriate and respectful to clients, sponsors and relevant stakeholders
4. Abides by the ICF Code of Ethics and upholds the Core Values
5. Maintains confidentiality with client information per stakeholder agreements and pertinent laws
6. Maintains the distinctions between coaching, consulting, psychotherapy and other support professions
7. Refers clients to other support professionals, as appropriate

Important Note: Familiarity with the ICF Code of Ethics and its application is required for all levels of coaching and the standard for demonstrating a strong ethical understanding of coaching is similar for an ICF credential at any level – Associate Certified Coach (ACC), Professional Certified Coach (PCC) or Master Certified Coach (MCC).

An applicant must demonstrate alignment with the ICF Code of Ethics in the performance evaluation. An applicant who commits a clear violation of the ICF Code of Ethics within a performance evaluation recording would not pass this competency and would be denied a credential.

An applicant must also remain consistently in the role of coach within the performance evaluation. This includes demonstrating a knowledge of the coaching conversation that is focused on inquiry and exploration, and a focus based on present and future issues. An applicant would not pass this competency if they focused primarily on telling the client what to do or how to do it (consulting mode) or if the conversation were based primarily in the past, particularly the emotional past (therapeutic mode).

If an applicant is not clear on basic foundation exploration and evoking skills that underlie the ICF definition of coaching, that lack of clarity in skill use will be reflected in skill level demonstrated in some of the other competencies listed below. For example, if a coach almost exclusively gives advice or indicates that a particular answer chosen by the coach is what the client should do, trust and safety, presence, active listening, evoking awareness and facilitating client growth will not be present and a credential at any level would be denied.

2. Embodies a Coaching Mindset

Definition: Develops and maintains a mindset that is open, curious, flexible and client-centered.

1. Acknowledges that clients are responsible for their own choices
2. Engages in ongoing learning and development as a coach
3. Develops an ongoing reflective practice to enhance one's coaching
4. Remains aware of and open to the influence of context and culture on self and others
5. Uses awareness of self and one's intuition to benefit clients
6. Develops and maintains the ability to regulate one's emotions
7. Mentally and emotionally prepares for sessions
8. Seeks help from outside sources when necessary

Competency 2: Embodies a Coaching Mindset serves as a foundational competency for coach practitioners, focused primarily on the "being" of the coach. The related behaviors are typically demonstrated across a coach's practice, more so than in any specific coaching session. This competency area is therefore more difficult to consistently assess within the performance evaluation process. As a result, there are no behavioral or skill statements in this competency area that are used for assessment purposes. Rather, an applicant's knowledge of and ability to apply Competency 2: Embodies a Coaching Mindset are more directly evaluated in the ICF credentialing written exam.

3. Establishes and Maintains Agreements

Definition: Partners with the client and relevant stakeholders to create clear agreements about the coaching relationship, process, plans and goals. Establishes agreements for the overall coaching engagement as well as those for each coaching session.

1. Explains what coaching is and is not and describes the process to the client and relevant stakeholders
2. Reaches agreement about what is and is not appropriate in the relationship, what is and is not being offered, and the responsibilities of the client and relevant stakeholders
3. Reaches agreement about the guidelines and specific parameters of the coaching relationship such as logistics, fees, scheduling, duration, termination, confidentiality and inclusion of others
4. Partners with the client and relevant stakeholders to establish an overall coaching plan and goals
5. Partners with the client to determine client–coach compatibility
6. Partners with the client to identify or reconfirm what they want to accomplish in the session
7. Partners with the client to define what the client believes they need to address or resolve to achieve what they want to accomplish in the session
8. Partners with the client to define or reconfirm measures of success for what the client wants to accomplish in the coaching engagement or individual session

9. Partners with the client to manage the time and focus of the session
10. Continues coaching in the direction of the client's desired outcome unless the client indicates otherwise
11. Partners with the client to end the coaching relationship in a way that honors the experience

Key Skills Evaluated

1. The clarity and depth in creating an agreement for the session
2. The coach's ability to partner and the depth of partnering with the client in the creation of agreement, measures of success, and issues to be addressed
3. The coach's ability to attend to the client's agenda throughout the session

At an MCC level, the minimum standard of skill that must be demonstrated to achieve a passing score for Competency 3: Establishes and Maintains Agreements is that the coach fully explores with the client what the client wants to work on. The coach partners with the client to thoroughly explore the importance of the topic to the client, measures of success, and any changes in the direction of the coaching conversation. Through a partnering discussion, the coach ensures that both the coach and client are clear about the agenda, the measures of success, and the issues to be discussed, and the coach attends to that agenda and those measures throughout the coaching, unless redirected by the client. The coach regularly checks with the client throughout the session to ensure that the client's goals for the session are being achieved and that the direction and process are supporting the client in moving toward their desired outcome.

Specifically, MCC applicants are assessed on the following skills within Competency 3: Establishes and Maintains Agreements as part of the performance evaluation process:

- Coach partners with the client to explore the topic or focus of the session at a level that is meaningful to the client
- Coach partners with the client to keep the desired outcome as a guide to the coaching conversation in a flexible, gentle and natural manner

APPENDIX 4

- Coach notices subtle shifts in the conversation and invites the client to change direction if the client desires.

A coach will not receive a passing score for Establishes and Maintains Agreements on the MCC performance evaluation if full partnership with the client is not demonstrated. Full partnership will not be demonstrated if the coach chooses the topic(s) for the client or if the coach does not coach around the topic(s) the client has chosen. The evaluation for this competency will also be negatively impacted if the coach does not explore the measures of success for each topic with the client to a degree that achieves clarity about the client's intent or direction for the session, does not allow the client full input into the issues that should be discussed relative to the client's stated objectives for the session, or does not check with the client about whether the client is moving toward what the client wanted from the session.

4. Cultivates Trust and Safety

Definition: Partners with the client to create a safe, supportive environment that allows the client to share freely. Maintains a relationship of mutual respect and trust.

1. Seeks to understand the client within their context which may include their identity, environment, experiences, values and beliefs
2. Demonstrates respect for the client's identity, perceptions, style and language and adapts one's coaching to the client
3. Acknowledges and respects the client's unique talents, insights and work in the coaching process
4. Shows support, empathy and concern for the client
5. Acknowledges and supports the client's expression of feelings, perceptions, concerns, beliefs and suggestions
6. Demonstrates openness and transparency as a way to display vulnerability and build trust with the client

Key Skills Evaluated

1. The coach's depth of connection to and support of the client

MINIMUM SKILLS REQUIREMENTS FOR MCC CREDENTIAL

2. The coach's depth of trust in and respect for the client and the client's processes of thinking, creating

3. The coach's willingness to be open, authentic and vulnerable with the client to build mutual trust

At an MCC level, the minimum standard of skill that must be demonstrated to receive a passing score for Competency 4: Cultivates Trust and Safety with the client is that the coach demonstrates complete and open trust in the client and the process by engaging the client as an equal partner in the coaching, and by the coach's willingness to be vulnerable with the client and to create a safe space for the client to be vulnerable in return.

The MCC-level coach demonstrates a complete confidence in self, the coaching process and the client as a whole, and a genuine curiosity about and respect for the client's perceptions, learning style and personal being. The client is treated as an equal partner in the relationship with a full invitation to participate in the development and creation of the coaching process and their own new learning and behaviors.

Specifically, MCC applicants are assessed on the following skills within Competency 4: Cultivates Trust and Safety as part of the performance evaluation process:

- Coach engages the client as an equal partner in a collaborative coaching process

- Coach exhibits genuine curiosity about the client as a whole person by inviting the client to share more about themself or their identity

- Coach provides space for the client to fully express themself and share feelings, beliefs and perspectives without judgment

- Coach acknowledges the client and celebrates client progress.

A coach will not receive a passing score for Cultivates Trust and Safety on the MCC performance evaluation if the coach does not treat the client as a full partner, choosing not only the agenda but also participating in the creation of the coaching process itself. Lack of full partnership will be demonstrated if the coach exhibits an interest in the coach's view of the situation rather than the client's view, does not seek information from the client about the client's thinking, does not seek information about the client's goals, or the coach demonstrates a lack of interest in or disrespect toward the client as a whole. In addition, the evaluation will be negatively impacted if the coach does not invite the client to share their thinking on an equal level with the coach or if the coach chooses the direction and approach without significant input from the client. Any indication that the coach is teaching rather than coaching will also result in a score below the MCC level for this competency area.

5. Maintains Presence

Definition: Is fully conscious and present with the client, employing a style that is open, flexible, grounded and confident.

1. Remains focused, observant, empathetic and responsive to the client
2. Demonstrates curiosity during the coaching process
3. Manages one's emotions to stay present with the client
4. Demonstrates confidence in working with strong client emotions during the coaching process
5. Is comfortable working in a space of not knowing
6. Creates or allows space for silence, pause or reflection

Key Skills Evaluated

1. The coach's depth of focus on and partnership with the client
2. The coach's depth of observation and use of the whole of the client in the coaching process
3. The coach's ability to create space for reflection and remain present to the client through both conversation and silence

At an MCC level, the minimum standard of skill that must be demonstrated to receive a passing score for Competency 5: Maintains Presence is that the coach is fully partnering with the client in the coaching dialogue and is a connected observer to the client, holding both objective and emotional perspectives simultaneously. The connection is to the whole of the client, who the client is, what the client wants, how the client learns and creates, and how the client leads the coaching conversation. The coach evidences a genuine curiosity in the client. As with Cultivates Trust and Safety, the coach is in a complete partnership with the client where the client is an equal or greater contributor to the conversation and direction of the coaching than the coach. At the MCC level, the conversation between coach and client is equal and easy, even in uncomfortable moments.

Specifically, MCC applicants are assessed on the following skills within Competency 5: Maintains Presence as part of the performance evaluation process:

- Coach responds to the client in a manner that keeps the conversation flowing with the client leading the way
- Coach remains curious and attentive to the client, exploring what the client needs throughout the session
- Coach engages in the coaching conversation with ease and fluidity
- Coach leverages silence to support the client and the client's growth.

ICF notes that Cultivates Trust and Safety and Maintains Presence are quite related competencies. Therefore, a coach will not receive a passing score for Competency 5: Maintains Presence with the client on the MCC performance evaluation if the coach does not treat the client as a full partner, choosing not only the agenda but also participating in the creation of the coaching process itself. Such lack of full partnership is demonstrated if the coach exhibits interest in the coach's view of the situation rather than the client's view, does not seek information from the client about the client's thinking, does not seek information about the client's goals, or if the coach's attention seems to be on the coach's own performance or demonstration of knowledge. In addition, the evaluation will be negatively impacted if the coach does not invite the client to share their thinking on an equal level with the coach.

6. Listens Actively

Definition: Focuses on what the client is and is not saying to fully understand what is being communicated in the context of the client systems and to support client self-expression.

APPENDIX 4

1. Considers the client's context, identity, environment, experiences, values and beliefs to enhance understanding of what the client is communicating
2. Reflects or summarizes what the client communicated to ensure clarity and understanding
3. Recognizes and inquires when there is more to what the client is communicating
4. Notices, acknowledges and explores the client's emotions, energy shifts, non-verbal cues or other behaviors
5. Integrates the client's words, tone of voice and body language to determine the full meaning of what is being communicated
6. Notices trends in the client's behaviors and emotions across sessions to discern themes and patterns

Key Skills Evaluated

1. The coach's depth of attention to what the client communicates in relation to the client and the client's agenda
2. The coach's ability to hear on multiple levels, including both the emotional and substantive content of the words
3. The coach's ability to hear underlying beliefs, thinking, creating and learning that are occurring for the client, including recognizing incongruities in language, emotions and actions
4. The coach's ability to hear and integrate the client's language and to invite the client to deeper exploration

At an MCC level, the minimum standard of skill that must be demonstrated to receive a passing score for Competency 6: Listens Actively is that the coach listens as a learner and demonstrates an ability to listen at the logical and emotional level at the same time. Responses from the coach evidence learning about the client at multiple levels. The coach's responses evidence that the coach is hearing the client's intuitive abilities, the client's energy, when the client speaks of important things, when new growth is occurring for the client, how that growth is related to the client's stated objectives and agenda, and when the client is finding, creating and using a more powerful sense of self. The coach is also able to hear the client's current thinking and growth and relate it to the future the client is trying to create. An MCC-level coach hears the totality of the client's greatness and gifts as well as limiting beliefs and patterns. The coach's listening is cumulative from session to session and throughout each individual session.

Specifically, MCC applicants are assessed on the following skills within Competency 6: Listens Actively:

- Coach responds to the client with an invitation into a deeper exploration of client thinking and behaviors
- Coach's responses to the client demonstrate an understanding of the client's emotions, energy, or learning and growth, in alignment with the client's agenda
- Coach reflects what the client communicates in relation to the context of the whole person.

A coach will not receive a passing score for Listens Actively on the MCC performance evaluation if the coach does not demonstrate listening that is based on the whole client and an ability to hear the client's thinking, learning and feeling at multiple levels. The coach will not receive a passing grade at this level if the listening is filtered only through the coach's methods of thinking, learning and creating, and does not actively hear and use as a significant coaching tool the client's methods of thinking, learning and creating. The score for this competency will also be negatively impacted if nuances of the client's language are not reflected in the coach's responses, or if the coach does not respond to what the client communicates, the coach's response is not related to what the client is trying to achieve or the coach's listening is primarily focused on the client's problems or weaknesses. The coach will not receive a passing grade on the MCC performance evaluation if the coach appears to be listening for the place where the coach can demonstrate their knowledge about the topic or tell the client what to do about the topic.

7. Evokes Awareness

Definition: Facilitates client insight and learning by using tools and techniques such as powerful questioning, silence, metaphor and analogy.

1. Considers client experience when deciding what might be most useful
2. Challenges the client as a way to evoke awareness or insight
3. Asks questions about the client, such as their way of thinking, values, needs, wants and beliefs
4. Asks questions that help the client explore beyond current thinking
5. Invites the client to share more about their experience in the moment
6. Notices what is working to enhance client progress
7. Adjusts the coaching approach in response to the client's needs
8. Helps the client identify factors that influence current and future patterns of behavior, thinking or emotion
9. Invites the client to generate ideas about how they can move forward and what they are willing or able to do
10. Supports the client in reframing perspectives
11. Shares observations, insights and feelings, without attachment, that have the potential to create new learning for the client

Key Skills Evaluated

1. The coach's use of inquiry, exploration, silence and other techniques that support the client in achieving new or deeper learning and awareness
2. The coach's ability to explore with and evoke exploration by the client of the emotional and substantive content of the words
3. The coach's ability to explore with and evoke exploration by the client of the underlying beliefs and means of thinking, creating and learning that are occurring for the client
4. The coach's ability to support the client in exploring new or expanded perspectives or ways of thinking
5. The coach's invitation to and integration of the client's intuition, thinking and language as critical tools in the coaching process

At an MCC level, the minimum standard of skill that must be demonstrated to receive a passing score for Competency 7: Evokes Awareness is that the coach's invitation to the exploration of important issues precedes and is significantly greater than the invitation to a solution. At an MCC level, the coach's way of being is consistently curious; the coach is willing to not know and allow the exploration to evolve based on the client's thinking, learning and creating. The coach asks mostly, if not always, direct, evocative questions that are fully responsive to the client in the moment, to the client's agenda and stated objectives, and that require significant thought by the client or take the client to a new place of thinking. The coach makes frequent and full use of the client's language and learning style to craft questions, insights or observations that provide a space for a client to use and expand their own style of thinking, learning and creating, and to discover their power, gifts and strengths. The coach provides sufficient space and encouragement to allow the client to integrate and use new awareness to identify patterns of thinking or behavior, resolve current challenges, achieve current goals and think how the new awareness may be used in the future.

Specifically, MCC applicants are assessed on the following skills within Competency 7: Evokes Awareness as part of the performance evaluation process:

- Coach partners with the client to explore the client's stories, metaphors and imagery that support growth and learning
- Coach stimulates new client insights with minimal, precise questions
- Coach asks questions that challenge the client to explore more deeply or to go beyond current thinking and feeling
- Coach shares with fluidity insights, observations or questions from the client's words and actions, to foster awareness.

A coach will not receive a passing score for Evokes Awareness on the MCC performance evaluation if the coach does not demonstrate an ability to use questions, insights, silence or other techniques that encourage the client to deepen their thinking in a larger, more reflective space related to the client or the client's agenda. The evaluation will be negatively impacted if the coach frequently asks questions that keep the client in the past or in present detail of a situation rather than in forward thinking, or if the coach drives the client toward solutions without fully exploring issues that may be important to gaining complete solution or accomplishment for the client. The evaluation will also be negatively impacted if the dialogue does not provide sufficient space for the client's full participation in creating awareness; if the coach's communication reflects an agenda or directing of any kind by the coach; if the coach does not evidence frequent use of the client's language, learning, thinking and creating styles; or if the coach does not often create an easy place for the client to engage in deeper thinking, learning and discovery. The coach will not receive a passing score for this competency area if the coach's communication limits the thinking and learning direction for the client without specific interaction with, discussion of and assent by the client to the limitation.

8. Facilitates Client Growth

Definition: Partners with the client to transform learning and insight into action. Promotes client autonomy in the coaching process.

1. Works with the client to integrate new awareness, insight or learning into their worldview and behaviors
2. Partners with the client to design goals, actions and accountability measures that integrate and expand new learning
3. Acknowledges and supports client autonomy in the design of goals, actions and methods of accountability
4. Supports the client in identifying potential results or learning from identified action steps
5. Invites the client to consider how to move forward, including resources, support and potential barriers
6. Partners with the client to summarize learning and insight within or between sessions
7. Celebrates the client's progress and successes
8. Partners with the client to close the session

Key Skills Evaluated

1. The coach's ability to support the client in exploring their learning about themselves and their situation and the application of that learning to support the client's goals
2. The coach's ability to partner fully with the client in designing actions from their new awareness, which may include thinking, feeling or learning, that support the client in moving toward their stated agenda or goals
3. The coach's ability to support the client in developing measurable achievements that are steps toward the client's stated goals or outcomes
4. The coach's ability to partner with the client to explore and acknowledge the client's progress throughout the session
5. The coach's depth of partnership in closing the session

At an MCC level, the minimum standard of skill that must be demonstrated to receive a passing score for Competency 8: Facilitates Client Growth is that the coach fully partners with the client to explore the client's learning about their situation and themselves, and ways to apply new awareness to support the client's agenda, desired goals and future growth. The coach partners with the client throughout the session to explore the client's progress and learning, and supports the client in reflecting on what the client is discovering about themselves. The MCC coach demonstrates trust in the client to develop actions and accountability structures that are reflective of the client's agenda and broader learning or accomplishment that the client wants to obtain, to integrate the client's strengths as well as the best of the client's learning and creating methodologies.

Specifically, MCC applicants are assessed on the following skills within Competency 8: Facilitates Client Growth as part of the performance evaluation process:

- Coach checks in with client and their progress, learnings and insights in natural and spontaneous ways throughout the session
- Coach invites the client to sense and reflect on what they are learning about themselves

- Coach cultivates an environment for the client to intentionally apply their own learning.

A coach will not receive a passing score for Facilitates Client Growth on the MCC performance evaluation if the coach does not invite full client participation or does not encourage client leadership in planning strategies, actions and methods of accountability, or if the coach dominates in any way the actions or applications of learning that are created. The evaluation will also be negatively impacted if the coach does not invite or partner with the client to explore what the client is learning about themself and possible applications of that learning, or if applications of learning do not reflect a clear potential for forward movement by the client related to the client's agenda or desired outcomes, or to some other learning that the client has defined as necessary for their growth. The evaluation will also be negatively impacted if designed plans and goals and/or discussion designed actions involves only physical activity with no attention to the thinking, learning, being and creativity structures of the client.

APPENDIX 5

ICF Code of Ethics

1. Introduction

The ICF Code of Ethics describes the core values of the International Coaching Federation (ICF Core Values), and ethical principles and ethical standards of behavior for all ICF Professionals (see definitions). Meeting these ICF ethical standards of behavior is the first of the ICF core competencies for coaching. That is, "Demonstrates ethical practice: understands and consistently applies coaching ethics and standards."

The ICF Code of Ethics serves to uphold the integrity of ICF and the global coaching profession by:

- Setting standards of conduct consistent with the ICF Core Values and ethical principles
- Guiding ethical reflection, education, and decision-making
- Adjudicating and preserving ICF coach standards through the ICF Ethical Conduct Review (ECR) process
- Providing the basis for ICF ethics training in ICF-accredited programs.

The ICF Code of Ethics applies when ICF Professionals represent themselves as such, in any kind of coaching-related interaction. This is regardless of whether a Coaching Relationship (see definitions) has been established. This Code articulates the ethical obligations of ICF Professionals who are acting in their different roles as coach, coach supervisor, mentor coach, trainer or student coach-in-training, or serving in an ICF Leadership role, as well as Support Personnel (see definitions).

Although the Ethical Conduct Review (ECR) process is only applicable to ICF Professionals, as is the Pledge, the ICF Staff are also committed to ethical conduct and the Core Values and Ethical Principles that underpin the ICF Code of Ethics.

The challenge of working ethically means that members will inevitably encounter situations that require responses to unexpected issues, resolution of dilemmas and solutions to problems. The ICF Code of Ethics is intended to assist those persons subject to the Code by directing them to the variety of ethical factors that may need to be taken into consideration and helping to identify alternative ways of approaching ethical behavior.

ICF Professionals who accept the Code of Ethics strive to be ethical, even when doing so involves making difficult decisions or acting courageously.

2. Definitions

- **"Client"** – the individual or team/group being coached, the coach being mentored or supervised, or the coach or the student coach being trained.
- **"Coaching"** – partnering with Clients in a thought-provoking and creative process that inspires them to maximize their personal and professional potential.
- **"Coaching Relationship"** – a relationship that is established by the ICF Professional and the Client(s)/Sponsor(s) under an agreement or a contract that defines the responsibilities and expectations of each party.
- **"Code"** – ICF Code of Ethics
- **"Confidentiality"** – protection of any information obtained around the coaching engagement unless consent to release is given.
- **"Conflict of Interest"** – a situation in which an ICF Professional is involved in multiple interests where serving one interest could work against or be in conflict with another. This could be financial, personal or otherwise.
- **"Equality"** – a situation in which all people experience inclusion, access to resources and opportunity, regardless of their race, ethnicity, national origin, color, gender, sexual orientation, gender

identity, age, religion, immigration status, mental or physical disability, and other areas of human difference.

- **"ICF Professional"** – individuals who represent themselves as an ICF Member or ICF credential holder, in roles including but not limited to Coach, Coach Supervisor, Mentor Coach, Coach Trainer and Student of Coaching.

- **"ICF Staff"** – the ICF support personnel who are contracted by the managing company that provides professional management and administrative services on behalf of ICF.

- **"Internal Coach"** – an individual who is employed within an organization and coaches either part-time or full-time the employees of that organization.

- **"Sponsor"** – the entity (including its representatives) paying for and/or arranging or defining the coaching services to be provided.

- **"Support Personnel"** – the people who work for ICF Professionals in support of their Clients.

- **"Systemic equality"** – gender equality, race equality and other forms of equality that are institutionalized in the ethics, core values, policies, structures and cultures of communities, organizations, nations and society.

3. ICF Core Values

The ICF Code of Ethics is based on the ICF Core Values and the actions that flow from them. All values are equally important and support one another. These values are aspirational and should be used as a way to understand and interpret the standards. All ICF Professionals are expected to showcase and propagate these Values in all their interactions.

4. ICF Ethical Standards

The following ethical standards are applied to the professional activities of ICF Professionals:

APPENDIX 5

Section I – Responsibility to Clients

As an ICF Professional, I:

1. Explain and ensure that, prior to or at the initial meeting, my coaching Client(s) and Sponsor(s) understand the nature and potential value of coaching, the nature and limits of confidentiality, financial arrangements and any other terms of the coaching agreement.

2. Create an agreement/contract regarding the roles, responsibilities and rights of all parties involved with my Client(s) and Sponsor(s) prior to the commencement of services.

3. Maintain the strictest levels of confidentiality with all parties as agreed upon. I am aware of and agree to comply with all applicable laws that pertain to personal data and communications.

4. Have a clear understanding about how information is exchanged among all parties involved during all coaching interactions.

5. Have a clear understanding with both Clients and Sponsors or interested parties about the conditions under which information will not be kept confidential (e.g., illegal activity, if required by law, pursuant to valid court order or subpoena; imminent or likely risk of danger to self or to others; etc.). Where I reasonably believe one of the above circumstances is applicable, I may need to inform appropriate authorities.

6. When working as an Internal Coach, manage conflicts of interest or potential conflicts of interest with my coaching Clients and Sponsor(s) through coaching agreement(s) and ongoing dialogue. This should include addressing organizational roles, responsibilities, relationships, records, confidentiality and other reporting requirements.

7. Maintain, store and dispose of any records, including electronic files and communications, created during my professional interactions in a manner that promotes confidentiality, security and privacy and complies with any applicable laws and agreements. Furthermore, I seek to make proper use of emerging and growing technological developments that are being used in coaching services (technology-assisted coaching services) and to be aware how various ethical standards apply to them.

8. Remain alert to indications that there might be a shift in the value received from the coaching relationship. If so, make a change in the relationship or encourage the Client(s)/Sponsor(s) to seek another coach, seek another professional or use a different resource.

9. Respect all parties' right to terminate the coaching relationship at any point for any reason during the coaching process subject to the provisions of the agreement.

10. Am sensitive to the implications of having multiple contracts and relationships with the same Client(s) and Sponsor(s) at the same time in order to avoid conflict of interest situations.

11. Am aware of and actively manage any power or status difference between the Client and me that may be caused by cultural, relational, psychological or contextual issues.

12. Disclose to my Clients the potential receipt of compensation, and other benefits I may receive for referring my Clients to third parties.

13. Assure consistent quality of coaching regardless of the amount or form of agreed compensation in any relationship.

Section II – Responsibility to Practice and Performance

As an ICF Professional, I:

14. Adhere to the ICF Code of Ethics in all my interactions. When I become aware of a possible breach of the Code by myself or I recognize unethical behavior in another ICF Professional, I respectfully raise the matter with those involved. If this does not resolve the matter, I refer it to a formal authority (e.g., ICF Global) for resolution.

15. Require adherence to the ICF Code of Ethics by all Support Personnel.

16. Commit to excellence through continued personal, professional and ethical development.

17. Recognize my personal limitations or circumstances that may impair, conflict with or interfere with my coaching performance or my professional coaching relationships. I will reach out for support to determine the action to be taken and, if necessary, promptly seek relevant professional guidance. This may include suspending or terminating my coaching relationship(s).

18. Resolve any conflict of interest or potential conflict of interest by working through the issue with relevant parties, seeking professional assistance, or suspending temporarily or ending the professional relationship.

19. Maintain the privacy of ICF Members and use the ICF Member contact information (email addresses, telephone numbers and so on) only as authorized by ICF or the ICF Member.

Section III – Responsibility to Professionalism

As an ICF Professional, I:

20. Identify accurately my coaching qualifications, my level of coaching competency, expertise, experience, training, certifications and ICF credentials.

21. Make verbal and written statements that are true and accurate about what I offer as an ICF Professional, what is offered by ICF, the coaching profession and the potential value of coaching.

22. Communicate and create awareness with those who need to be informed of the ethical responsibilities established by this Code.

23. Hold responsibility for being aware of and setting clear, appropriate and culturally sensitive boundaries that govern interactions, physical or otherwise.

24. Do not participate in any sexual or romantic engagement with Client(s) or Sponsor(s). I will be ever mindful of the level of intimacy appropriate for the relationship. I take the appropriate action to address the issue or cancel the coaching engagement.

Section IV – Responsibility to Society

As an ICF Professional, I:

25. Avoid discrimination by maintaining fairness and equality in all activities and operations, while respecting local rules and cultural practices. This includes, but is not limited to, discrimination on the basis of age, race, gender expression, ethnicity, sexual orientation, religion, national origin, disability or military status.

26. Recognize and honor the contributions and intellectual property of others, only claiming ownership of my own material. I understand that a breach of this standard may subject me to legal remedy by a third party.

27. Am honest and work within recognized scientific standards, applicable subject guidelines and boundaries of my competence when conducting and reporting research.

28. Am aware of my and my clients' impact on society. I adhere to the philosophy of "doing good," versus "avoiding bad."

5. The Pledge of Ethics of the ICF Professional

As an ICF professional, in accordance with the standards of the ICF Code of Ethics, I acknowledge and agree to fulfill my ethical and legal obligations to my coaching client(s), sponsor(s), colleagues and to the public at large.

If I breach any part of the ICF Code of Ethics, I agree that the ICF in its sole discretion may hold me accountable for so doing. I further agree that my accountability to the ICF for any breach may include sanctions, such as mandatory additional coach training or other education or loss of my ICF membership and/or my ICF credential.

www.ingramcontent.com/pod-product-compliance
Lightning Source LLC
LaVergne TN
LVHW051216070526
838200LV00063B/4913